A Can of Madness

By Jason Pegler

1

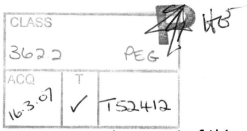

Published by
Chipmunkapublishing
PO Box 6872
Brentwood
Essex
CM13 1ZT
United Kingdom

www.chipmunkapublishing.com

Copyright © 2006 Jason Pegler

A record of this book is in the British
Library
ISBN 0 9542218 2 6

Fifth Edition, this book has sold over
250,000 copies

Love to my family and friends and everyone who cares about the mental health of others.

This book is dedicated to Tom Robertson and Ali Priestly

Chipmunkapublishing

In 2002 Jason Pegler set up Chipmunkapublishing, which quickly became a social phenomenon helping thousands of people with mental health problems worldwide. A new generation of mental health sufferers could now force the world to listen to their plight and therefore accommodate them in a humane manner just like Martin Luther King had led black Americans to equality in the United States of America. As Chipmunkapublishing grew it reached out to carers, the medical profession, the media, politicians, celebrities and society. The Chipmunka vision illustrates that we are in a transitional period in history where mental health will essentially be "normalised" and broken down as a taboo. This is inevitable in a world where mental health suffering is on the increase. As global communication improves in the consumerist generation of the 21st Century it is inevitable that we will all be more sensitive to the mental health of others.

Chipmunkapublishing is a social enterprise that drives its resources back into the community.

About the author

Jason Pegler is a freelance journalist, inspirational speaker and consultant. He is CEO of Chipmunkapublishing and also the Co Founder and driving force behind the Chipmunka Foundation and the Chipmunka Group. The Chipmunka Foundation was set up in August 2004 to further the Chipmunka vision and become the world's largest mental health charity. For more details please go to www.chipmunkapublishing.com.

A Can of Madness is Jason's autobiography up until the age of 27. He was born in 1975 and lives in London. He intends to direct A Can of Madness as a blockbuster movie and then work on the inside of Hollywood to change the way the world thinks about mental health thus reducing the pain, suffering and humiliation that people with mental health issues experience on a daily basis. In March 2006 his second book Curing Madness was published and he is currently writing his third book 'The Ultimate Guide to Well Being'.

Foreword

This is a strong book: full of strong language. But the hard words are not just the superfluous, value-added expletives of gangster rap there to make the writer feel hard. These are the natural expressions of a young man trying to make sense of experiences that can only be fully understood from within. They resonate with anger, sometimes with bewilderment and, always, with knowledge and understanding. By grounding his descriptions of madness in the emerging story of his life, Jason Pegler makes his story accessible to anyone with hopes, fears and compassion.

Jason's story draws frankly on his childhood, upbringing and experiences at school; it marks his intellectual and physical developments; and it acclaims his passions and desires. In common with many young and talented people, Jason's story mixes the conventional, socially desirable successes and achievements – examinations, rugby matches, university – with the risky and audacious exploits of youth: booze, brawls and sex. But the central theme is his battle with his personal madness, and the humiliations with which this brings him in contact.

For those of us who work in the healthcare system, many of Jason's descriptions should be a warning; this is not the way it should be. His recurring experiences of lack of time, lack of training and, worst of all, lack of compassion on the part of healthcare staff provide a mirror in which we must hope *we* are not reflected. For people who share some of Jason's experiences, and for their friends and families, the book is hopeful that its message, that seemingly devastating circumstances can be overcome, helps.

This is a strong book. Read it and gain strength.

Teifion Davies

Senior Lecturer, editor of *The ABC of mental health* and Consultant Psychiatrist at St Thomas' Hospital, Lambeth, London, United Kingdom.

Preface

What follows is intended to help people understand the condition of manic depression and similar mental illnesses. And I hope that sufferers, their families and friends will gain an enormous amount of strength from reading it. My own experience is that it's possible to emerge at the other end of adversity and live a decent life. Admittedly you may have to make changes in your life and behaviour, but that's a small sacrifice compared with the alternatives.

The first step is to accept that you've got a problem, or rather, that there *is* a problem, the exact cause(s) of which, more often than not, will forever remain unknown. The second is to deal with it, and the sooner the better.

When writing this book, I often thought back to how long it took me to accept my own illness. I have discovered that I have helped many people cope with their illness better than I did. This alone makes the pain of writing it and talking about it worthwhile.

Prepare for a journey that will take you close to the edge as you read the most honest account written about manic depression that you have ever seen. For those of you who find it a page turner read on and once you have finished telling people about it encourage them to be more open about their own mental health. For those who may be offended I apologise beforehand and urge you to read on.

Writing this book made me a better person as I got all the pain out of my system. To make it more politically correct at this stage I would feel like I am not being true to myself as the words you are about to read explain exactly how I felt at that moment in time. 'Writing about my experiences saved my life and publishing the work of others has enabled me to help more people'.

Chapter 1 – In the beginning...

As I was being driven off in the back of a police van in a space suit, I thought I was Donovan Bad Boy Smith being driven to a rave. I could hear music in my head and flashed back to another night at the Brunel Rooms in Swindon. *The Brunel Rooms, a hardcore Mecca for druggies from Gloucester and surrounding areas in the early to mid-nineties.* Donovan was so hard core when I saw him there that he'd refused to turn off his set at 3am. He'd carried on until 3.30am when someone finally turned off the electricity mid flow.

Talking of flows (as opposed to stable mindsets), just how the fuck do you live with a mental illness? Don't ask me, I'm still trying to find out now. After all, it's not something you plan let alone something you'd ever expect to have. As we all say: it won't happen to me. But it can. And in this case, it did.

And if Hercules and Ajax couldn't hack it, how the hell could I? Unsurprisingly, I didn't – and that's why I wallowed in self-pity for so long.

So, do you want to know what it's like to be crazy, mad, and loopy? Well, I'm about to tell you. I'm also going to tell you how it feels to be suicidal for months on end – the fate of the manic. One thing, however, is for sure: the sooner you kill mania the better because you're a danger to yourself and other people when you don't know what you're doing. The longer mania is allowed to continue the longer and more severe the inevitable depression will be.

The problem is that mania is a unique and sometimes beautiful experience, even though its genius is flawed and must be quelled. The irony is that it draws strength from imperfection. Think of the Mona Lisa without her eyebrows. She's more appealing because there's something that's not quite right. She is in some way different, contrary to the norm, and thus fascinates the observer.

I also draw strength from Van Gogh, as I imagine him painting just down the road from me in Stockwell. Slipping in and out of consciousness when writing, I try to summon up his 'madness'.

Finally, I take comfort from the poet and composer, Ivor Gurney. Like me he was manic, and like me he came from Gloucester and moved to South London. Apparently, he would often walk from one to the other, singing folk music and sleeping in barns along the way.

...

Hucclecote, one of the more pleasant areas of Gloucester (although still with its fair share of pingheads and run-of-the-mill crims loitering outside the Wagon and the shops), is about a mile, mile and a half outside the town centre on the Cheltenham side. We moved there because my parents were keen that my brother, Harvey, and I did well at school – Hucclecote is a bike ride away from the renowned grammar school, Sir Thomas Rich's, in Longlevens. The plan was that we would each would pass our Eleven Plus and get in.

Green Lane, where I lived, was quiet, (lower-) middle class and had a huge green at the end of it. Because it's right on Hucclecote Road, access to either Gloucester, or its more upmarket neighbour Cheltenham located only seven miles away, is easy. But that's enough on Gloucester for now. Let's meet the family.

My dad. A senior fireman, often under stress, worked extremely hard all his life (saving two lives in the process) and was the best snooker player in the district for the best part of his life, as well as a pretty good golfer. In fact, he still is. My mum. More maternal than perhaps is the norm, liked staying at home (although always had a part-time job) tidying up and drinking tea. Imaginative and strangely fond of teddy bears. Harvey. More complex – see below.

...

When I was seven, my parents were advised to put me up a year as I was streets ahead of everyone else. I didn't want to because I was scared of being bullied. There again, at the same time, two boys were bullying me in my own year so what the hell – they'd pick on me when the rest of the class

14

were in orchestra and insult me by calling me *brainy*. They'd also hit me and once, when I kicked one of them in retaliation, I missed all my lunchtimes for a week because I was too scared to tell the headmistress that I was provoked. The timing was ironic because, the very same morning she'd reprimanded me, she'd made an announcement in assembly that there was to be no kicking in the school. As things turned out, my parents were undecided as to whether to put me up a year (they were unable to discuss anything rationally) so I stayed put.

When I was nine, I won the Gloucester Chess Congress – out of 243 entrants. I won all eight of my games which, as far as I know, was and still is a record despite most of the competition being a year older than me. I also had the highest reading age throughout my school years and when everyone else was struggling with their 1-12 times tables I had already finished my 12-20s. I finished the year's maths cards in about four weeks so they forced me to do comprehension for the rest of the year. That was after I'd completed another load of maths cards ordered specially for me. In hindsight, there was little to keep my buzzing brain occupied. A pity, because I loved learning. But not only at school.

When I was little, I enjoyed playing the map game with my dad. He'd place a big wooden map on the floor and I'd learn every capital in the world. He would then test me not only on capitals, but on flags too. I even learnt all the American states in alphabetical order.

And when sport was on the TV, or when he'd tuck me in, he also used to pretend he was the greatest sportsman in the world at everything. Which to many, it seemed he was: he had about a hundred trophies for sports but wouldn't display them in the lounge. He was reserved, certainly no show off; a man of action, not of words who slogged his guts out providing for his family. This was my dad and I was proud of him. He would always work overtime or play golf, volleyball or snooker. He was extremely competitive and a perfectionist in everything he did. I knew I possessed his natural doggedness in competition with my success at football, chess and rugby.

My greatest achievements had been winning the County Under- 11, 15, 18 and Southwest Under-16 Chess Championships. This was my life and it was unique. It would become more and more unique but unfortunately not in the way that I had once envisaged.

I had some very unhappy moments in junior school. This was largely because the other kids were jealous of my intelligence. I didn't feel very popular although I discovered that the best looking girl in the school fancied me after I dropped a Valentine's card round her house. My mum drove me round there and I placed it in the letterbox then darted off as if I had just stolen someone's bag from a pub. Eventually, I ended up 'smooching' with her at the junior disco only to ruin things by proceeding to beat up another kid who interfered. That was not how the junior school social clique led by Cheryl Long worked, and once I'd blown it there was no way back in.

When I was nine our school went away on camp. I won a moonie competition with two other boys in my class. We were trying to shock the girls and I won hands down as I went one step further than my classmates, showing the four prettiest girls in the school my cock in private. In return they agreed to let me see their bare arses – they didn't let me down. Not a bad day's work, all the more so for the fact that nobody else had had that privilege, at least as far as I knew. However, one of them said my dick looked like a sausage and for the rest of the excursion proceeded to sing "Moonie Addict" at me in place of "Sister Addict".

I spent the last two nights of that particular holiday experiencing my first "breakdown". I spoke to one of the teachers in charge of us who had never taught me. Mrs. Knight was a scary looking woman with black curly hair and always wore funny scarves that made her look older than she was. She had a reputation for being strict but was quite sympathetic with my situation. I told her that my parents were separated. My mum was living round my Nan's and they were going to get a divorce. They were also planning to drag my older brother and me through the courts. She understood and said something like: "Unfortunately it's something that happens, but I'm sure the worst is over ... Just hold on tight, and everything will be OK. You'll see my dear." I told her that I didn't mind if they got divorced. In fact, I wanted them to. I was just sick of the arguing and sick of being used as a go between. I was fed up with being dragged through shit.

There were psychologically traumatising incidents at school. The other boys didn't like me because I would score more goals than everyone else put together in every football match – during breaks and for the school team. I beat them all at chess, spelling, reading, writing, and even Top Trumps – I had a photographic memory for learning numbers so knew which category to pick on each card.

One week, however, they got their own back on me. Because I was a Man U supporter, every lunch and break time they paraded round the school singing: "We all hate Man United, they're not gonna win the league, and we'll really shake them up when they lose the FA Cup 'cause United are the crappest football team." They would follow me round whenever I was in the playground and some of them would push me. Sometimes this made me cry; at other times it made me angry but the chanting would continue irrespectively.

The experience reminded me of my first day in junior school when kids from the upper year picked on me because my brother and his mates had picked on them in their previous years. Now, though, he had left and was at a different school unable to protect me. As for the bullies in my year, I was stronger than they were individually but not collectively – although with one exception: a boy from Canada who marched on his own singing. He supported Norwich City. Now that took guts and stupidity. It got to me so much that I told the teacher who rounded the ringleaders up. He went ape shit and, with the whole year in a specially arranged meeting, demanded that they all apologise to me. They did, but the scars are still there somewhere in my subconscious. One teacher used to make me come in early at lunchtimes because I sweated so much. *Fucking bitch. I'd slit her throat if I ever saw her again. Who the fuck did she think she was? Was she some kind of Dominatrix or something? Now that would have been more interesting.*

One consolation for the unhappy moments in my childhood was my dog, Ben. I'd asked for a dog when I was nine and for once my dad caved in. When we took him home, he stank of shit so my mum and dad gave him a bath. The first night, he shat all over the house and whined incessantly. My dad wanted to take him back the next morning so I slept with him the next night to try and keep him quiet. He stayed in our house by the skin of his canine teeth and everyone eventually came to love him. He was so cute as a puppy with his big head and his big paws. We'd take him for walks down the green and he was dead happy running around, chasing balls and sticks, and wagging his tail. He became very loyal and my mum and I took him to training classes. He finally became house trained and a good guard dog. He was part of the family and stayed with dad, Harvey and me when mum left.

For various reasons, he fell into my mum's hands in 1995 and she projected her love for everyone else onto him. Ultimately, though, he was still my dog and acknowledged that with the look he sometimes gave me. The last time I saw him as a manic I made him head police dog of the world to stomp out crime, once and for all. His back legs weakened and grey fur appeared round his face as he reached old age. His acceptance into the family seemed to symbolise my parents staying together until I was 15. Then my mum left home and, after moving out of her mother's went to live with Michael, now my step dad. I liked him a lot and made a speech supporting them at their wedding. The only wedding I have ever been to is my mum's. Michael would always be the joker and liked rugby. Once he watched me play and I scored the only try of the game. He had taken my mum to Wales and I didn't think I minded because she was happy.

My grandfather died when I was 14. His was the first dead body I ever saw. He died of angina in 1989. I kissed his cold forehead on my Nan's request in the funeral parlour and watched my brother do the same. It was a peculiar moment. I tried to comfort myself by thinking of an afterlife but was beaten by what I saw: he was dead. What was more distressing was the way my Nan was behaving: "Doesn't he look nice and smart in that suit? He was always smart, Colin, his hair and his clothes; always immaculate." My Nan started to cry and I hugged her tightly as she cracked up.

Aware of her devastation, I cried too. They had been happily married for 52 years and now she was alone: nobody to cook for, or to snuggle up with by the fire during cold, wet and windy nights; nobody to make those special cups of tea; nobody to talk to when she was happy and nobody to talk to when she was sad; nobody to cuddle and, worst of all, nobody to sleep with at night. That's if my Nan would ever be able to go to sleep again. For six months after his death she slept downstairs in the lounge, too scared to sleep upstairs without him, and lived in that big house alone. He had provided for her, paid the bills, protected her and given her life a purpose. He had given her everything.

All that remained were memories of the time they had spent together, objects they had obtained over the years and photographs they had taken of one another. Today, a picture stands in the lounge of my granddad when he was young. My Nan always shows it to new visitors and has told me a thousand times that I have the same eyes as him and that I am as kind as he was. Well, I'm happy for my Nan to recognise a likeness between us but I know that I'm not as kind as he was.

He was a bit of a saint. Everyone liked him. For 25 years, he worked for Morses and was the top local salesman. If people couldn't afford what they had ordered, but he could, he would pay for them out of his own wages so they wouldn't get into trouble. What's more, he would never ask for the money back. As the vicar said at his funeral: "I didn't know Colin personally, but I am struck today by what a special person everyone I have spoken to says he was."

The only time I ever saw him angry was when it came to my dad. Let's just say they didn't get on. Despite this, he still let my dad boss my mum around when he could have easily stepped in. If I was in his shoes, I know I would have.

He was passive; a true gentleman. He was the sort of man who would not speak during dinner because it was rude. He was no coward but someone who did things by the book. He was the youngest of 13 brothers and sisters and times were hard when he grew up. They would have to ration their food and yet he managed to break away, find a steady job and pay off a mortgage. He had bettered himself and was content. My saddest memory of his life is that he never went abroad. He always wanted to but my Nan was scared of flying so they never did. He didn't want to upset her so that was the end of that.

I never had the opportunity to talk with him at great length: he was always ill when I was growing up and couldn't speak very well either because of chronic bronchitis or a sore throat. He was no intellectual but would read detective novels every evening by the fire. The only practical things I learned from him were not to have gravy on a Sunday lunch and not to smoke like he had. Through him, though, I learnt something very important: that it's OK for a man to have a sensitive side, especially with a woman – and that most women actually prefer it.

...

I had experienced violence in my life but never saw myself as a violent person, except for the odd bit of vandalism when I'd drunk too much. There again, I was always fighting on the rugby field and was banned for two months when I was 16. However, although this was aggression, at least it was in a controlled environment. As for fights on the street, I never started any of them, I just seemed to be in the wrong place at the wrong time. I was also never a bully, and would even stick up for the geek in my year at school. He used to be tormented for peeing his pants and I stopped him from being kicked and teased on several occasions. Strangely enough – or not as the case may be – he went to Oxford and read biochemistry.

Anyway, back to the rugby. I played rugby for Gloucester Under- 16s, when even the fantastic England hooker Phil Greening didn't make the team. Mind you, he was a year younger than everyone else at the trial. I reckon I could have gone far if someone had taken me under their wing. One of the teachers at school, Mr Goddard, wanted me to play for Berry Hill and be captain of a team he was coaching. If I'd taken the weights more seriously and stayed off the drink I could have made it. I don't need anybody else to tell me that. From the age of 15 I was playing for Old Richian's Colts who were one of the best Under-19 teams in the country. In the three seasons I played for them, we won 58 games, drew one and lost one. I scored loads of tries and would often have write-ups in The Citizen, Gloucester's paper.

…

Despite having freckles and some fairly bad acne I always seemed to attract girls. When I was 16 I had a girlfriend for a few months but we never had sex. I tried to at my mum's house one time but I was drunk, had taken speed and magic mushrooms, and couldn't get it up. Our relationship was absurd – she never said a word. We two-timed each other and eventually split up. A few weeks later, though, I heard she still fancied me so I asked her out again with the sole intention of dumping her to get revenge. It worked but I still never fucked her. I mean, what was the problem?

I also remember having an aching hard-on with several naked girls when I was 14 but they wouldn't let me have sex with them – either because they didn't want to get pregnant or because they didn't want to be called slags. There again, I did manage to push it in to one of them but she wriggled off. In the event, I started fucking one who had passed out but she woke up barfing on my shoe. Her friends broke in and gave

21

her a bath to sober her up.

It was frustrating. When I was 14 I started getting drunk and was forever snogging girls. It was easy. Then it became more difficult. I think I got a bad reputation for drinking a lot – perhaps some girls had heard that I didn't finish the job off properly; or maybe I was getting ugly, unlucky or turning into a homosexual.

The first time I came in a pussy I was 15. It was with this really sexy French brunette. She screamed a lot and kept saying "Oui", obviously enjoying it, which was exciting, but at the same time rather vacuous. My problem was that I was too proud. For example, when I was 14 a girl I had been getting off with who was older than me asked if I was a virgin. I tried to be cool and said no. Her reaction was to think I would be unfaithful to her if we had sex. I'd made the wrong decision and would see my first shag put back for a while.

By the age of 14 I'd been to my first rave but I didn't go regularly until I was 16 or 17. Fantasia was the most successful legalised rave in 1993, and I went to one at Castle Donnington. Twenty-eight thousand people were there and I had three rhubarb and custards. After all, I hadn't had any tea. I didn't have a ticket but told the bouncers that a gang in the queue had stole mine. The second security guard I told this story to must have bought it or at least admired my audacity as he gave me a ticket. Two girls who were friends of my brother drove me there and I didn't see them until seven the next morning. I spent 11 hours walking around hiding my t-shirt which had a huge "E" on it under my jacket – a raver too terrified to dance in case anybody laughed at him for being the worst "mover" there. Thing is, I knew I was a great dancer. That's how paranoid pills can make you. Every hour I'd go to meet my friend Peach at the fairground, but he wasn't there as we'd arranged. I found out later that a group from the rock- head tent had mugged him.

The only people I saw who I knew I steered clear of including MC Al'n and his posse. He was a dodgy bloke who sold fake acid and walked off with people's cash. Mind you, he'd always been all right to me. I also saw DJ Spider who was a major drug dealer in the Forest of Dean. I'd taken my first E at the age of 15 when I was round his house. I also saw this huge guy called Steve, who I had beaten up previously, with his crew. This was seven months before my manic depression first surfaced.

Steve exemplified what I hated about Gloucester. It was full of small-minded people who would judge you without reason. There was no reason for him to fight except for his rotten ego. I was outside Fifth Avenue with my brother, Dom and his sister Tara when Steve approached us with an accomplice.

"What are you doing here? Get off my fucking road. I'm going down this alley and if you're still here when I get back, I'm going to kick the shit out of you – all of you."

My brother and Dom were sat cross-legged wearing headbands. They said that they didn't want any trouble and were ready to leave. I wasn't, I was sick of being bossed around. I mean I might have let my parents, the bullies when I was little, and some hard nuts in the past bully me, but nobody else. No way. I had to make a stand. Steve returned from the alley and I had just about convinced everyone to stay put.

"What, you still here?"

"Who do you think you are?" I calmly replied.

I could feel butterflies in my stomach. I was 6'3" and 14 stone but this guy was 6'5" and 18 stone. We stood opposite each other, and I couldn't resist it when he took a swing at me. I dodged out of the way and swung my hips giving him a right hook to the side of his head. He dropped straight to the floor. As I kicked him in the head a few times, Dom prevented his friend from intervening and Tara urged me to stop. The fat slob on the deck eventually managed to get back up. He put his arm round me and congratulated me saying that he had wanted a pop at me since he met me at a party a few years back. He said he had a knife in his pocket and that he could have killed me.

I remained quiet as he left praying for some more action.

But what for? This was one of so many fights that I had and so minor in comparison to others I had already had and would have in the future. Believe me, the great brawl scene in Scorsese's *Mean Streets* was a weekly occurrence in Gloucester. It was a rugby town where everyone thought that they were bigger and better than they were. Small-minded and arrogant locals drank shit-loads of booze after a mind numbingly boring week. That's how they let themselves go, by picking on some poor sod or group of sods. To make things worse, they were never held accountable for anything, the police were often too scared to intervene. Meanwhile, less than a mile from where I decked Steve, Fred West was rearranging his house and proudly adding to his collection of dead bodies. I wasn't surprised when the story broke out because I always felt there was something odd and perverse about Gloucester – a sinister undercurrent if you like.

...

On the subject of oddness, mad people in Gloucester were sent, for recuperative purposes, to Coney Hill hospital – the butt of much local humour. I'd never known anyone who had gone there despite the fact that there was a history of mental instability in my family. I knew that my Grandma's brother had killed himself just after World War II, thinking the Germans were still after him. I also knew she had been institutionalised herself before. She'd attempted suicide by filling the house with gas and putting her head in the oven. Her ex-husband, my Uncle Tom, had returned to find her unconscious and took her to hospital.

My grandmother would always tell me a story about her conquering her mental breakdown and compare it to how she had given up smoking. The thing is, years later, she started smoking again. The story goes something like this.

"I tried to kill myself twice – not once, but twice. The first time, I was depressed because my ex-husband Tom had left me. He'd been having an affair. Anyway, I don't want to talk about that. It won't cheer you up. No, listen to this ... (Prodding my forearm with her finger and then sipping some gin.) I let gas off all over my kitchen and stuck my head in the oven. Somebody called for the ambulance and I was barely conscious. Lucky to be alive, I can tell you, at least that's what the nurse at the hospital told me afterwards (laughs, gulps down some more gin then regains her composure). They took me to a mental hospital and it looked like hell on earth. Remember, suicide, or rather attempted suicide, was illegal in those days so they could have arrested me... I could have been arrested. Anyway, back to what happened. As soon as I saw the state of the patients in there ... the poor sods ... I immediately decided that I was not going to stay there and demanded to see the doctor. I remember the doctor; he was a lovely man. I told him that I wasn't mad and wasn't staying with those people in there. They weren't well and I wasn't going to feel any better by being there.

The doctor held me by the hand and said: 'What you did, Mrs. Best, wasn't a cry for help. You really meant it didn't you?'

"You bet I did. By God, I meant it. I wanted to end my life. "'Well, that's a very brave thing you did Mrs. Best,' he agreed. You know, Jason my darling (reaching for my hand and squeezing it), that same man, the doctor – I can't remember his name – told me that I was one of the most intelligent people he had ever met. You see kid, that's where you get your intelligence from – not your mother or your father or your Nana. It's me kid.

"You see, Jason, that was the first and only time that I have been in a mental hospital. From that moment on I decided that I would never go into one again. It was as simple as that. I suffered depression for years after that, mind you. But I will never go back to a place like that. Only to see you, and I don't want to see you in a place like that again dear boy."

One or both of us would cry when she told me this story although the more senile she became the more she repeated it and the more disillusioned I would get. If she told it to me when I was really depressed I would think that I was a weaker person than she was ... If she told it me at any other time I would think she misunderstood my situation. No two circumstances were the same and I thought my illness was clearly worse than hers ever was. It had been diagnosed and she had never had to experience mania or the coming to terms with it. Although she cared a great deal in her own way, she could only offer comfort on the rare occasion when I was so depressed that I would have believed anything she said. In those states of mind, I would even have listened to a vicar.

That was the version of being mentally ill my grandmother told me when she was drunk. When she was sober, it was a less dramatic but more detailed story. You see, she was depressed whenever she was sober unless she was playing scrabble with her friends or touring round the Lake District. Her sober narration went something like this.

"In 1953 or 1954 (I can't remember which) I was admitted to Lancaster Moor Hospital. My name was Mrs. Crichton then. The Doctor summoned me and offered me coffee. Now, that was unheard of in those days. He told me never to allow anybody to tell me that I was mentally ill, and that just because I was in for the so-called 17-day section, didn't mean I was crazy.

However, I wished I was dead. I was in love with a married man named Bobby, but he said that he would never divorce his wife. He was a farmer. He had fourteen farms and three slaughterhouses. Farmers didn't want to divorce in those days because they didn't want to split the land. Divorce was a dirty word, I can tell you. I became really depressed and got a chopper from the kitchen in my house in Barrow and breathed in gas out of the hole I made in the tube. I can't remember anything else. All the doors were locked. The next thing I remember was your Great Nana sat on top of me pumping my arms up and down. I never wanted to be saved and wished – and still do wish – that I was dead. An ambulance and doctor came and took me off to Lancaster Moore Mental Hospital. It took 40 minutes. I arrived at nine and that morning was like an unending desert of time. They gave me some aspirins, which I'm allergic to, and some other drugs – I can't remember their name.

"I kept myself to myself and always sat by a window. I always wanted to see outside. Bobby came to see me out of guilt and gave me 200 Players cigarettes. I had known him five years.

"My mother was very cruel to me. She'd even thrown my father, Joseph Henry, out when I was nine and my brother, Jack, eight. I hate her for that. He was a man who loved his children and was nicknamed "Snowy" because of his silver white hair. He worked for Vickers. They were in Barrow and built warships, submarines and cruisers. He'd fought in the World War I – which was enough to drive any man mad. The last time I saw him was in court. My mother had taken him there for non-payment of rent which didn't really affect her because I paid most of it anyway. She just did it out of spite.

"Your Great Nana, that's my mother, was always jealous of all of my friends. She was always away when I grew up. I lived with my Auntie Nellie from the age of 11 until I was 16 or 17, I can't remember exactly. I didn't see much of her when I was growing up and it was upsetting to see her jealous. She even became jealous of Auntie Nellie. I mean, I loved Auntie Nellie but that never compared to the love I had for my mother. I mean, that was different. Everyone knows that. One other thing, Jason, simple people don't go mad. Brainy people do. Remember that, Jason my darling. Come and give your Grandma a big hug. There, there."

I asked my grandmother about two other members of our family that had suffered from mental illness and was disturbed by some of the things she told me. I knew about her brother and thought I'd leave that until last so I asked her first of all about Auntie Ethel Thomson. My grandmother was a great storyteller.

"My Auntie, Ethel Thomson, killed herself in 1932, maybe three or even four, I can't remember. She was a depressive. She was terribly sad. Now, I was born in Barrow-in-Furness, on 29 December, 1919 so I was about 14 when it happened. The poor woman. She was better off for doing it though, I can tell you. She was always crying, and ran a corner shop with her mother. Hospitals were very strict in those days. She had an illegitimate child. This was seen as a terrible thing to do back then. They wouldn't let her out of the hospital, but somehow she managed to get out and she ran under the railway line and flung herself under a train. This was in February. They found her foot a mile down the line. They found her head stuck to the end of the train. They left patients in there for years and years. Some of them were in there for the rest of their lives. They didn't know what to do with them then; there was no treatment for it.

"It was my Jack who told me that Ethel had killed herself on a Sunday morning. I used to visit her in there. It was at Lancaster Moor Hospital – the same one that Jack and I were in. People used to jeer at them and make fun of them but it wasn't their fault that they were ill. That's not right. They were still human beings just like you and me."

I saved talking about Jack in detail until last because I knew it would upset my grandmother the most. "Jack Crichton Thompson, my brother, God bless him, was born on 14 October, 1917. He worked on a machine in Vickers in Barrow. It was semi-skilled factory work that concentrated mostly on shipbuilding. He suffered from severe depression and used to cry all the time. It struck him in his late 20s or early 30s, I can't remember exactly. Before then, we'd always be joking and laughing not like all the miserable sods today. In 1936, King Edward V11 gave up the throne. Your Great Nana and I had a fish and chip shop.

"Jack was very popular. He would go for a drink with other young lads at the Plaza in 1936. They went ballroom dancing. Oh, there was less crime then; the world was less violent. People fought the enemy then, not each other. At the age of 22, he was married with three children. He kept working somehow and joined the army of occupation in 1944, in Belgium.

"I moved to Gloucester, and sometime after that, Renée, my brother's wife, wrote to me and told me that Jack was unwell. She explained how he had sat on the wall in Cavendish Square in Barrow laughing to himself. Then

Renée threw Jack out. They split up sometime between 1960 and 1964. Jack probably knew that she was having an affair but nobody else found out until later on. He worked for a few more months but was finally admitted to Lancaster Moor hospital. I went up and spoke to the psychiatrist. Jack was so sad. I gave him a sandwich and he wolfed it down. I took him back to Gloucester to the wine shop with me for a few days. I remember that his face lit up when I said that I was going to take him out of that horrible place. Soon after, I decided to take him out for good and look after him.

"Tom was wonderful with him. Jack went off and Tom went looking for him.

"Jack had a funny appetite. He didn't eat. He couldn't walk. He badly needed treatment and we didn't know what to do with him so, as a last measure, we took him to hospital in Gloucester on a Sunday. Jack wandered off and moved to live with your Great Nana on Stanley Road. I had my own shop where the big Debenhams is now. It was a wine shop at 15 St Aldgate Street. I paid the rent for the wine shop and the rent for your Great Nana's mortgage. Tom was the meanest man in the world when it came to money. Jack lived at Stanley Road for a year. He saw doctors and took pills. He was on medication.

"A week after he died a man came in the shop. I was Mrs. Pegler then. The doctor said that he would have killed himself if he was in the same situation and his words gave, and still give, me great comfort whenever I think about your uncle Jack, and my brother, God bless him. Jack was taking pills, you see, and had overdosed. All that day, I remember as if it were yesterday. I had been extremely worried. I was manager of the shop and couldn't leave it, but I wish I had. By God, I wish I had. Your Great Nana and I watched him die in hospital. It was a relief. He couldn't suffer any more pain that way. He had suffered enough, you see.

"He had schizophrenia not manic depression like you. It was down on his record. He would hallucinate. He would open curtains an inch and see thousands of soldiers in the street thinking they were coming for him. He was terrified. I would go along with it. I didn't want him to feel that he was on his own, you see. 'Don't worry, they're nothing to do with us,' I would say. 'They're from the council,' or something like that, I would say. I used to make it up as I went along. One of the symptoms of his illness was suspicion. I made sure never to contradict him. Oh my poor brother. He missed his children."

I was very touched by what my grandmother had told me about members of our family and their illnesses. I felt sorry for the fact that she'd witnessed so much suffering in her life. I knew that she would have been very good working with the mentally ill. She understood them and empathised with them, you see. I know my mum would be good at that too – especially now she's experienced so much of what it is like with me. It takes special people to be good mental health nurses and there should be certain additional prerequisites to qualify. For example empathy, understanding, a specifically trained knowledge of mental illnesses, and the social skills necessary for this type of care.

I asked my Grandmother to think of one happy memory of her brother and she immediately mentioned one time when he had come home on leave from the army. "He'd put on weight, looked fit – like a proper soldier – and said that he would have loved to have been in the army for the rest of his life." That made me feel more at ease when I put my pen down after our heart to heart. At least we'd ended on a positive note.

I had a bit of a headache, felt a bit anxious and thought of how my Grandma told me that she loved nothing more than walking across Walney beach in Barrow with the wind on her face. She loved the wind and the freedom of the lakes and, despite her depression, idiosyncrasies and unpopularity within the family, was actually a remarkable woman. I hoped that I would always remember her as that. A remarkable woman who had worked until she was well into her seventies and who had led an interesting life travelling all over the world.

Thing is, there had been a lot of problems in my family

life and a lot of people felt that she was to blame for them. She had helped my mum and dad out of debts when they were younger and paid for my dad to go to America where he met my step mum Clare, but she always wanted something in return. She was an interfering woman but cooked me a lot of meals after my mum left and gave me a lot of money to go out with my friends. After I left for university, it would upset me seeing her. She had senile dementia and I couldn't handle her mood swings. Maybe she was a manic-depressive – I didn't know and most of the time I didn't want to think about it. If she wasn't then she was a moaner. Always moaning about what she had given people and that she had got nothing in return. She wasn't making herself any happier by moaning about everything but she could never snap out of it, and that was the most tragic thing in her life. Not that she had tried to kill herself, or that Bobby never left his wife, or that she was unpopular but that she was unable to forget about things and move forward. If she could have done that she'd have been a lot happier, as would have everybody she came into contact with. Because of her, other members of the family had to try harder to get along.

However, I am very grateful to her and always will be for a number of reasons – for example she supported me emotionally when mum left, and took me on my first aeroplane. I was 12 and Harvey was 16. The three of us went to Greece on a historic tour. We went to Athens, Corinth, Olympia and Delphi. It gave me a unique insight into the classical world. I stood on running tracks at the awesome amphitheatres and imagined the competitors in the ancient Olympiads. I stared out from under the Acropolis in the intense heat with a sense of nostalgia that I had never had before. I would always remember the amazing view of the Gulf of Corinth. The classical world was closer to me than it had ever been and led me to study classical civilisation at A-level.

Chapter 2 – I've lost it

My first episode occurred when I was 17 – possibly a result of drugs – and hospitalised me for six months. There were no warning signs before the avalanche of mental illness engulfed me although certain factors doubtless played a role: unhappy marriage, divorced parents, domestic violence, heavy alcohol intake and, of course, cannabis, LSD, speed and ecstasy.

This was nothing out of the ordinary, though, and was standard for someone growing up in the 1990s. Take my brother. He was studying a philosophy degree in London and took drugs for "intellectual reasons", as he put it. For example he wanted to know what it was like to listen to Sgt. Pepper on LSD. He did that and was proud of that. I was just as curious about taking drugs as he was, that's why I took acid before he did, but the fact was that everyone was doing it. Meanwhile, I was becoming obsessed with the rave scene. I would steal from my father and sell drugs at school to feed my habits for amphetamine and alcohol. The pleasant rural area that I lived in was notorious for pingheads residing in various squats. These special-brew addicts would do anything for a bag of billy. They just loved cooking up and, while this repulsed me, I actually thought they were quite cool. Now I just feel sorry for them.

A part of me regrets getting ill so soon as I never got round to taking as many drugs as my friends. I loved to go raving. I loved dancing to the hardcore. I loved the rush and the way the girls danced. It really turned me on. The whole movement gave me an identity during my adolescence.

I first "officially" went mad – experienced the unexplainable phenomenon of mania – in Gloucester in November 1993, aged 17. It's impossible to say when it started exactly, it may have just surfaced then, but nobody can prove that is wasn't there all along. Just because I was diagnosed then didn't mean that I didn't have it before. As I remember it, I'd gone to stay with my best friend, Dominic, at the university in Swansea and we went to a few clubs. He's medium height, pretty stocky, has dark hair, extremely intelligent, has a sick sense of humour like me and always looks a bit worried except when he's laughing.

I took a White Calais and a Pink New Yorker in this hardcore club called Martha's on the Kingsway. That night, DJ Lomas was making a special appearance. I stomped around until ten in the morning but seemed to get higher and higher for the next two weeks. One minute I was an aspiring clubber along with my friend and his acquaintances; the next minute things had got completely out of control.

I first remember completely losing the plot at school in an English A-level lesson. We had a double lesson on Ursula Fanthorpe and her poetry. This lesbian had inspired our overweight but raunchy English teacher into reaffirming her feminism. My mind was racing far quicker than it could do in a sane state. I wouldn't let anybody voice their opinions. I recall being drawn into one poem as it mentioned Lechlade. Only a few weeks before there had been an illegal rave there that the police had been unable to stop. Twenty-five thousand people turned up and in my confusion I thought the revolution had come. As Lechlade wasn't far from Gloucester perhaps I was needed to front it? A madman makes links in this way and in the early stages of mania can have extraordinary confidence.

After having informed the class what it had been like to be at Lechlade, I proclaimed and repeated several times that everything was a paradox. Nobody, outwardly at least, disagreed with me. Either they were in shock or they were scared to be sparked out by a psycho. When I was asked to define the word "paradox" my immediate response was to say that the question was a paradox in itself. Alas, the mania only had its own internal logic you see. One eccentric member of the class who had been put forward to sit the Oxford entrance exam with me interrupted my Virginia

Woolf-like stream of consciousness monologue, to which I responded: "Shut up Mr. Lockwood", which he did straight away.

My mind had been bordering on the absurd since I'd stayed, along with my English class, in the middle of the Yorkshire Moors a couple of weeks previously. The night before I had gone to a rave club and spent the entire night paranoid and lunched out on three trips. I had had no sleep and was fucked for the next four days. I hardly said a word on the five hour minibus journey and was just as paranoid with my classmates as I had been in the club. I remember the trip extremely well. We were studying the novel Wuthering Heights and spent the weekend at a grand and beautiful cottage. It was completely isolated just like the two houses in the novel *Wuthering Heights* and *Thrushcross Grange*. The weekend turned out to be a pilgrimage into the world of the Brontës and each of us recorded the events in a diary as they happened. We went to the Brontë museum, saw Penistone Crags where Heathcliff and Cathy professed their love for each other, and even walked through the graveyard where Emily Brontë is buried. I found the latter disturbing and remember the weather being particularly foggy.

After having a fucking strong Lebanese joint that I had picked up from a traveller the previous week I told my entire life story to a member of the class, Chris. He was black, very kind and intelligent, and his dad was a lawyer. He also knew a lot about the rave scene so I had respect for him. Once, he sent me a Christmas card with a poem he'd written about Mciing and getting off his head – and this guy was drug free. Now that was the sign of a tough cookie. I admired that. All his friends were on drugs and most of them dealt, but he was clean.

I was totally off my head as we sat on a fence in those bucolic surroundings and ranted on about everything that had gone wrong in my life. He would listen and on the odd occasion give words of advice. Sometimes in life he said it is "good to take three steps forward and then a step back". I thought of his interesting words but it was already too late. I had stepped too far forward and my legs would soon buckle under the pressure and be scarred forever.

In the club, two of my friends, Dom and Tim, were just as paranoid as I was. We sat cross-legged in the chill out room too scared to dance and too afraid to talk to each other. I broke the silence by asking someone to give me some Vicks Vaporub. He took the nasal stick out of the tube and rubbed it around my eyes. I sat down blinded, fearing that I would never be able to see again. One of my friends asked me what I had been talking about. My only response was to say that there was a guy in Swindon who had taken over 500 ecstasy tablets so far that year, 1993. My heart rate increased, and I struggled to handle a dozen Es. I felt weak psychologically as there was a simple philosophy in club life: the more Es, coke and ketamine you've taken the cooler you are perceived to be. It was a mad week which started with 15000 watts of hardcore pumping out and it took its toll, but it was nothing compared to the madness which had started to poison me during that English lesson. The only surprise was that I hadn't gone mad during a lesson on the manic-depressive Sylvia Plath's *Bell Jar* whose text I was also studying at the time.

My mind became more and more complex. My English teacher asked to see me after school on the day I lost it in her lessons. As I walked in to greet her I felt on top of the world. For whatever reason, although possibly because I felt secure in the knowledge that I was top of the class, I confessed everything about my drug taking to her. I was satisfied in the knowledge that I would form a sexual relationship with her although I anticipated that I would be the submissive one.

"Jason, before you say anything come and sit next to me and tell me what's going on." I replied in what I thought was an assured manner.

"There's going to be a nuclear war and I'm going to stop it. Look at these books… It all makes sense…"

"Are you on drugs?"

I was proud to inform her of my previous antics. "I've been smoking hash since I was 14, and have had speed, acid and ecstasy loads of times. Some of it's mixed with coke, smack and ketamine (that's a tranquilliser used on horses). I've had opium as well but never injected anything. Some of my mates do that, down the squat. (Mrs. Barnes proceeded to burst out in buckets of tears.)

"Oh you poor dear. Drugs are bad for you (now holding my hand). Don't you realise that? You've got to stop taking them. Will you promise to stop taking them for me?"

"Yes, miss."

"That's a good boy. Is anyone else taking drugs in the school?"

"At the end of the fifth year, 40 of my year had taken acid. There's a few in our form now. Chris, Nick, Ali, Paul, Mark, Gary and Emma, but none of them have taken as much as me. There's a few on acid in the fourth year, like Hanks, and they're all good recruits in helping to stop the nuclear war… I'm setting out a plan… got to succeed…"

"No more outbreaks in class, Ok? Go home and get some rest. Try to get some sleep tonight. Promise."

"Promise."

Meanwhile, I was positioning myself to be head of the European Hard core Committee. I mean, what the fuck was that? My intention was to create world peace by having everybody take drugs and dance as "one family". What a crock of shit. All I had done was take a rave anthem and attributed grandiose thoughts to it. I might as well have been one of the pingheads down the squat jabbering their heads off on billy. I wasn't changing the world. I wasn't making any difference whatsoever. Yes, I could have been staring out of a window at a tree for four hours without moving a muscle as one of my friends told me he had done. I would realise several months later that my thoughts were on a different level. At least when cooking up, you know when to expect the hit. I was permanently buzzing on another level.

I became fascinated by my untheorised theory that a nuclear war was imminent and proceeded to inform my friends of the phenomenon. First, I visited my good friend Brad (he was a pinghead so was therefore definitely on the

36

level). We knew each other so well he would understand. He told me that he would buy me any reading material if it would help prevent the war. In my manic state, I manoeuvred everything in my room into a strategic position planning an unplanned course of action.

I set about organising a trip to Cheltenham to see Macbeth ... I wanted to reserve 12 seats and sit people in particular positions so they could discuss in detail which role they would take in my anti-nuclear war alliance. I rode round to see friends who showed apparent interest, but before the performance intense paranoia had set in. My closest friend was actually my worst enemy ... Everybody in Gloucester was plotting against me and I had to get out ... The only escape was to stay with another friend at Littledean in the Forest of Dean ...

My father's girlfriend, Claire, drove me to Gloucester bus station although I felt as if I was in a space shuttle ... From there I took the bus. The bus journey was ludicrous. I spent 25 minutes on the top deck of the double decker, at the back, speaking to a 14 year-old about my mission. *In my rucksack I had 30 or so books all of which were of significance and could be placed in strategic orders, coloured pencils, and several hardcore tapes each of which contained messages of prophecy ...* I told the boy that I was going to stop a nuclear war and that he should thank me ... I talked about rave culture and how it was taking over the world. During the entire journey he watched me intently but didn't utter a word. In hindsight, I think he was probably scared out of his wits and thought I was crazy. At the time, I thought he knew the score. I thought he was hard core and understood my mission. Maybe I should have listened to my brother who always said that repetitive music melts your brain and classical music enhances it. This is an intriguing point with some scientific evidence. Nevertheless, it was too late for me as the mania was too strong.   …

On arriving in Littledean, I was greeted with a cup of tea and a spliff and told to stop talking bollocks by my hippy and

37

magic mushroom-selling friend, Ashley. This was the same person who I had comforted for hours on the phone several times when he was scared he had astroprojected into another world. Maybe he did have an outer body experience or maybe he just couldn't handle his acid. He went to sleep while I went downstairs. The old house was dark and quiet. His hippie mother and father were asleep as was his 13 year-old sister.

I performed some kind of manic ritual in the kitchen taking all my clothes off and rolling my wrist around very quickly while keeping my thumb forward. This was a habit that I had acquired having taken four grams of speed when dancing to hardcore at a club called Brunel Rooms in Swindon. I stared at the digital time on the microwave and intelligently waited until 4.44am… Then I could transport myself into the future… My paranoia had turned into ecstasy, or so I thought.

In my eyes, my friend's mother was the healer of the world and it was my duty to make Stoic love to her… Then I would have prevented Armageddon and been initiated as head of the European Hard Core Committee by her husband… I thought back to those times when he let me pick magic mushrooms from his land. I looked back with pride on the day he chose me. This was when he asked me, in his kitchen, how many magic mushrooms I had picked. He had an endearing smile on his face with a sense of natural goodness, honour and integrity.

Now it was time to act on my manic impulses and bring about my destiny… I walked around the house entirely relaxed and stepped into the young daughter's room. She saw me naked and yawned in what seemed like a totally relaxed and expectant manner. I left with a feeling that I had conquered the world and given this Virgin Mary what she had been waiting for… I rested in the spare room feeling a cross between a king and Little Red Riding Hood … I opened the window expecting the wolf to come and was prepared to give it a beating. The monster would be followed by one of my many new female servants who would perform the sexual gratification that their master desired...

These rambling thoughts are typical of any manic episode and can never be properly understood unless you've experienced mania first hand. There are so many and they are so frequent that it is only possible to mention and recall a few of them. From the dominant master, I then focused on turning myself into an abject slave. I now took the line held by my English teacher. The first cultures were matriarchal and I sacrificed my mind, body and soul for the goodness of women and therefore mankind.

I can remember performing a ritual for my new mistress. I took a metal pole about two feet long out of the fireplace and placed it on the little finger of my right hand. There was some metal cord attached to it that I tied around my finger several times. As I did this, I relented my eternal craving and became the abject slave of a domineering woman.

By morning, I was still naked and from where he was feeding the horses her husband could see me in the spare room. In a firm manner he told me to get dressed. My friend saw the pole on my hand and told me to put it back before his mother got angry. I coyly replaced it and several minutes later I was watching television downstairs when my mistress asked me if I wanted some honey on toast. I was delighted – all the other times I'd stayed round there she had never offered me anything. I thought back to Jacques Lacan – live the language of your dreams. Therefore, in my mind, as soon as she uttered those words I had fucked her. I would never tell anyone as I feared my punishment for hubris would be too great... My imagination decided that her son and I would be treated like kings and would be given a different beautiful girl every night to copulate with... *Through this household world peace would begin to spread ...*

Her husband drove me home safely and quickly. Neither of us uttered a word. He arrived at my house, spoke to my father and left thick mud all over the carpet. Then I thought it was a compliment ... Now I know it was a sign of disrespect.

Soon after, two of my friends asked me to come out and smoke some spliff. I declined on my dad's advice. I think deep down I knew that something was wrong with me as I usually ignored what my father said. To this day I do not know what my father's conversation with the old hippie was about and am still too embarrassed to ask.

I tore up magazines and displayed them on the two single beds in my room. Some of them were pornographic, and I organised material thinking that I was a sexual guru ... The sister of my friend in Swansea was my next conquest ... I read her a love ode from Horace over the phone when she asked for my brother. I could tell she was turned on although she didn't admit it ... After all, she was still just about seeing my brother and I was four years younger than them.

She was a woman and according to my interpretation of Lacan I had made love to her along with every other woman on the planet. The only difference was that I had given this one special treatment.

I went to the bathroom and realised another part of my destiny. Unfortunately, I wasn't to be an Aeneas founding Troy but would settle for being the Head of English at Balliol College, Oxford. I was also destined to be the most respected poet in Britain. I searched through a Sylvia Plath book and noticed that I had bookmarked a page. It was the poem entitled "The Graduate". My rediscovery of this marking meant that I was going to graduate with flying colours and I had not even applied for university at this stage.

This elation was similar to an epiphany I had experienced while I had been on ecstasy the previous week. The lemon and lime I had consumed was mixed with ketamine, smack and acid. I was in a nightclub with my best mates, Brad who was pinging up speed at the time, and Dominic. We all necked one along with a virgin E taker who disappeared and later told us amazingly that he did not feel a thing except for the alcohol he was drinking. I was higher than a kite within half an hour and after five minutes of insane dancing I decided to watch the dance floor telling Dom that I would be the greatest writer in the world.

He was so off his box that he kept nodding his head and raising his eyebrows. The three of us walked home, and the ketamine made me feel five years old. Or was it the smack? Even now I don't know, I never mixed it whatever it was – but it was mind boggling. Dom walked home. Later, to my great surprise, he told me that he had gone straight to sleep. Brad and I talked until 9.00am about life, people, relationships, the universe and how we were going to pack the next spliff even more full of gear than the last one. We were stood in the local public toilets which were a common meeting point for pingheads. We shared the same cubicle once in a while taking it in turns to sit on the toilet seat. This was a crazy night, and I'd probably had the strongest pill I'd ever taken. There again, it's sweet fuck-all compared to mania.

Things were becoming more and more blurred. Somewhere in between my conscious and subconscious I believed that I had passed the next day's Oxford entrance exam without even sitting it. The exam was due the day I went into hospital and I was in no state to sit it. Despite correctly anticipating that Hardy's poems, and not his prose, were to be discussed, another manic realisation would be in vain.

I was to experience a journey that was to be way beyond the realms of normal consciousness. The indescribable and extraordinary links occurred more frequently and became more severe. By morning, I had demolished my room pushing all my books and everything else off the shelves. My dad heard me yelling from the garden. He saw me planning to throw my electric guitar out onto the patio from the first floor and urged me to put it down. In a sudden flash, I became jealous that I couldn't play the guitar as well as Hendrix and hurled it through the window.

My father shrieked "no" in despair. What had caused this outrage? Drugs no doubt. I find it hard to think about although I do recall an incident that had occurred earlier in that week with my brother. I interrupted his revision for the same entrance exam that I had missed in fits of tears. I had read *Wide Sargasso Sea* by Jean Rhys and had broken down. Was it that I cared too much about the human race and took it upon myself to endure the suffering of others? Was I hyper-intelligent? Was I genetically inferior to others? The answer was probably a combination of all three.

I told my brother that it was not fair that black people had suffered so much, but at least, I continued, the problem was being dealt with. He agreed and I thought once again about the happy black raver at school, Chris, who had showed me some dance moves, didn't take drugs at all and danced for Fantasia.

After I had thrown the guitar out the window in my manic state my dad sent my grandmother into my room to try and calm me down. She asked me if I wanted some honey on toast. I gleefully accepted it as if it were some kind of reward for being her precious grandson. When she returned she said that my brother wanted to see me. I asked my brother to listen to the tape that I was playing. It was Phantasy and SS, Fantasia Summertime 1992. The MCs, Joe Peng and Robbie Dee, were fucking intense.

"To those of you who know the score ... how's about a little bit of hardcore ... Speaker box climbers get off the stage - you are distressing it for everyone ... Get off the speakers ... For the last time get, off the speakers."

Instead of reacting and trying to comfort me by putting his arm round me my brother, who was eccentric at the sanest of times, stepped on my bed and started dancing. I shouted for him to get down. My dad came down and hearing my plea told him to do the same. As soon as he did I head-butted him. It was badly misplaced, and my brother dragged me to the floor putting me into the same stranglehold that he put my dad in when he threatened to hit my mum several years previously. Eventually my dad persuaded him to let go after crying out that we were brothers and that we shouldn't be doing this to each other.

Within five minutes my dad had called the police and an ambulance. Because my brother didn't want to press charges they said whether or not I went with the ambulance was down to me. Meanwhile, I thought this was all a test, perhaps part of the Oxford entrance exam, and that I still was destined for a life of psychological, emotional and physical ecstasy. I chose the ambulance and started to fantasise again. This time I was to meet the heartthrob of my youth, Alena Campbell. We had been close from the age of 14–16. Her brother went to my school and was tragically run over on his bicycle. We had been friends ever since. I was convinced that I would soon meet up with her and be the only man in a never ending mass eternal orgy of which she would be the head. I was destined to escape from an everyday life that always had a sad edge to it.

I sat in the ambulance alone and was quite excited about my forthcoming adventure ... They took me to the hospital and lay me down on a bed. They asked me my name and a few other questions and gave me a brain scan. I thought that the 20 or so staff who were watching me believed that I was the most intelligent person in the world and that they were examining a brain which had worked out the way to bring world peace and happiness... (They were all dressed up as if they were going to perform an operation. This is no bullshit.) I thought I was going to be ruler of the world and that this was a historic moment... Jesus was my son and I was God ... I was on top of the world...

The ambulance then drove me to the police station. I thought that I was being kept in a safe haven as it wasn't yet the time to deliver the news to everyone. Everything seemed to make sense. Even the policeman who offered me a cigarette in the car park of the police station seemed to have a perfect cameo role... He was a clone of my stepbrother Paul... His spirit belonged to a family that had given my mother a happier life. He was a member of a family that had healed one of the suffering. In the reception at *Bearland* I thought I was playing the Commodore 64 computer game *Footballer of the Year*. Now even someone on heroin couldn't have a thought as fucked up as that. If they ever have, I can only offer my condolences – not my sympathy. You see, I never needed to put a needle in my arm to become manic and get suicidal afterwards. I had no choice. That's the difference between them and me. They can go to rehab and get off. Whatever pills I take, or relapse prevention work I go through, I'm stuck with it and that's the difference. They're more fortunate in that they don't get a life sentence. Sure, bad luck and unforeseen circumstances may have driven them to it, but everyone goes through shit at some point in their lives and most people carry on regardless. Sometimes it just boils down to a battle of will-power. That's what settles many differences between people – along with luck and opportunities or a lack of them. Ultimately, a drug addict or addict of anything becomes an addict by choice. Not me. I had no choice and I still have no choice. I fight every day to conquer my affliction and the best I can do is to minimise its effect or postpone the inevitable. It was not the experience itself that was always the most disturbing but the coming to terms with it afterwards.

At the police station I was taken to a cell and locked up. There was graffiti scratched all over the cell. I immediately noticed the rapper's name, Ice Cube, that had been carved on the door. I then started to think I was Ice Cube and that I was *Amerikkka's Most Wanted* ... I proceeded to kick the cell doors and walls for four hours. Soon I was smashing the cell window as hard as I could. This really hurt as my forehead was catching the top of the steel door.

There was only one interruption. A policeman entered with a cup of tea and placed it on the bed. Nothing registered, he might as well have poured it over my head. He must have noticed my new bruising but left without giving a fuck. What sort of inhumane treatment was this? By the time I saw another copper I had a bruise on my head the size of a melon. I continued to bang my

Head on the steel door and scream AAAAAAHHHGGGGGHHHH for a good half an hour. A pig came in and led me to an open room. He told me to get undressed and put the shower on for me. Taking my clothes he left a white suit for me to put on and walked off. I happily had a shower and thought that all the pain and suffering was over. I thought that I had to endure twice the pain that Christ did, as I was God ...

After my shower, I was locked in the room and started to plan my escape. I sat on the floor in the break dance position for a back spin and, in various yoga poses, worked out how I was going to climb the ceiling. I thought of DJ Spider and how I had my first E round his house – a White Calais. I had felt great. My eyes saw different things, everything sparkling, glimmering. I remembered that I had seen him at Fantasia. I remembered how I had not danced at Universe when I went with Brad the year before. I tried dancing for 10 seconds but felt so uncoordinated on the acid that I sat down in an even more paranoid state than I had been in before. We had a trip, two grams of billy and two and a half E's each. Brad was dancing all the time while I was lunched out and chain smoking, furious that I didn't have the courage to dance and bring the Ribena raver posse together as I had done so well in the Brunel Rooms before.

As I positioned myself to climb the wall, I revelled in the fact that the whole world was waiting for me to dance ... All these DJs were just waiting for somebody who knew the score ... A messiah, a prophet, a bringer of peace – and that was me, who would have believed it, a 17 year-old from Gloucester.

I'm not sure to this day how far I climbed. I seemed to have got suspended on the side of the wall somehow when my dad and stepmother approached looking at me through the clear door. In my naked state I felt proud and proceeded to put the white body suit on.

Now, the French psychoanalyst Jacques Lacan had taught me how to conquer my stepmother. At that time, she was the last woman on earth that I had to conquer. She had seen me naked and that was enough. I thought back to how, the previous night, I had woken her up when my dad was on nights. I had entered their bedroom wearing my father's fire uniform – fully equipped with his boots, waterproofs, jacket, helmet and gas mask. She screamed as I turned the light on. What happened after that I fail to remember. Maybe one day, if our relationship improves sufficiently, I will ask her.

My dad told me that he was going to take me to a place

where they would take care of me. This was great, and was all in line with my theory. I found his tears comforting. It must have been a very emotional experience to realise that he was the father of God ... I mean, that is a pretty important role in life. I felt unique in the body suit.

As he left, he said that he loved me. This was the first time that I remember hearing those words from a father who I had always respected for his hard work and sporting expertise.

As I was being driven off in the back of a police van in a space suit, I thought I was Donovan Bad Boy Smith being driven to a rave. I could hear music in my head and flashed back to another night at the Brunel Rooms in Swindon. *The Brunel Rooms, a hardcore Mecca for druggies from Gloucester and surrounding areas in the early to mid nineties.* Donovan was so hard core when I saw him there that he'd refused to turn off his set at 3am. He'd carried on until 3.30am when someone finally turned off the electricity mid flow.

...

I arrived at Coney Hill mental hospital very late at night. A nurse greeted me with what I interpreted as open arms. I thought that she was a subservient witch who was going to join the aforementioned orgy. She gave me some pills to swallow. Pretty quickly I began to feel hazy. I went to the toilet in my pyjamas and started to cry when I attempted to urinate. The pain was excruciating – as though Satan himself was inflicting pain on my penis.

In bed I studied my book on Ursula Fanthorpe's poetry, scribbling all over it. I was still convinced that I was destined for stardom in some way and was comforted from the presence of what I believed to be an old school friend snoring in the bed opposite. It was Adam Rimmer, the only member of my year who had psyched me out. We were once very close until, when quizzed, I told his girlfriend that he had got off with another girl. A fight ensued that was pretty even but he made me think he was harder by threatening to get his mate Linden to beat me up. Linden was a few years older and was clearly harder than both of us, but lying in that bed I felt that Adam had forgiven me.

There were about 20 patients in all. I went round calling staff, patients and visitors alike different DJ names, while quoting the words of MCs. The ward consisted of a large lounge with a dining area, a small hall with a phone, a quiet room for visitors to see the person they were visiting in private, and a staff room strictly out of bounds to the patients. There were also two lock-up rooms at the end of the corridor.

Eventually, my mania began to wane. This was due to the drugs that had been administered, in particular the anal injection of Haliperidol that I had received on my arrival. For years, I was furious with these people for curbing those moments of internal magic. Mania had given me something in life that others could only strive for. I was perfectly happy. It didn't matter that I wasn't actually making any sense. I knew afterwards that it didn't last forever and that depression always ensued. I would long to have those moments of mania back, but instead I had to realise that I was actually in a mental asylum. I was living in a place that was meant for other people not for a chess champion and Gloucester rugby representative, and especially not for the person who believed he was the most intelligent pupil in his grammar school. This was not the life that a talented, but essentially normal, person should be leading.

I was surrounded by patients who were far older than me. I could see why some of them belonged there, but to me it didn't make any sense at all. I used to speculate on what I had done wrong. If I could find out, I would know never to make the same mistakes again. There were too many things to cope with: returning to sanity, realising that all my thoughts were incoherent, putting up with the humiliation of being in there, seeing how it affected the people around me and most of all being so unstable that I suffered from fits of rage and depression.

After a month, they released me from Section 1 and discharged me. I had calmed down and was somewhat depressed although this, apparently, was to be expected given what had happened. On Christmas Eve, my mum drove me to her house for the "festive" period. I didn't sleep and had her up all night writing poetry. Christmas day arrived, and to avoid ruining it my stepfather, brother and mum put up with my mania. They drove me back to hospital on Boxing Day. As we went down one empty road I tried to climb out of the back window.

I was admitted back into the ward and given some drugs, notably Benzotropine, that had an adverse effect. This period marked a black hole in my life. From 27 December, 1992 to 1 February, 1993 I suffered from complete amnesia. On 1 February, I remember standing on a bed and urinating on top of some newspapers when my mum walked in, similar to a scene in the film *Made in Britain*. I noticed that I now had my own room. My mum told me that I had been given the only individual room so that the staff could keep an eye on me because I was particularly ill. My mum cleaned up the newspaper by going to the toilet and returning with lots of tissue. To this day my parents, who visited frequently, have told me little about my behaviour during that period. My mum told me how I threw a chair through the common room window when I caught sight of my dad visiting. Dad proceeded to tell me that they then put me in a straight jacket. I presume that was because I threw the chair. My mum said that it took a group of five male nurses to restrain me. It was a shock to have no recollection of such a violent incident.

The depression of my first episode remains confusing. The experience was new and it's still hard to quantify. Above all, I was numb – sleeping all the time, avoiding any kind of social contact, lacking any kind of motivation to do anything. Nothing made me happy – whether seeing my friends, family or even playing music. You could have given me a million pounds and, although it would have registered, it would have meant fuck all to me at the time. It's hard to describe. You just have to fucking sit and wait or kill yourself if you can't hack it. Thing is, killing yourself takes thought and effort, and when people are massively depressed they lack motivation to do anything except perform natural acts like breathing, pissing and shitting.

I feel really shit. There's no future. I'm so unhappy and I'll never be happy again so I'll fucking kill myself. I'll jump off a building. That would kill me. Thing is, I'm too depressed to even fucking stand up let alone walk, and walk all the way up a fucking tall building. You must be fucking joking. I could get a lift but I don't want to see anyone. They'd only be wankers anyway and they wouldn't understand the shit I'm going through. I'll have another cigarette and kill myself that way. Shit, that's too slow. If I had some pills now I'd take a fucking overdose. I don't give a fuck. Thing is, I don't know what would kill me and I'm too depressed to go anywhere. Just want to stay here and feel like fucking shit. There's no future anyway so it doesn't fucking matter.

The thing about feeling suicidal is that it lasts for fucking ages. The thought process above repeats itself endlessly, and often on different levels. During the low parts of an episode, you think of all the possible ways of killing yourself: hanging yourself, shooting yourself, running in front of a tube (the latter has often been a very tempting one for me). The list goes on: drowning yourself, slitting your wrists, beating yourself to death, poisoning yourself, getting someone to shoot you, etc.

In hospital, I have seen lots of people who have tried committing suicide. Some were readmitted to stop another attempt, some were let out and tried it so came back in again, and others had tried it in the past. Some do it because they crave attention. These ones aren't really attempting suicide. Like my friend from uni, Roger, they merely inflict pain on themselves. If someone knows that they tried to kill themselves, they'll feel sorry for them, and that will give the attention seeker someone to talk to.

It's hard to spot the difference between a genuine suicide attempt and a cry for help, although if anything, the ones who are quiet about it are usually more serious. It's a personal thing and not something you usually go bragging about to other patients.

49

The saddest thing is that the staff don't seem to give a fuck about it. I mean, they detach themselves from it. I guess they have to though – otherwise the daily routine would be too hard to bear. Also, if they always discussed it, wards would be more like uni philosophy tutorials on ethics. Sometimes though – and it really pains me to say it – they're not properly trained in these matters. A lot of them seem more interested in reading the fucking sport in the paper and bossing people around – quoting what patients are not allowed to do and shit like that. They don't give a fuck. Sometimes I wish the strictest and unemotional ones – because there is the occasional caring staff member – could swap places with a suicide candidate for life. They wouldn't be so fucking insensitive then, would they? No, they'd be curled up on the floor of the corridor like those other poor fuckers you see in the mental hospital trying to talk about their problems, or completely avoiding social contact with anybody and sleeping all the time. Some may be OK one minute and fucked the next, especially if they're receiving ECT (electro convulsive treatment) i.e. electroshock therapy.

When I first told my family that I felt like killing myself there were different reactions. My grandmother's was the most comforting. She would cry and say: "You poor little boy. I've felt like that you know. Just like that. And it's a terrible thing. It's a bloody terrible thing. But I don't feel like that anymore. You've gotta fight through it kid." My brother would either analyse why I felt like I did by interviewing me with carefully thought out questions or, if that failed, to make me feel better would tell me that it was a selfish act. It would be selfish because it would affect the rest of the family and he would be unhappy if I wasn't around at Christmas time. My dad would simply say: "Oh, bloody hell" in disbelief and then give me a slap on the head, telling me that he was there for me at any time of the day or night if I wanted to talk.

As for my mum, I think that it affected her the most. Her first response would be to try and snap me out of it by saying that "things will get better. The worst is nearly over now. You've got plenty of time to get well." When that didn't work, she would say: "I feel like that sometimes." She would often repeat this and would wonder what she'd done wrong when bringing me up. When I sensed this, I would become less self-obsessed and think of how terrible her life would be if I killed myself. Maybe it was a selfish act. I think the only reason why I haven't killed myself in the past is that I would feel guilty if I killed myself: guilty for hurting those close to me, especially my mum, dad and brother.

I'm lucky that I've never heard voices. Schizophrenics put up with a level of shit most of us could never imagine. They really have to get their stuff together and exert their willpower to reconnect with society. Take Winnie, for example, a black girl in Coney Hill. She was forever hearing voices that instructed her to kill people. She was a very strong-minded and caring individual and insisted that everyone read the bible and love each other – although for many people on the ward who were almost catatonic, along with the staff, she was the most disruptive patient there. She had been brainwashed by somebody or something and was now preaching the bible. One day, she was alone in the lock up room as she had been noisy on the ward. She kept on asking me to save her but I couldn't. She told me to stay strong and said that she loved me. I said that I loved her and I did, in a funny sort of way, but I also knew that she was the most disruptive patient there.

My strangest memory of assessing my manic state in Coney Hill was when I went for a brain scan. The nurse on duty told me that I was going to have a haircut. I still believed her when wires were being stuck to my head and a machine placed over my head and everywhere. What a nutter.

Routines exist even in mental hospitals. In hospital, there are the morning, afternoon and evening calls for medication. People generally smoke excessively, drink large amounts of tea, look depressed and sit down together for meals. Other activities include watching television and playing table tennis, which I became pretty good at. Few patients have sufficient concentration to read for long periods. Some go for walks around the grounds if they are allowed to and are up to

51

it. I found refuge in the quiet room. Whenever I had a visitor I would take them in there and we would get some privacy away from the germs and bacteria in the main room. I could play my tapes in there and try and forget about what was happening to me. Time stood still for a moment until a visit ended. As time went on, though, the visits were less help because I was sinking into a deep depression.

I was exhausted by what had happened. I was tired of being ill, worried if I would recover or not and scared that I would be ridiculed if I returned to the outside world. My dad told me on one visit that he thought I was going to be a *cabbage* for the rest of my life. I couldn't feel comforted by what he said as my mood was too low. Now I can see that other people are less fortunate and that helps me keep my balance. Where was I going? What was happening to me? How was I going to explain this to everyone? How was I going to recover? I didn't care much anymore. I had gone through too much to be positive.

Time became the only real healer. It took time to accept the situation and time to adapt to it. I'm not sure how therapeutic psychiatric hospitals are. I mean, all they do is put depressed people together. How are they going to cheer each other up? They just add to the misery. The other patients might have helped me gain a perspective but it was not a positive one. It was still the loonies on the inside and everyone else on the outside. It felt like being in prison when I was innocent. I'd been caught but had not done anything wrong.

They had stolen my free spirit. My soul would have been better off wandering around on an island designated for people experiencing mania. Years later, one of my university professors agreed with me. Once I'd left, he told me that he had experienced similar problems. This didn't surprise me as he was very sharp and quite eccentric. I would be able to reach my manic potential on this island that I imagined myself on. Who knows, I could have come up with moments of inspiration and genius there and even acted upon them? I would have been special and capable of changing the world for the better. And if saving the world was beyond me, then at least I would have maintained my humanity and dignity. My free spirit would have thrived and blossomed.

I planned to try and be positive. I would fight this plague. I was glad that I wasn't normal. Ignorance may be bliss as Socrates once said; perhaps that was why I was so unhappy. I turned to epigrammatic poetry to raise my spirits. I would read them to everyone on the ward even those who were in a trance. They evoked a lot of rhetorical questions and assessed my mood better than I could in reality. I wrote hundreds of them only to throw them away in anger when I was trying to adjust back into society. Could I come back from the abyss? If I could then how could I fit back in, be told what to do by the system and suffer new burdens? I wasn't going to be a modern-day Sisyphus – pushing a stone up a hill all the time only for it to fall back down again wasn't my idea of fun.

I spent my eighteenth birthday in hospital. It was one fucked up occasion. About half a dozen patients were well enough to have some cake with me and we finished one bottle of buck's fizz in under three minutes. There was a celebration at my grandmother's house where my mum and brother were present. My mum and grandmother took several photos of me. My eyes were more dilated than they were when I was E'ing my bollocks off. They were worn out, beaten by all the medication that had gone through my mind and body. I felt nauseous whenever I thought of my mum and Nan's photo albums so I asked them to take those photos out. My mum wrote "Jason's eighteenth birthday" next to it. It was a loving but futile attempt to pretend that everything was normal. I feel that I looked like I'd injected an ounce of ketamine through my forehead with a syringe the size of a baseball bat. People's eighteenth birthdays are meant to be special or fun, not utter humiliation like that. It wasn't anyone's fault though, just how I felt.

I was to spend another three months in Coney Hill. I spent a lot of the time writing poems, playing the ward guitar, chain smoking, watching TV, playing table tennis, speaking to visitors, going for walks and participating in general ward activity. As I regained consciousness, the routine of the ward helped me to focus and the occupational therapy I undertook, along with mixing with patients and staff, helped me to regain a morsel of my self-esteem.

I had lots of visitors. My mum and dad would come near enough every day. My dad would often bring me a Mars bar and say that he loved me. My mum left her job in Wales for as long as was necessary and moved in with my Nan so that she could visit. This really helped me. She would try and be strong when seeing me and cry when she got back to her mum's house. My brother would come a couple of times a week and ride up after work and be positive. I know that it really upset him but never really knew what to say to compensate for all the suffering he endured because of me. What could I do? I was no Houdini. I couldn't stop him feeling this way.

I noticed that my mum and dad never came at the same time. This must have been planned. They still hated each other at the time and probably blamed each other for my being in there. They knew that any confrontation on their part would upset me. I guess it was also nice to see them separately as that meant that the time I spent with visitors was far greater. I wouldn't have wanted them to come together anyway. I couldn't have handled it.

It really helped when I had a visitor. It broke up the despairing monotony of ward life. I looked forward to seeing Brad the most. He was recovering from injecting speed by going to the gym most days and coming to see me. His presence made me feel that I could cope with returning to society as he was doing exactly the same thing. I remember him visiting me when I was particularly manic. As soon as I saw him I ran into my room and put all the clothes on in my wardrobe. I put on about a dozen tops, four pairs of trousers, half a dozen pairs of socks, two hats, gloves, shoes on my hands and feet and packed my rucksack full of the rest of my belongings. He laughed.

"Jase, what are you doing?"

"I'm getting out of here man. I've had enough of it here."

"Do you fancy a game of table tennis?"

"All right."

I kept trying to smash every point for a winner and Brad laughed throughout the game. He won pretty easily because of this. Afterwards, we went back to my room, stuck on a hardcore tape, sat down and lit up a cigarette.

"What are you doing now?" asked Brad.

"I've decided to stay here for a while."

Brad is in stitches and I have a grimace-like smile because of the high dose of medication that I'm on.

I also looked forward a lot to Tim coming. He was in my original year at school and visited me almost as much as Brad. He saw me at one of my lowest moments. We were sat in the living room one time when my jaw started to twist. I had not been given enough Procycladine and was unable to speak. I was crying because of the extreme pain. My jaw would wind down, rest for a moment and then start up again. They gave me some Procycladine that worked very quickly.

Years later, Tim told me that after that visit he burst into tears. He couldn't believe what had happened to one of his closest friends. This made me realise what it must have been like for others that had watched me suffering. I was so lost in my own depression and self-pity that I didn't stop to think of the lasting effect it had on my family and friends. My dad never said how it affected him but he was very calm and positive about it all. He understood that I had had a rough time but encouraged me to get on with it. My mind was often in a state of flux so any positive comments I heard would be mixed in with the negative effects of my depression.

A handful of people came to visit me once. Derek Gabb, Nicholas James and Paul Kingsbury, Kerry Tamlyn and Jenny Tomlinson, Helen Cosgrave, Petal and Sam Checkitts. They either came because I asked them them to, because they were concerned or because they were simply curious. People are generally curious about what it is like to be mad but don't want to get too close. I had a card delivered to me sent by Denmark Road High School for girls. That was very moving

– dozens of girls had signed it. I knew most of them.

Chris, the dancer from school, and his friends came to visit but were turned away. The staff thought that they were going to give me drugs. Fucking hypocrites. They wanted to see me, not give me drugs. Anyway, the drugs the consultant had given me had fucked me up more than anything else. They had given me amnesia and caused me to have a serious relapse. I had no energy to fight anything. My will was weak, and I was tired, worn-out and ill. My confidence had been shattered and my sense of reality was permanently altered. Nothing would be the same. After a brief recovery period, though, my attitude to life changed. I was tougher and didn't want to take any shit from anyone anymore.

One day, my classical civilisation teacher, Mr. Moss, visited. This was a pleasant surprise, and he told me that he looked forward to me coming back to school when I was back on my feet. He was a wonderful man who gave me the confidence and inspiration to become a writer. He apologised on behalf of my French and English teachers who couldn't come but sent their love.

I was gutted that my English teacher couldn't make it. I had only known her for a few months but she had been an inspiration to me. I guessed then that she just couldn't handle the drugs thing. I felt that she had let me down as I had heard that she had intended to visit. For a while afterwards, I regarded her as a selfish bitch that talked the talk but didn't walk the walk. Eventually, I forgave her.

I clung anxiously to Coney Hill's recreational activities to try and stop the depression taking over. I somehow had to escape the monotony of the ward. The first activity I tried was football at 8.00am in the morning. This forced me to change my sleeping pattern at the time, which was to hide in bed until at least one in the afternoon. Sometimes, I was pressured into getting up by the staff. At other times, I was prodded but they often gave up after a few attempts. They wouldn't physically force me out of bed but would draw the curtains or steal my sheets. When I was sunk in depression their actions would make no difference and I would sleep without any covers. During the most severe bouts, I lay in bed for 20 hours a day. I would only get up for food, to go to the toilet or if a visitor came in and coaxed me out of bed. Then I would return to bed as soon as they left. However, when I started playing football I had recharged enough to consciously make up my mind to get back into society, and this seemed the appropriate place to start.

We had to do warming up exercises in a group. I found it rather embarrassing as I was a sporty type and knew of better warming up techniques. I felt like I was in a junior school games lesson. Then, to my despair, we were issued with a foam ball. For fuck's sake. Anyone who's played with a sponge football knows that it's impossible to achieve power and fluid passing. There again, the exercise was good so I went a few more times during the weeks that followed. Not many people turned up and the opposition was rather poor but it did my self-confidence some good.

I soon took up another class. Relaxation classes were more popular than the football, probably because everyone was depressed and just wanted to sit there like cabbages. Also, the room was only 20 metres away from the ward whereas the gym was a 10 minute walk.

During relaxation classes, a group of up to 15 people would sit upright in chairs. Soft music was played in the background and the co-ordinator would ask us to close our eyes. She would tell us to make sure that our backs were straight, our feet and knees together, and our palms and elbows resting on our upper legs. Then she would ask us to follow her, breathing in deeply and slowly, and breathing out in the same manner.

The first few times I went I found it refreshing and relaxing. Then I lost interest. I would start to cheat and see if everybody actually did close their eyes. They did and were unaware that I was looking at them. The last time I went, I even fell asleep. I didn't see that as especially relaxing as I could fall asleep back on the ward. What's more, when I was on the ward I could have a cigarette when I wanted to. Fags were a great comfort for putting up with the endless boredom and the periods of anxiety that I so often felt. Most of the patients were heavy smokers and you were permitted to smoke anywhere apart from the lounge, dormitory, kitchen or staff room. That left the main room and outside – if you were allowed to go out for a walk, that is. Some patients were voluntary and could go out if they told the staff where they were going, while those on section had to wait until a member of staff was available.

There were other forms of occupational therapy, but I didn't participate in any apart from pottery, which I went to only once. I was a great fan of sixth and fifth century BC, Attic Black and Red Figure Pottery. I was most impressed by the magnitude of the *François Vase*, and was impressed by the fact that after it had been dropped somebody had managed to put over 1200 pieces back together. All I could think of when in the pottery room was the love scene in *Ghost* where Patrick Swayze and Demi Moore get covered in clay. This love scene made me feel lonely. Five months before I had thought that I was the most attractive man in the universe and the most appealing to all women. Now I was living in a mental hospital in the company of grannies who were knitting and sewing; and despite having seen a dozen or so naked women and received some good blowjobs I had only had sex properly a few times. Maybe this was why I was ill. Maybe I lacked the emotional support that a caring relationship would have given me.

I had one vaguely sexual experience in hospital. I went to have a bath and, passing the unlocked door, saw a girl called Karen lying in it. She was demented and cried out my name so I left the room worried that the staff would come in and put me on a six month section. I didn't want to be trapped for longer because of one incident and I was too shy and considerate to make a move on her.

It took the approval of three professionals to put me on a month's section – the whole process being quite thorough. There was a ward round once a week that was intended to discuss anything on the patient's mind. Unfortunately, these are often overcrowded and full of student doctors whose presence can often intimidate the patients. They are also rushed and the patient will usually come out of one even more stressed unless represented by an advocacy worker. If you're ever in this situation make sure you get one. It's unlikely, however, that you'd be told that you have a right to one if you are in hospital. Apart from the ward round, there is no contact with the consultant who prescribes your medication unless you persistently beg the staff to make an exception.

The nurses keep an eye on you and are sometimes pleasant. However, they're careful not to get too friendly as it's deemed to be unprofessional. In any case, the patients don't usually want to get too close either as they are generally not in the mood to make friends and deep down resent the authoritative figures that wake them up every morning, figures from hell that keep stepping on your toes. Such views are, of course, unfair in a way but commonplace nonetheless. These nurses were genuine people who chose to help others for a living. Still, I will always be a bit sceptical about this. Nobody can deny that the job involves a kind of power trip. This is most resonant when medication time is called. Every patient is given their medication in a particular order and is expected to be grateful. Only the charge nurse is permitted to give out the medication in case any mistakes are made, and sometimes they dish out crushed tablets to the patients. I know some people who've said that it's fine to eat crushed tablets when probed. But if they ever read the little notes accompanied with Lithium or Sodium Valporate tablets, they'd learn that this is not the case.

Why should we be grateful about taking pills anyway? It's a bloody nuisance having to take lithium every night for years, I can tell you. When taking the pills they feel uncomfortable, get caught in the throat, give you a dry mouth, make you wake up to go for a pee and then sometimes you can't remember if you've taken them or not. Because they are so important, however, your lifeline in fact, you get stressed out about it and confused.

Some patients would spend the whole week demanding to speak to the consultant and as soon as they'd finished talking to him or her they would demand another consultation. These psychiatrists were busy enough. Patients would revere them and think that they could cure not only their illness, but their emotional problems too. It was as if the consultant ruled the world. Well, then I guess they have the same power cravings as the nurses, probably even more so. But then doesn't everyone have these tendencies? We all want to be in control of something or someone. Why do so many of us have pets? To have a loyal companion? I don't buy this assumption and I never will.

To help me adjust back into society from hospital I was allowed weekend leave. My first night out I went into town with two of my friends, Kevin and Brad. We went to the pub and got slaughtered. People knew where I had been and greeted me with a simple "Hello Jase" or "All right Jase". We then went on to a nightclub. As I hadn't drunk any alcohol for five months I was legless by the end of the session. My two friends rang my dad's doorbell, propped me up against the door and made a quick getaway. My dad answered the door, stopped me from falling and put me to bed. I spent the rest of the weekend sobering up. As time went on, I would spend more and more time at home. I felt embarrassed as I recalled manic thoughts that I had had in the house. This was very difficult for me as my dad and his girlfriend were both acting as if everything was normal. I'm sure it was extremely difficult for them as well. I mean how were they supposed to act? There were no guidelines for them to follow.

I had started to see a counsellor regularly towards the end of my stay in hospital. He was helping me establish a firm footing with the outside world. I would continue to see him once a week for the next 12 months. He was a polite, perceptive and reasonably intelligent man but was a bit robotic and always gave the impression that he was telling me what I wanted to hear as opposed to the truth.

I would sometimes feel patronised, paranoid, humiliated and belittled. This was hardly surprising considering I was relaying my innermost thoughts to a complete stranger. I don't really feel that he ever got to the bottom of what was wrong with me. No matter what I told him about my past, my family or my mania he would never actually know what it was like to be me. What's more, he didn't really understand me. When I told him that I wasn't going to see him again, he didn't believe me. He still made an appointment for the following week. It was as if, despite his intelligence, he was somehow artificial, too squeaky clean and incapable of true empathy.

Maybe it was the nature of the profession itself, being too regimental, too organised, too out of touch. I know that I left at the right time because I was becoming too self-analytical, too honest and too engrossed in my own psyche. I would leave school when everybody else was having lessons and go and speak to my psychologist about things that I had only just found out about myself. This was part of my weekly routine and it was absurd. I felt different, an outsider.

I would never be able to return to being normal after living in Coney Hill. No matter how secure my recovery was I would always have the knowledge that I had lost my sanity completely and the people sat next to me in class hadn't. They knew what had happened but never uttered a word. They covered everything up by just saying "All right Jase." That was fine with me, as I would have felt uncomfortable talking about it.

One of the last days I spent in hospital I had a long talk with my key worker. His name was Alan and his role was to follow my progress on the ward. He was a nurse that I was allocated to for special attention. He was a very chirpy chap who always tried to reassure me that everything was going to be all right.

I asked him if a diagnosis had finally been reached. At last, he told me it was called "manic depression". He told me not to worry, though, as it may never happen again. I was relieved because I wasn't sure I would be able to cope with another breakdown. I wish that Alan had got his facts straight or been more up front with me at the time and informed me that 95% of sufferers have another relapse – if he had, maybe I would have taken better care of myself in the years ahead.

Chapter 3 – Back to reality…?

Because I only made it back to school a month before the end of the year I ended up dropping down to the lower sixth for a re-run. I also switched from A-level French at school, which wasn't going too well, to politics at Gloscat College on Tuesday evenings in Cheltenham.

In my new year, I had only one real friend, Kev, who'd visited me in Coney Hill a couple of times despite his dad telling him not to. I didn't really question his dad's reasoning – after all, I could understand that, as a parent, he didn't want his son hanging around with a card-carrying loon.

I appreciated the fact that Kev had ignored his old man. Here was someone who was really making an effort to get closer to me. As a result, we became close friends. He accepted my madness and found it intriguing – exciting even. This helped me relax when I was in his company and I even made a joke or two about myself.

At weekends, I'd usually go out with Kev, although sometimes Brad would come along too. We drank a lot of alcohol but steered clear from drugs. Christ, drugs had put me in hospital, made Brad lose the plot and turned Kev paranoid.

Anyway, it was pretty depressing seeing everyone from my old class leave Gloucester for university when I had to stay. I mean, it wasn't as if I'd failed my exams – I'd just been, how do you put it, held back. When I was in hospital I was told that the whole school had prayed for me to get well. This was a comforting feeling as I thought that I was going to be expelled for taking and selling a few drugs. But why?

I'd put loads of effort into extra curricular activities over the years, had been a member of the school chess team from the start and was even about to be school Chess Captain for the second year running just before I got ill. I was also a key member of the 1st XV having scored loads of tries over the years, even in a Schools' Cup Final. Fuck, I should have been made school captain but I ended up in the loony bin.

I'll always remember what it was like to play, win and

score a try on Gloucester's infamous rugby ground, Kingsholm. Twenty minutes had gone in the first half of one cup final and we were getting hammered by a tough comprehensive school called Saintbridge. We were lucky to be only one try down. Hundreds of their pupils had taken the afternoon off school and we got booed when we went out onto the pitch. It seemed to intimidate the whole team as we only had a couple of dozen supporters, if that. Anyway, I was so pissed off with the way that our team was playing that I ripped the ball out of my scrum half's hand and ran forward yelling, like a man possessed. I was so proud of Tommy's that I simply couldn't envisage losing this match and not holding up the trophy. As I ran forward I broke one tackle, then two, then three, then four using my famous hand off every time. When I was eventually tackled, I managed to stay on my feet until reinforcements arrived. I'd run from my own 22 into their 22. We were awarded a scrum and two minutes later we scored our first try. My run had totally changed the impetus of the game – until that moment we were fucked. We ran out deserved 23–11 winners and I scored one of our three tries. After the game, Bilous, one of our toughest players along with me, came up to me for the first time ever and congratulated me on the way I'd played. He mentioned the run and called me a psycho. I knew that he meant it as a sign of respect. The scrum half also mentioned the run I'd made and both of them knew that it had changed the psychology of the game.

I was the only pupil from the school to represent Gloucester at Under-16 level and got into the county squad. I proudly wore my tie at school which was different to everyone else's. I also competed for the school at chess, cross-country – and even on the streets. When anyone from another school, be it state or public, put Tommy's down for being full of pompous geeks, I put them right, sometimes verbally, sometimes physically.

However, one thing that really pissed me off when I left school was that I wasn't in the hall of fame – unlike my black friend, Panji, who played for England at basketball. I was also surprised that I wasn't chosen to play for England Under-18s at chess.

I hadn't really got to know Panji that well at school despite the fact that we'd been mates in the first and second years. As he moved through the years he became increasingly introverted, playing his Walkman all the time. However, Panji was fucking hard. In the first year, he'd even make some of the kids cry when we played "stinger" – a game in which whoever had the tennis ball threw it as hard as they could at whoever they wanted to. With Panj, you could hear a real sting when the ball made contact.

In our year, Panj and I were the best at that game – the hardest throwers – although he was probably more accurate than me. Maybe that was why we were good mates. He had a lot of willpower and endured a lot of racism at school. He took it all in his stride until he was about 16 then started beating the crap out of everyone who'd taken the piss out of him over the years. It was fucking great. I remember a big group of us about to play football one day when this fat kid called Stuart Finch said: "We're not going to let the nigger play, are we?" Panj went over, decked him and kicked him in the head once, in a clinical fashion. I said: "Nice one Panj, come on, let's pick teams." One thing that always amazed me was that Panj said he could never remember the incident. Well, I did: it was a classic moment of justice, of freedom beating years of oppression. After that, and after he'd beat up the other ringleaders, people finally shut up. Not only did they respect him but they feared him and that gave everyone a buzz whether they admit it or not.

...

The day after my A-level examinations I flew to New York with Kev. We were going on holiday for six weeks and staying with acquaintances of our families. For the first half of the trip we stayed with Bill and Francis Spicer. Bill was the chief of Woodbridge fire station which was about a half an hour drive from the centre of Washington. Basically, my dad had worked as a fire officer for 30 years and had organised several exchanges between families and fire fighters of Woodbridge and Gloucester fire station, so knew Bill quite well. For this trip, he had planned everything: the flights, excursions, who was staying with who, etc.

When he heard that I was keen to go to America he wrote to Bill asking if we could stay with him for a couple of weeks and Bill was happy to oblige. My dad said that he had written instead of phoning because he wanted to give Bill "thinking time", as he put it. I'm always amused when I hear my dad repeat this story, partly because I like the way he tells it, and partly because I appreciated it and I knew that he was pleased that he'd helped me out.

When we finally got there our accommodation was great. We had a huge downstairs apartment with a five-foot square TV, a fridge full of food and refreshments, an outdoor basketball court and a hot tub. They made us feel very welcome, taking us out to restaurants, bars and malls. Kev wasn't really into the tourist stuff so we spent a lot of time drinking and chatting up girls – although we did go to the Whitehouse and even saw the President. That day there were about 50 people queuing up by the entrance. They stopped the traffic and then a convoy emerged. There were four huge black limousines and the president of the time, George Bush Senior, was in the third. The entourage consisted of a dozen police cars and motorbikes.

Everyone was really friendly and loved our accents. We even went on a firemen's training exercise where real buildings were burnt down. We put on all the equipment and went into two different fires. I was positioned near the exit and was told by one of the fireman to put my thumbs up when I wanted to get out. As the fire was lit, the tops of my feet were the first part to heat up. Then I could feel my knees, the palms of my hands and my face stewing. I was in there for about a minute but got out safely. I took my helmet off and wiped the sweat from my forehead. I handed the helmet to Kev – it was his turn next.

His experience was far more dramatic. He said that when he was inside a huge part of the ceiling smashed on the floor right next to him. He couldn't believe that it hadn't hit him. He thought that if it had landed on him, he would have been dead for sure. He was fucking relieved to get out of there.

Bill took Kev and I to our first ever baseball game. It was a minor league team and there were 6000 spectators. It was a much friendlier environment than at a football match in England. One thing that struck me was how Bill and his second son Patrick stood up and put their hand on their hearts as they sang the American national anthem. For as far as I could see everyone was stood up and singing it, and this was only a small domestic match. It showed that the Americans have a great deal of pride in their nation.

Maybe this is one of the reasons why they're so successful economically. Christ, every person we met, car we went in, house we visited, restaurant we ate in, shop we looked in, whatever, was bigger and better than its English counterpart. Even Big Macs, which came in at just under a dollar, were twice the size of the ones back home.

One great day out with Bill and Francis and their three sons (Billy, Patrick and Billy Junior who were fifteen, nine and six respectively) was when we went to a huge amusement park. There was one roller coaster that went upside down three times and even underwater. Another great afternoon was when Bill, Kev and I had a go on the automatic baseball machines. We took it in turns to go in a cage with a helmet and bat and hit balls at different speeds. It was cool, and so was America. It was a great place to be.

The next family we stayed with lived in the posh fishing town of Annapolis. This, like Woodbridge, is a half-hour drive from central Washington. The mother was an old friend of Kev's mum, and her husband was a former admiral in the American navy. It was like living in Fort Knox. We couldn't stand them. We weren't allowed any alcohol in the house and they said that they wanted us back early each night to sit down and have a formal lunch with them. We wished we were back at Bill's making huge sandwiches from his enormous fridge.

We were also being hounded by their stuck up eight year-old daughter who was trying to follow us everywhere. She was even bossier than her parents were. After a few days of suffering, we met a local lifeguard called Drew and told him about our dilemma. He was a few years older than us and said we could spend the rest of our holiday chilling out with him and his friends.

We'd stay round their houses most nights, get pissed and stoned and have a wicked time. We bought loads of crates of beers, with the fake driving licenses we'd picked up, and drank them at gatherings and parties. One night we went to see an American legend in concert. We were part of Drew and his mates' convoy. There were about 20 of us all together. We bought a shit-load of Bud and other lagers on the way. We got there six hours before the show started and parked the cars up next to each other. We must have had the loudest stereo system there. It was four hundred watts and we blasted out Guns and Roses or chilled out to Bob Marley as the sun shone down on us. Spliffs and beers were being passed around left, right and centre.

It was a beautiful day. The weather was so hot that summer. Hotter than anything I had experienced before. I remember walking out of a mall with Kev one day and it was so extreme and humid that neither of us wanted to walk to the phone box to ask for a lift. I loved the sun like most people and realised how much I had been deprived of seeing it by living in a country without a sunny climate.

The man in concert, Jimmy Buffet, was a cross between Bob Marley, and Country and Western, and could really play the guitar – although I've never met anyone in England who's heard of him. 15,000 Americans sang to his famous song which started: "Come on, let's get drunk and screw." To get into the concert we all climbed over a 15-foot wall. There was a middle bit that you could rest on and people were pulling their friends over from the other side. There was a lot of fighting after the concert, though, because people were getting squashed crossing a footbridge on their way back to their cars. This dampened the occasion somewhat but I had still had a great day.

When hanging round with our new friends during the day we'd play a lot of street basketball with the local black kids. I became a pretty mean player by the end and could even do a one-handed slam dunk, although I admit that the basket was a foot lower than professional height. At parties people would be taking helium, swimming, fucking and getting wrecked.

One game that was often played was called "asshole". It was a brilliant drinking game. You'd basically play a game like whist and each player would be ranked: there would be a first in command, say a general, then a second in command, a few other ranks and finally the asshole. Each player could tell the players below them what to drink at any time within limits agreed before the start of the game. Positions would alter depending on the outcomes on the next hand. So the asshole could become the general in the following round. The game livened everybody up and people would team up against others and get revenge when they could. Lots of people would throw up and everyone would cheer when somebody had a good swig of beer or downed a big shot. The funniest thing was being able to say "drink up asshole." It was such a humiliating experience but so funny when saying it to somebody else.

Kev and I got really drunk at one party and had some powerful bongs. We ended up having an argument in which we threatened each other and I suggested taking it outside. This guy, who was 6' 5" and 18 stone, declined. The next day, we had an in depth discussion while relaxing at an outdoor private swimming pool. He said that he could have beaten me up when I was asleep. I don't think we would ever have hit each other, though. I mean, I could never imagine hitting Kev – we had been through too much together. He'd become a close friend when Dominic was at university and I owed a lot to him. He'd basically befriended a madman and risked his own sanity and reputation in the process. Not many people would have done that. I also admired his ambition and respected him as a rugby player. I would still have returned to school if he hadn't been there but he seemed to make the transition back easier.

Back to the States. One bloke called Butler, who knew Drew, drove us down to stay with his aunt in a place called Ocean City. It was here that I was to discover the beer bong – a funnel joined to a tube resulting in an accelerated form of drinking. His aunt was an alcoholic so we got on well. She lived in a trailer that looked identical to the other 5000 trailers that surrounded it. Later that night, I split up from Kev and was wandering round pissed out of my mind looking for the trailer until five in the morning. I only found it because a policeman ended up driving me around looking for it. All I knew was that there was a brown Pontiac parked outside and that the trailer was green or blue.

...

On returning from America I worked full-time as a summer holiday 'Play Scheme Leader' for two months. Dominic had got me the job. It was fun and we were responsible, with two other staff, for the safety and entertainment of 40 five to eleven year-olds. I also started back at the video shop that I'd had worked in since September 1993. I would open the shop on Saturday mornings and work Saturdays and Sundays. I was the only person working in the shop and would study when it was quiet. The job helped restore my communication skills with people after my stay in Coney Hill and helped nurse me back to having a structured life. It also gave me a bit of extra money.

I'd spent a week in Manchester on a politics course in the January before my A-levels and had been shown around by some of Dom's mates from university. I knew I wanted to go there. I helped them shift loads of fake designer clothes by telling all the kids at school. They gave me a fake jacket and took me out for a drink. That was fucking tight considering I must have made them over 500 quid for less than half an hour's work. One of them lived in Manchester and his name was Oliver. He was the biggest drugs dealer I knew. He would buy and then shift 10 kilos of weed and 2,000 E's at a time. I was taken in by his flash Volkswagen GTI, designer clothes and slick personality. Thing is, I knew he was a bit of a wanker at the same time, happy to rip off his mates and all that. Once, he sold me loads of fake designer clothes to sell at school. I knew they were fake but I trusted him and gave him the money before I could work out how much I could reasonably sell them for. I had to rip off another mate to make any kind of profit. In just a few seconds, Oliver had help to ruin a friendship that I had had for several years and which didn't heal until I got back in touch and apologised in January 2002.

I was embarrassed that I had been so gullible. I can't believe I never beat him up. Kev only met him once and swore that he would beat him up if he ever saw him again. I was attracted by Oliver's charm and wealth and thought that if I hung around with him then I'd get rich like him. Instead, I just allowed him to be cheeky. He got his dues though. A couple of years later he bottled somebody outside a nightclub in Swansea and did some time. I wrote him a letter while he was inside saying that I knew what he was going through as I'd been sectioned and I made comparisons between the two then wished him luck. I've seen him several times since and he's never even mentioned it. These days he's a very successful and legitimate businessman. He always had that drive to do something different. I guess we were very similar in that way. As for me, back then, I was clearly living a risky life and I was lucky things hadn't got worse.

One fight, when I was 18, was a close call. It was on the way back from college and was pretty ugly. Kev picked me up with two local crims. They were working on a pure commission basis but we had no intention of paying them. We drove them around for an hour and they stole about eight stereos. One of them became restless and said he wanted some speed. Kev took his friend aside and I refused to pay him. It was dark and he tried to make a grab for the bag that contained the stereos. I pushed him away and he hit me on the side of my eye with a screwdriver. I went into a frenzy like Agave when tearing up her son in Euripides' Bacchae. He could have blinded me, that fucker. That motherfucker. I grabbed him and smashed his head against the car bonnet. He kept falling down but I kept pulling him back up and doing it again. As I smashed his head against the side window he somehow managed to slice me with a Stanley knife across my forehead. I got him in a headlock and punched him in the head about 200 times. He had a broken nose and a lump on his forehead the size of a tennis ball. He wriggled himself free and I kicked him as he ran off. He started to cry, saying to the other two that I was fucking crazy. We ended up keeping the stereos and made some cash, but I nearly lost my eye in the fucking process. I cleaned myself up round Kev's house. His mum and dad were very concerned and helpful. Then Kev's dad took me home and explained to my dad what he'd been told had happened. We told our parents that we'd been trying to prevent some men from stealing Kev's car in the college car park in Cheltenham. My dad said that it was lucky Kevin was with me, otherwise I could have been even more injured. What little he knew about my life, I thought. The irony was that it was Kev's great plan that nearly led to me losing the sight of one eye. My dad's remark made Kev sound like a hero and there is never one when violence is concerned. It's hypocritical to use violence to stop violence – anybody knows that. It takes a braver man to walk away. The guy I beat up didn't come out for three months after the fight, and at the same time his girlfriend started wanting to go out with me. I got off with her once or twice but by the time I came back from America she was being fucked by another thug.

When I got back from America I was to get my A-level results. I'd set my heart on Manchester confident that I would get the grades. When I found out that I'd got in, I was over the moon, all the more so for the fact that my grades hadn't been great – I'd got four C's in English, politics, classical civilisation and general studies. It was a phone call from my classics tutor that had made the difference. He became a character reference and said that my grade C was a great disappointment given the fact that I'd had an "A" in my mock. I've never seen or spoken to him since but sent him a thank you postcard the first week I was there. I stayed in Whitworth Park during my first year. It was situated close to town and on the borders of the infamous Mosside estate. There were 1,500 students in these halls and in the whole of Greater Manchester a total of 50,000 students. This total consisted mainly of students from Manchester University itself, UMIST, and the Metropolitan University which was really a Polytechnic.

Manchester was much bigger than Gloucester. It would be a challenge living there and a whole new experience. I knew living there would broaden my mind and give me a university life to remember. I could go to a new city and forget about being a madman. In a strange way, though, I was somehow proud of it as it made me unique.

Chapter 4 – Mad for it

In September 1994, about 15 months after leaving Coney Hill, I went to live in Manchester to study a BA (Honours) in Classical Studies. In April of that year, I'd visited a friend there with Kev and we'd both fallen in love with the place. On one of the nights we got tanked up and went straight to the Hacienda. Inside, Kev told me that I was a really good dancer. Quite a compliment really: this wasn't one of those cheesy nightclubs in Gloucester. The Hacienda was hardcore – and I fitted in because I'd seen the dark side of life.

My attendance of lectures was poor from the start although, in hindsight, I suppose I was simply fulfilling the fresher's role: students, in particular freshers, try to make themselves look intelligent and try to show that they can get the best possible grades with the minimum amount of effort. It was all part of the game.

Anyway, I was so excited about being in a big city and having a grant and student loan that I didn't really think about studying. This was compounded by the fact that I'd actually intended to read politics at Manchester, rather than classics, and was probably in the wrong state of mind from the start. I also kept postponing my work because I knew I could write good essays and easily catch up when deadlines started to loom.

There was also a lot less discipline at university than there was at school. If you didn't hand in a piece of work most of the tutors failed to chase it up. What's more, I'd already studied a lot of material on the first year's syllabus at A-level and found it boring, so much so that I even tried to make my thoughts known. During the second week, I even went to see my personal tutor and asked her to advise me on writing an essay. Basically, a lecturer had set me an essay but he hadn't discussed the length of it, etc. I wanted to know the difference in quality between a good A-level essay and a good university essay. I wanted to get ahead. I also wanted to know the difference between a good first year and a good second year essay and the difference between an "A" in the second and an "A" in the third year. Then I could set my benchmark and go for it when everyone else had hangovers. Me? I had the answer to hangovers: Lucozade, and lots of it.

I really wanted to tell her about my illness although this urge was more subconscious at the time. You see, I needed to trust somebody first before I could open up to them. She just brushed me off saying that she couldn't write the essay for me and looked shocked to see me taking my studies so seriously.

That same week, I went to the University Counselling Service and spoke to a receptionist and told her of my illness, but there was a long waiting list and I didn't feel comfortable. Instead of having a discussion in private we were in the middle of a room where other people could hear what we were talking about. I never went back there and my university life was markedly worse as a result.

My first few weeks at uni were spent in a drunken haze like most freshers but afterwards, and unlike the others, I failed to settle down. I started drinking more and more. There were the usual distractions at first – selling speed, ecstasy and hash to students, nightclubs, meeting new friends, and women. And then, a few days before Christmas, things took a downward slide and I really started to throw it back. I arrived in Gloucester just in time to see my dad having lunch with his girlfriend and her daughter and boyfriend. That upset me even though I'd told them I was having tea round Dom's. But then the shit really hit the fan. Running upstairs and into my room I noticed that it had been turned into a guestroom. This really sparked me off. Yes, I'd felt guilty removing my brother's stuff from his room, when he was in London, but now it had happened to me.

At that time, my brother lived with my grandmother down the road. Now my dad was doing the same thing to me. As I ran down the stairs he shouted "Jay" but I slammed the door and jumped into the car with Dom. Ten minutes later, at Dom's, I called him on my mobile and said that I wanted to kill him and hung up. He shouldn't have taken my room from me and given me the small room, and put most of my stuff in the loft. I'd planned to catch up on my work during my break. How could I do that without a desk and, above all, with this mental trauma? Wasn't my head already fucked up enough? And now I had to go through this shit. I mean, he didn't even warn me. How did he think I was going to react? Happily? For fuck's sake!

A few nights later, having stayed round my grandmother's and at Dom's, I saw my dad. He apologised and said he'd give me some money to help me through uni. He would give me £50 a month which amounted to one drinking session and entrance into a club, or 50 litres of cider. I didn't want to talk to him at all so I went out and got pissed.

…

On 23 December, after going out in Cheltenham, I went to one of the local pubs, The Wagon and Horses, with Dom. A girl that I was seeing, Karen, met us there with some of her friends. Around closing time, Dom and I were chatting up some other girls when we got into an argument with a gang of blokes. Or rather, they started an argument with us.

There were two of us and about twelve of them, most in their mid twenties. We were arguing with this one bloke who said we should watch who we were trying to pull. It turns out that one of the girls we'd been talking to had been the girlfriend of one of his friends. He told me that I'd better keep hold of my pint glass. I didn't think anything more of it until, a few minutes later, this huge bloke threw Dom over the fruit machine. Straight afterwards he punched me in the face. I just fucking stood there and instinctively smashed my pint glass in his face. He fell to the ground and I kicked him in the head shouting: "Mosside, motherfucker you're dead."

Meanwhile, Dom had regained his composure and had started to kick him in the head too. This all took place in the middle of the pub. Fifty people must have seen it. We proceeded into the games room. A little crook I knew was congratulating me when five of them picked Dom up and threw him against the light on top of the pool table. As I ran over and decked one of them I cried out. Despite the fact that I'd been drinking for several hours I could feel a throbbing pain on my knuckle. Whenever I raised it the pain was agonising. Anyway, because of this somebody had got me into a headlock and three or four other drunks were trying to punch me in the face. I was hitting the guy who had me in a headlock in the head with a pool ball when he shouted for me to stop. When I stopped they all punched me in the face. In response, I grabbed a pool ball and knocked another one of them out. I then threw one – which, thank God, connected – until Karen screamed for me to stop. She took the pool balls from my hand, but then our assailants started hitting her too.

By this time Dom's dad and some of his local drinking friends had plucked up enough courage to try and stop the fight. The only way we could escape was to hide in the women's toilets and phone the police on my mobile, but it needed recharging. Several peacemakers came between us and the gang, and after a few seconds I realised that the police were on their way and that I could come out.

On leaving, one of the gang shouted: "You're dead" to me. At the same time, Karen asked me if I was "all right", but as she said this somebody punched me straight in the face. I ignored the misplaced punch in the jaw and told her to go home and that I'd call her the next day. A police van was already there and a car was approaching.

I got into Dom's dad's friend's car and, with his wife, he drove me to the hospital. I ended up with several stitches in my knuckle caused by glassing the bloke whose teeth I'd helped remove with my size twelves. I'd been waiting there for a while when, as luck would have it, the guy I glassed came in propped up by two girls and wearing a headband with blood all over it. He sat next to me, apparently not knowing who I was, and as I motioned to punch him, Mark who had given me a lift, suggested that I sit on the other side of the room which I reluctantly did.

The fight had taken place less than 500 yards from where I grew up and where my dad still lived. One of the gang phoned my house the next day and pretended to be the landlord of the Wagon asking to speak to me. My dad knew it was one of them as he had just spoken to the real landlord himself to see what had happened. The event marked another scar on me that grew and grew. It wasn't necessarily the fight itself but what I felt to be the injustices afterwards. I was banned from the pub and they weren't, and I had to watch out that I wasn't on my own around town or I'd be in trouble. Basically, the only fight scene in any movie with as much panache as the one I've just described is when the gangsters in De Niro's *The Bronx Tale* lock the bar door and smash the bikers and their bikes to bits.

...

In my second term at university, in January 1995, I decided to bunk off lectures – I hardly ever made it in with my hangovers anyway – and go to see Dom for a week. Four of us headed off in a brand new Mazda to Pau, at the foot of the Pyrenees in the south of France, where he was spending a year abroad. I went with Todd, a mate of mine from uni, and two of his mates from Chester – Sharif, a complete nutter who drank hard and gambled most of his money on the boat over and Hung, the driver, a short, excitable, possibly crazy nip whose family were apparently triads.

I went skiing for the first time and was a natural. I remember seeing the snow-capped Pyrenees when we were driving across to Pau. It was an amazing sight and a frisson of freedom pulsed through my body as we all sang along to the DJ SS and Seduction lyrics: "Like a bird in the sky, flying so high." It was one of the most amazing sights I had ever seen.

Going up the ski lift and skiing down the mountain, through the clouds, was beautiful. I felt as if I was in a different world and that wasn't even due to the bottle of Archers and spliff I'd had in the cable car on the way up. After successfully negotiating the learner slope Dom led me onto a blue slope. I picked up speed and after I had snowploughed well out of control, began to fall for what seemed like ages. I fell for about a minute. It must have been nearly a mile. I lost my shades that I'd bought that morning and ended up about 20 yards away from falling off a cliff. Fucking hell, and I thought crashing through the line and scoring a try at rugby gave you a rush.

At night, we all hung around the bars, although they were full of pretentious English university students, and got shit-faced. One night when we were drinking flaming vodkas or some other drink, Dom and Sharif got arrested for kicking off dozens of car wing mirrors. I gave up after a couple – I'd done enough of that when I was 14. My record with a couple of assailants was about 30 in a night. We only went skiing twice but I loved it and knew I wanted to do it again sometime. One time, Oliver went with us. That's right; the flash guy from Manchester was now living with Dom in France. It was good to see Dom though and I left feeling human even though I was still just as hooked on alcohol as I had been when I had arrived.

When I returned I found out that Kev, who was also at Manchester and lived only 10 yards away from me in halls, had been beaten up with a baseball bat and had received 50 stitches to his head. Craig, also from Gloucester, had been stabbed in the leg and smashed over the head with a bottle of vodka. They'd been doormen in Manchester for three or four months and with their boss, Terry, had beaten up the wrong doormen. They were unprepared and attacked during a lock-in.

My drug dealing was by now non-existent. I'd refused to pay my dealer some money as some of the speed that he'd laid on was dodgy, but ultimately I couldn't organise anything anyway because I was drinking too heavily. I was sceptical about being ripped off and didn't have the right contacts to get a big deal. Also, I think I'd just grown out of it. So I turned to 8.4% cider instead. I would knock it back with a fellow alcoholic called Roger.

Roger was fucked up but right on the level. He knew what it was like to be on the edge. He used to cut himself all over his body with razor blades and once claimed that it was better to hurt himself than hurt somebody else. I guess there's a certain kind of logic to that, albeit pretty warped. The first night I met him there were a dozen people at a gathering and he didn't utter a word. He was just sat there drinking a couple of bottles of neat vodka until he threw up.

All this drinking wasn't doing my lithium level any good but I tried not to care. I tried to blot it out. I couldn't accept that I needed medication to be normal. I couldn't face up to the fact that I was a loon. Anyway, fuck it. I forgot to take it half the time. It had toughened me up and, as Alan had told me, it probably wouldn't happen again. I assumed that because I was well at that particular time I didn't have to stick to a strict regime with the medication. I was at university enjoying myself, or at least trying to, and I tried to take comfort time and time again from the words of the key worker: "It might never happen again."

I was fucking this medic, Sarah, for about two months. If I hadn't had her as an outlet I'd have probably ended up in prison or something. We had sex every night, usually three times, and it was good, but we always seemed to have the same conversation. The night I met her there was a party at her flat. It turns out that Kev had scared a few lads he was arguing with and armed police had burst into the flat. They were wondering what was going on.

Apparently, somebody from Mosside had threatened the people in the flat and pulled out a gun. This somebody, in fact, was Kev, but the fact is, he had really put the shits up them. Sometimes he was brilliant; he could be so convincing. It changed him when he was attacked. He was more angry, defensive, paranoid and even wanted to kick-off with me.

This was largely my fault because when we were still at school he brought his new girlfriend Karen round and in a drunken stupor I got off with her in front of him. He went to the toilets in the pub and when he returned, saw us snogging. This was a tragic moment as we were very close up to that point. He said that if it were anybody else he would have hit them. I said that he could hit me and I wouldn't retaliate as I felt so bad for what I had done. As misfortune would have it, this Karen was the same girl I'd been with on the night of the brawl in the Wagon.

There were also practical reasons for me not kicking off. Not just that we were good friends but also the fact that he was actually massive. All this was before he became a doorman and then he went really crazy. Fuck! Was this guy, the mate I spent most of my time with, as crazy as I was? What was going on? Our lives were spiralling out of control and, instead off calming each other down, we were both playing on it. It was as if we would rather be feared, than liked, by people.

We would hang around with thugs and proper gangsters although it was always hard to tell the difference. There was no pattern – you don't really know who's really crazy until something happens. That's when the men are sorted out from the boys. Of course, they're all muppets at the end of the day. There are many better things in life than becoming a gangster – being a writer; being an entrepreneur, as Kev always planned to be; or even being a monk as my brother sometimes daydreamed about.

Soon, Craig and Kev were turning into bigger head cases after every shift. As Kev said, this wasn't *Goodfellas*, this wasn't a movie; it was real life. They even made me want to become a doorman.

One night, I had some Italian girls round cooking us dinner. We'd met them in a snowball fight the previous week. Half a dozen of us were pelting everyone who went past with snowballs and nobody tried anything, as they were scared of Kev, Craig and me. One bit of eyeball and a stare, grunt or "All righteey then" from Craig and anyone would shit themselves. Craig punched a huge hole in my lounge wall one night. It was plasterboard, but he was massive. He was on steroids and built like an ape.

Once, when we went to Leeds, I remember him swinging metal lampposts from side to side. You could see them swaying all down the road when we walked off. This remains to this day the greatest example of brute physical strength that I have ever seen.

Smashing my wall in Manchester pissed me however. It angered me so much that I pretended not to be in my room when they knocked later on. They kept banging and then ran at the door, knocking it off its hinges and taking a big chunk out of the bottom. What kind of animals had they turned in to? Deep down I was pissed off because they'd acted violently towards one of their best mates but really, in my warped drunken haze, I was upset because they'd done something more violent than I had. They'd done something that had rivalled the madness of Jason Pegler, certified nutter from Coney Hill. I didn't want to give up my reputation as the class "A" nutter. I was proud of it. I was one warped motherfucker.

Mind you, I could talk. I had already threatened two of my flat mates and was later to threaten another two. I had smashed several windows with a golf club, smashed every plate and glass left in the lounge, urinated on Kev's flatmate's eggs, and persuaded Hung to menace two of Kev's flatmates with nunchukkas – but Kev never minded. At least, he never said he did. I'd only met Hung twice and I'd persuaded him to be something that could have got him into trouble. This Chinese youngster who, although he was a bit flash like Oliver, essentially had a friendly and passive nature, turned into the devil when I told him to. Everyday, it seemed that I would do something vile or morally corrupt. I reminded myself of Juvenal's description of Rome which was of a place full of "stupidity, ugliness, vice and crime".

The only sane part of my life was giving Sarah a mindless fucking. She was pretty square and one day I think I went too far for her. I had veered away from the drugs apart from the very occasional spliff and the few E's I had taken when Dom came to visit once, but this time it was Roger's birthday. My drinking partner had never taken any drugs apart from speed once and hash now and again so I bought us a couple of trippy E's each, some billy and the regular White Lightning cider. I bought eight litres which didn't prove quite enough. We sat in his room and had some erudite conversations about life, the world, the universe and what song we were going to play next. I was also trying to teach Roger how to dance but the pills were so trippy and full of strictnine that I was stumbling all over the place.

By early evening the following day I was wasted. Roger was sat in the living room trying to drink some more cider that somebody had brought him. I kept telling everyone that I felt very odd and drank vast amounts of water. I must have drunk 20 pints in a little more than an hour. I phoned Sarah and asked her to come over. I said that I was wrecked and was desperate to see her. She came and we went to my flat and had sex. I told her that I was dying. She said that I would be OK, and the fact that she was a medic made me believe it; she was bound to know the score. She led me back to her flat where we had sex again. During it, I felt very hot and breathed very slowly. I thought that I was going to pass out but the sex did feel good; it was the only tonic for my ailment.

A few days later I went to Tenerife with Kev. Before I left I tried to see Sarah but she said that she was busy. She did, however, leave me a nice note on my door saying that she hoped I had a great time, and sent her love. Now that's the sort of open relationship that I want, I thought. Fuck, she must have known that Tenerife was a pulling joint – all my mates certainly did and most of them had never been there. Did she want me to pull other women or stay with her? I analysed the message and showed it to Todd. Was it a nice message or did it have a hidden meaning? After all, she had never said that she didn't want to see me before.

She'd been really upset the previous week because she'd had to take the morning after pill. I'd said I was sorry but didn't really understand how cut up she was about it. I mean, I had said that I was sorry a few times and asked if she was OK, but I didn't offer her any support. I was no shoulder to cry on, just an alcoholic mess. That talented chess junior had transformed into a beer-drinking monster.

The week in Tenerife was really hot and I got a good tan. We stayed next to a brothel. I was really tempted but couldn't afford it. I thought back to when I was 17 in Amsterdam. I'd fucked this horny model-cum-Chinese prostitute, but her beauty was diminished by the seediness of the occasion, and my paranoia and inexperience. I walked into the Tenerife brothel a few times when drunk but was escorted out by the bouncers after refusing to buy women drinks. Kev and I pulled German and American birds. The night we pulled the German birds Kev threatened me. He said I was chatting up the bird he wanted. I didn't mind because I wanted the one he was talking to.

Our nights consisted of drinking Tequila slammers with Sprite, and lots of lager and cocktails. We had some great chats, good laughs and drank ourselves into oblivion. We would go to some bars and then a club until about six in the morning. We spent all day sunbathing and cooling off with brief swims. My illness was not apparent. I was often depressed but this was probably because of the amount of alcohol that I was drinking. I didn't feel that I was going high or low on a daily basis – Christ, I didn't even know that manic depressives could go high or low on a daily basis at that time in my life. I'd tried to forget the illness by drinking as much alcohol and acting as recklessly as possible. It worked to some degree because I was blotting it out and had made a conscious effort to drink more than anyone else.

I had had the same attitude to drink when I was younger. The problem now was that the stakes were higher. I had met Roger who got drunk every day and had beaten him. Now I was in a futile competition against myself. A slippery slope where all I lived for was alcohol. It got to a stage that nobody wanted to drink with me; I would pressurise everyone I met into getting out of control. I wanted them to be just like me.

...

After the holiday, in April 1995, I returned to Gloucester. I was about to enter a nightclub with my mate Duncan, who was in the marines, when a gang approached us. One of them asked me menacingly if my name was Jason. Wanting to avoid trouble, I said no and that my name was James. He said: "I know it's Jason Pegler" and took a swing at me. I moved out of the way and said I didn't want any trouble. As he took another swing I got him in a headlock and told him that I didn't want any trouble. Dunc was trying to stop the others from joining in. Some of them were in the same crowd that I had fought in the Wagon four months previously. I let the bloke go and repeated that I didn't want a fight. Then he got hold of a bottle and threw it just missing my head. My patience snapped, I grabbed hold of him and threw him through a car windscreen, dragged him out and punched him repeatedly in the face. Then I saw a policeman approaching and swapped places with him so that it looked like he had thrown me through the windscreen. I was even punched after a second policeman had arrived.

I was arrested for so-called Breach of the Peace and referred to as a "prisoner" by one of the officers. I protested that I shouldn't be called a prisoner as I was the one that had been attacked. He ignored me which enraged me. I was left in the cell for about 20 minutes and then two policemen interviewed me.

I told them that I was attacked and they said that the aggressors had said that I had glassed one of their friends a few months before. I owned up to it but said that I was attacked first that time as well. I said that I was just sticking up for myself. I was actually proud that I wouldn't let other people push me around. The police must have seen some validity in my argument as I persuaded them to give me a lift home. These types of brawls, however, couldn't have been doing my sanity any good.

…

I was released without charge and glad to return to Manchester a few days later. In Manchester, I could get drunk and nobody would notice. I could be my anarchic self and not be interrupted. I could be me. In Gloucester, people just got in the way and they knew about my past – they knew about my mental illness. I thought it made some people want to challenge me to a brawl.

The reality was, that as time went on, I played up to my

madness more and more instead of accepting it as a problem and trying to prevent it from happening again. When I was drunk, I was loud, obnoxious and acted like a muppet. I remember once being really pissed after having played snooker with Kev, Todd and a guy called Ronnie. What was meant to be a quiet night turned out to be an ugly one when for no reason, apart from my alcoholism, I threw a huge breeze block through a club window. It was the snooker club that we had just been in. I could see the irritation in all of my friends' faces afterwards. It was one step too far for all of my mates but I didn't give a fuck. I was the crazy one and I didn't give a fuck. I was the crazy motherfucker and I might as well have been born in fucking Compton.

I had gained a reputation for fighting, and playing rugby, in Gloucester which naturally made me a target for thugs. Living in quite an affluent area and being known as the County Chess Champion also made people want to take a pop at me. That was why I hated going back there; it was too violent. The narrow-mindedness didn't really sink in until afterwards. Gloucester was quickly turning into a place that I didn't want to go back to at all. It was absurd. I was becoming just as irrational and narrow-minded in my behaviour – probably even more so – than the thugs in Gloucester who I despised so much.

I spent my first day back in Manchester drinking Stella Artois and waiting for Sarah to return as Kev was working and Roger was still away. She didn't return until the next day and when I helped her carry her stuff in she was more interested in talking with her male friend than me. I asked her what was going on and she told me that she wasn't ready to have a relationship. I left calmly but felt rejected and gutted that I couldn't have a regular shag. I also knew that I had lost the only sense of stability in my sad and chaotic life. This was exaggerated by the fact that I was only taking my lithium sporadically.

A few days later I started fucking this girl called Harriet. She was fat and, although her face was reasonable, I only went anywhere near her because I wanted to sleep with her friend, Meredith. When I first met Meredith she was very obnoxious, conceited and temperamental. She had short bleached blond hair, was about 5' 4", slim and trendy. She looked like a pretty horror doll as she was very good looking but wore way too much make-up. Sometimes, after we'd got together, I felt like I was fucking Darryl Hannah in Blade Runner. I wanted to get into her pants, though, the moment I saw her.

Within a week, I managed that. We started to sleep with each other most nights. Some nights, I would walk into her flat and, when her flatmates said that they thought she was asleep, I would say it doesn't matter. I would walk into her room, half wake her up then fuck her senseless. She always seemed distant and I soon discovered that she was on Prozac. She was also a drunk like me. Interestingly, we would never speak to each other when any of our friends were around. I also felt that I had to humiliate myself to get her to say something nice to me.

One evening, for example, in front of Meredith and two of her friends, I drank a pint of their piss for 15 quid. It tasted horrible even though it was supposed to be full of vitamins, and I had to wash my teeth hard for the next few days. I can't believe that people used to clean their teeth with piss in the days before dental hygiene. I felt like Egnatius in a Catullus poem. Catullus laughs at him for cleaning his teeth with piss – imagine how he'd have laughed at me for drinking it in the modern age…

Although I wasn't officially crazy at this time, because I wasn't living in a mental hospital, I was certainly crazier than anyone else in my social circle and always would be. I was the loony and I was obsessed with it. I thought the experience of being in Coney Hill would feel like a noose round my neck for the rest of my life. It was something that I had to live with inside of my mind and it caused lots of problems. I had achieved my goal. I acted crazy to protect myself from going crazy. *As I saw it, if I was always crazy I couldn't go crazy again.* I was a manic-depressive with a classic case of denial. It became difficult for me to socialise with people on a normal level, my university work was being neglected and my overdraft was steadily increasing. The sporty fellow was now no longer sporty.

After I'd started to see Meredith I managed to settle my score with Sarah. I couldn't have her so in my jealousy and anger I set about enacting revenge on her through making her friends suffer. I went into my hall's bar, The Grovel, brewed out of my mind. I was with Kev and this guy Tom who tried to give the impression that he was as crazy as me and Kev. Well, that was one hell of an effort, man. Anyway, I went up to three of Sarah's friends who were sat down at a table and punched them all in the face with the help of Kev and Tom who were holding them down. I ran out as the bar manager came in, and was banned from the bar for the rest of the year. I later found out that one of the lads I'd punched left university for good the following week. I guess my beating him up was the last straw.

The next day, Sarah came to my flat and told me how nasty I'd been. I said that she hadn't given me a choice. Who did she think she was, screwing with my head like that? Fucking slut. My head was fucked enough as it was. However, after I listened to her moral argument, I agreed that I'd been out of order and apologised. What had I become? I had turned into a wanker. I was a monster.

This wasn't the life that my parents had expected me to live but parents can never predict how the lives of their offspring turn out. They can only do what they think is appropriate. It's often not enough, though, as we live in an imperfect world. We live in a place of survival of the fittest. There isn't enough sympathy for the madman, the homeless, the third world or humanity in general.

I was having more and more thoughts like this in my drunken state. By now, I was drinking at least four litres of extra strong cider every night – usually White Lightning or Wild n' White. I had also mastered my beer bong, which I was thankful to Butler for.

The physics of the beer bong is as follows. It consists of a funnel and a tube joined together. You pour, say, a can of

8.4% cider into it making sure that your thumb is at the bottom of the tube. You straighten the tube and wait for the bubble to hit the top. Then you put the tube in your mouth and lift up the funnel. The bong creates a vacuum and the liquid rushes into your stomach quicker than anyone can neck a pint. The concoction is lethal. I've even tried it with small bottles of vodka, whisky and the odd can of Special Brew – dangerous but a good party trick.

I frightened some people, excited others, but whatever their view only geeks would forget about the beer bong. Eventually, I got bored with it. For starters, nobody could stick me when I was using it. But it also made me violently sick when I overdid it – the beer would come out in a huge gush of puke. The world record, according to Butler, was somebody in Los Angeles. They apparently drank 40 bottles of Budweiser in two minutes and then their stomach exploded. Now that was a great urban myth. But I didn't believe it.

Once, I had 10 cans of Lowenbrau Pils, which is 6%, in 90 minutes and kept it all down. At one time, I used it every evening but now I was happy to drink my horrible cheap cider. Basically, I didn't have much money and needed to get drunk everyday so cider was the obvious choice. My first year at university had started by going out to three or four clubs a week and had finished with me sleeping with a girl that I never spoke to and becoming one of the best drinkers in Manchester.

I had managed to avoid hospitalisation, though, and, on the surface, even felt strong. My stream of consciousness went as follows: only a strong man drinks strong cider and I could drink more strong cider than anyone else. Now I look at tramps drinking the same shit and go through a mixture of emotions. First, I identify with them because I know what it's like. Second, I feel sorry for them because it's not a good state to be in. Then I think they're weak as they should choose to do something more positive with their lives. I feel relieved, as I'm not like that anymore, although I know that I always have the potential to go back to the drink. A leopard never changes its spots and neither does an alcoholic.

I hoped that I would never get ill again but I was risking my health by drinking heavily, and so far the gamble had paid off. Thing is, because alcohol's a depressant, there was nothing to win except for a short-term removal of inhibitions. Deep down though, I was terrified that it would return and was trying to forget somehow – via alcohol – that it had ever happened at all. As with most people, alcohol was a form of escapism.

Alcohol had taken over my life. On the plus side, it helped me chat up and fuck dozens of women. On one occasion, I had a brief relationship with a woman from Stockport. She was a 33 year old single mum and had a 12 year-old kid. I pulled her in a club called the "Boardwalk", although probably wouldn't have if the booze hadn't made me dance like a maniac. I was dancing so well I would have made James Brown raise his eyebrows. I had lightning quick hands and feet, and was bang in time with the music. I looked like a professional.

One night, at about 2.15am, Kev and I left the club where he was working. We were both smashed and he shouted at some black girl calling her an Afro. This was not like the Jean Rhys that I had pitied in a rare moment of manic lucidity and sensitivity. What was going on in my life? I was now hanging around with a racist. Sure, I used to call my white mates "niggers" but that was a joke. Panji even told me to call him "nigs" when we were at school together. I was not racist though. I was into rap and had a massive poster of Snoop Doggy Dogg holding a gun in my room. I had had a fight with Panji at school when I was 12 and called him a nigger. He had thrown a stone by mistake in my eye and had laughed when he did it. I kicked off although it's something that I regretted almost immediately. Soon after that, we became good mates and my prejudices faded away. I empathised with him. He had it hard enough as it was. Being mixed race, he had enough problems as it was trying to forge an identity for himself in a school full of white kids.

After the Afro taunt, two students starting punching Kev

in retaliation. I decked one of them and started to kick him in the head repeatedly. We then ran away from an approaching police van but were soon arrested. A few hours after being locked up I was told that I had a phone call. That was odd as I hadn't told anyone that I was there. It was my solicitor. He told me that the bloke whom I had allegedly assaulted was in hospital. As things turned out, we were released the following morning with no charges. I couldn't walk as my feet hurt from kicking the bloke who had hit me.

The next day, we were on the front page of the main student newspaper, *Mancunion*, and in the same paragraph as the BNP for "a racist attack". You see what newspapers do, distort the truth. Or was it actually true? After all, my friend had called her an Afro. However, we had been hit first even though Kev had made a clumsy comment. We certainly weren't in the National Front. To suggest so was absolutely ludicrous. What did these student journalists know anyway? They were all fucking geeks. They didn't have any balls like us, our gangster friends, or Snoop or the mob in those gangster movies. A part of me, as ashamed as I am to say it, felt some pride in what we'd done. I'd been victorious in battle and had had some publicity. I was turning into a twisted motherfucker. I also wanted to write at that point, but never got round to it. It was something I dreamed of. Anyway, you couldn't know a lot about life if you're always writing about it – you had to go out and live it, I thought. I got Meredith's address in London before I left Manchester for the summer and went back to Gloucester.

...

On my first night back in Gloucester, in the summer of 1995, I got into a fight with an old friend Daniel Roberts. I hadn't seen him for a while as he'd spent the previous two years in prison for burglaries, robberies and assaults. I'd started the fight by grabbing his pint out of his hand and drinking it in one. It was my way of celebrating seeing him and I was even prepared to buy him a drink afterwards. Moments later, I received a weighty punch on the side of my

91

face. Most blokes would have been knocked down by it, but not me. I just fucking stood there.

The punch was from Daniel. He'd been doing a lot of weights in prison. His hands were twice the size they'd been before he went down. By way of response, I punched him to the floor and started kicking him in the face. As Duncan tried to stop me, I strangled him. The bouncer pushed me out of the pub, as I was off balance, and closed the door. I regained my composure and tried to get back in. It was a futile task. Daniel had also been thrown out. Was this how I treated my friends? Were these the sort of people that I should be hanging around with?

The next day I apologised to Dunc and sort of did to Daniel. We were round Peach's house and I remember Daniel swinging Peach's eight year-old brother around and saying: "If I ever had a little brother like yours, Peach, I'd kick fuck out of him everyday so when he's my age he'd be hard as fuck." For God's sake. My life couldn't go on much longer like this without triggering other episodes could it? I declined my friends' offer to go swimming that day as I knew I was crazy enough without hanging around with them. One nudge too far and I might be pushed over the edge again. It wasn't as if I had to prove my madness as everybody knew I had been in Coney Hill. Sometimes, I convinced myself that I was proud that I had a reputation like that but really I knew that I pitied myself. I felt that there was something lacking in me: total sanity.

That summer I drank every night and after a week in Gloucester went to stay with Dom in Hossegor, in the South of France. He was with his girlfriend camping and they lent me a tent. Dom had become pretty good at surfing and, after trying it for a couple of days, I took his advice and bought a Boogie Board and all the extras including a summer wetsuit, fins, some surf magazines, and wax so I could stay on the board when riding a wave. I learnt to boogie board and doing that for several hours every day for six weeks makes you fit no matter how much you drink.

Going to France provided a much-needed break from the

grey, rainy climate of Manchester. Hossegor was beautiful, hot and sunny everyday. Temperatures got up to 33 degrees centigrade in the shade. It didn't feel as hot as it had been when I went to Washington though as the humidity was low. The campsite was huge and I stayed there rent free, doing a runner when we eventually left. We'd cook a barbecue every evening and eat chocolatines and French bread for breakfast.

I got my first great sun tan. The only time the three of us would argue was about who was going to do the washing up. We bought some plastic chairs and would often eat with a German couple. The man, Axel, had a long board and all the expensive gear. He went surfing every summer but I don't think he ever caught a decent wave. The beach was topless and there were some bloody sexy women there. Thing is, it was difficult for me to pull as Dom was happy with Paula and everyone else, surprise, surprise, was French. We drank Kronenbourg 1664 every night and cheap French wine called "Grappe" which was 12%.

We bought some metal boules and played most evenings on the sand. One time, in the middle of an argument, Dom threw the boule at me. I was 20 yards away and it went about 30 feet in the air smashing through the plastic chair and just missing my foot. Now that was close. He had a temper like all my friends seemed to. I think part of it was just male hormones, but I had always tended to hang around with charged up people.

Paula left after I'd been there six weeks and Dom only wanted to stay there a few days longer. The two of us flew back from Biarritz. I was never really into it but when Dom and Paula disappeared in their tent I would wander off to a large group of French puff heads nearby who were always happy to share spliffs with me. Most of them would sleep in hammocks and they all had huge bamboo bongs. That was the last time I ever had a spliff except for when I was manic once several years later.

A few days after flying back from Biarritz, I went to Newquay with Kev and rode the biggest wave that I've ever seen. Out of 40 people trying to get out back only two or three managed it. It took me several minutes, mind you, and when I did I had to sit on the crest until the cramp that had locked my leg went away. When I took off, it was one of the most intense and thrilling moments of my life. I rode the wave for what must have been a minute and had to jump off the board when I realised I was heading for the rocks at Fistral beach. I left unhurt and with a feeling of great freedom and exaltation that I had never experienced before.

Kev and Craig were working as security guards at Trevelgue campsite and tried to get me a job, but after a couple of weeks we all left as we ran out of money. I remember fucking a virgin in our poxy little caravan which Craig had broken into. Kev was sleeping on the floor and Craig slept outside. We hung around these Scousers and ate their food, borrowed their car and trashed their caravan. The Gloucester boys were back together again but there was always a sense of violence in the air that made everything so intense. Anyone who came into contact with us was lucky that we didn't knock them out for the sheer hell of it.

We made friends with some South African doormen. At least they were on the level. Kev and I had arranged to get jobs as doormen in a Newquay nightclub and one night, when Craig was working, we went out with the two South Africans to celebrate. We played pool all night in the pub blatantly using everyone else's money on the table. Nobody would dare ask to play as they saw that there were four steamed up lunatics playing doubles who were ready to kick-off at any moment. When we left the club Kev and I walked back and he must have threatened a hundred people. I'd never seen anything like it. He was crazy. He'd go up to a gang of four blokes and demand a fight. First, he'd demand a fight one-on-one and then he'd challenge them all. I was acting as a diplomat, but nobody was up to the challenge of having a brawl with Kev. He had fire in his eyes and something in his belly that night. The memories of the relaxing weeks in Biarritz were fading away as I got back in with the Gloucester boys. Soon, I would return to Manchester, move in with them and seek refuge with an alcoholic by becoming an alcoholic myself.

...

In August 1995, I returned to Manchester to sit two retakes. If I'd passed my philosophy coursework I wouldn't have had to take these exams, but I got no marks. I'd asked my brother to do an essay on Plato on Aristotle. He was a philosophical genius but was so unstable at the time that he ended up copying a big chunk of the essay straight from a book. Years later, I asked him to tell me how he could do something like that. He said: "I was so weak I didn't even know what I was doing... There was a time three years previously when I could have dictated the essay from the top of my head. I'd recently been kicked out of dad's and had to move in with grandma. I'd gone from having a study and planning on being a professor to sleeping on a couch and living with a geriatric old biddy. No one will ever know the psychological impact that having my room taken away from me had. I felt as though someone had ripped the floorboards from underneath me and I was sinking into the abyss." Dad and Claire had their reasons. Claire had done domestic chores for Harvey and I for a couple of years. She had already brought up two daughters. Wasn't it time we stood up on our own two feet? I could understand this. It was just the way things happened – without any consultation.

Back at uni I also felt let down by the department. I was fascinated by philosophy because of my brother's influence. He encouraged me to read Plato and Bertrand Russell when I was 11. By the time of my first class, I already knew about all kinds of philosophy from ethics and aesthetics through to epistemology and metaphysics. Afterwards, the lecturer said that there would be a tutorial the following week for those who were interested. I was really looking forward to it. Just as I had loved debating at school and hanging around with intelligent people, philosophy was also my forte.

In the event, nobody turned up apart from me. I was so angry. I couldn't believe it. In my view, the lecturer had shown a complete lack of responsibility. But maybe I had scared everyone off. Maybe I had been so engrossed in the class that people saw me as pretentious and didn't want to sit in the same room as me. They could have switched locations without telling me, but I wasn't that paranoid and knew I had the right time and place.

I was so pissed off I didn't go to a philosophy lecture until three months later and only then because I had been told to in a letter that said I must improve my attendance. The philosophy professor had destroyed my dream start at uni. I was like a time bomb waiting to go off and he had pressed the detonator.

I ended up passing the exams and did a week's labouring. Six of us lived in a house in Mosside: Kev, Craig, Roger, Chris, Todd and me. We moved to another flat in November as nobody could be bothered to clean the house. The backyard looked like it had gone through a nuclear melt down. The nearest anyone got to it would be to open the door, eyes closed, and throw the rubbish as far as possible so it wouldn't make you feel anymore sick the next time you opened it. I also didn't pay any rent which helped fund my drinking.

By now, I could drink six litres of 8.4% cider in a night – and each of the 12 pints in one go. I was proud of myself and thought that nobody watching the World Embassy Darts Championships at the Lakeside could do that. The new flat was in Victoria Park and we were burgled five times in six weeks. Everyone's stuff was taken except mine, as my room must have been mistaken for a cupboard (even though it was massive). I had a suspicion that we might get burgled as the area was a bit rough. I mean, we nearly had a fight with a group of Asian lads when moving in and that was in the afternoon. As a precaution, I covered my stereo and everything else that was visible with dark sheets so they couldn't be spotted by someone looking through the key hole.

I eventually moved in with Meredith as I knew I would get thrown out of university if I kept on drinking with Roger. My relationship with Kev had turned into a Jekyll and Hyde scenario. He was frustrated that I didn't want to go out and get drunk and pull. I mean, I was an alcoholic who could drink from the flat and had a regular shag that came round when I said. I didn't need anything else. I was becoming socially inept and couldn't deal with the violent moods of a doorman. He threatened me when we were in the new flat and that was the last straw. Kev told me how he hadn't got the deposit back from the previous landlord. I told him that he should have knocked the fucker out. I told him that he shouldn't have paid so much rent in the first place. I hadn't. Kev's response was to say: "Maybe I should knock you out." I was pissed off and we left the house two minutes later after necking some Stella. I would still occasionally start off drinking the same as Kev. It was a kind of bonding ritual when we went out. By this time, though, I was more prone to necking a bottle of wine in one through a straw.

Just after leaving the house, I saw an Asian bird that I had shagged some weeks before. I told Kev to cross the road as I didn't want to see her. After the girls crossed over, Kev shouted at me. "Who do you think you are telling me what to do? Nobody tells me what to do except my old man. You ever say anything like that again and I'll knock you out."

The drunken threat by Kev made me think where my life was going. My life couldn't go on as it was for much longer without disastrous consequences. I would fail university, certainly go mad again and probably end up in prison for any one of several public disorder offences: vandalism, GBH, ABH or even murder. What could I do?

A few weeks before the threat, I tried to get off with Meredith's flatmate, Lucy. She and Harriet, who lived with Meredith, treated Meredith really badly, took her money and food, and even left her locked out of her own house. I was so fucked up that I had initially gone round to have a go at Lucy. They were having a party which Meredith had not been invited to. The evil cow and me slept on the same bed with our clothes on but we didn't get off with each other. She wouldn't let me, as she put it, "score a hat-trick".

The next morning, I went into Meredith's room and told

her what happened the previous night. She said it was OK but I said I couldn't see her anymore because it wouldn't be right. I left kicking bins in the street and crying. It was the first scrap of sensitivity I had shown in a long time – months, possibly even years.

Five minutes after getting back home Meredith was at the door. I couldn't believe it. Was this the same girl who was so cruel to me when we met? Was this the same girl who had dared me to drink a pint of piss and implied that I had a small dick? Yes, it was. I told her it was too late. She left and a few minutes later I got a phone call from another girl that I'd been shagging. I told Roger to say that I wasn't in. He did but told me she'd said she wanted to see me. I'd ignored her previous couple of phone calls and it was the last time that I would get a call.

I called for Meredith a week after she left my doorstep in tears. I'd discovered that she had tried to overdose the night after I had split with her. We'd missed each other and for the first time talked to each other properly. All the bullshit had gone out of the window and it was evident that two incredibly fucked up individuals each needed a shoulder to cry on. She was clever and unique. We spent the next few nights and the New Year in London together. We really got on well and things were really romantic. Although Meredith decided to quit her degree in Art History, we agreed to move in together in Manchester. We moved to Chorlton-cum-Hardy, a friendly neighbourhood where the Bee Gees used to live. My relationship with Meredith improved and became more interesting as time went on.

We moved in with each other in January 1996 and were happy until October of the same year. I particularly liked not having a television for the first few months. It meant we talked to each other more, got to know each other better and used our imaginations. She was very artistic and we had her drawings framed on the walls in each room of the flat. We were both in a bad way when we moved in but gradually got our heads together and were grateful to each other for it. She was the first girl I loved.

My alcoholism had reduced to binge drinking about three to four nights a week. It was a fresh start. I started studying and my grades improved a lot. I actually became interested in my course. I admired the Roman race again and became absorbed in Greek tragedy. I even read Lucan's *Civil War* from start to finish. I liked the gruesome bits that described, in detail, blood splashing when heads were being hacked off. My life was more stable although I still had that violent streak in me especially when I was drunk.

This was evident on the day of my twenty-first birthday. I got drunk with a guy who'd lived with Kev in the first year. His name was Charlie. I drank ten Stellas, while he stopped at eight and met up with his geeky friends. I was furious and hurled an empty pint glass across the bar. It smashed against a bottle of spirits and I didn't look back when I walked out. Meredith had gone straight from work to meet me for a quiet drink but I guess I ruined her night by being shit-faced, moaning and being so fired up. Also, for my twenty-first, mum and dad had made a special effort to come and visit and buy us things for the flat. They bought us a toaster, some crockery, an ironing board, kettle and stuff like that.

In the summer, after comfortably passing my second year, I worked for Ladbrokes for two weeks and at Safeway for six weeks part-time. I didn't like the bookies: it was full of drunks, chain smoking and throwing their money away. They never said thank you, just grunted and were glued to the screens showing horse and dog racing.

The job at Safeway was OK to begin with. I worked 6am to 10am Mondays to Fridays and was responsible for assessing and reordering the stock in the store. It took a few weeks to be trained up and I could use my natural ability at mental arithmetic to count how many cheeses were on each shelf. If there were 13 rows and 13 columns then that would make 169 slabs of mature cheddar.

I also used a computer database and inputted my results. I was doing a job that was important to the store. Then, when my manager was away, the bureaucracy arrived. I was given a machine that would count the products for me. I told one of the senior managers that it was slower than my head and that it was a nuisance, but I was told to keep using it. That was the last straw. I left and never went back to get my P45.

Although I didn't stick the jobs, I had changed and was a human being again. I hadn't seen my friends for months. They no doubt felt I had deserted them. But I'd been brave enough to make a change. By leaving the hectic lifestyle with my mates I'd made a decision and stuck by it. This decision was proving to be beneficial.

In the month before my final year began, I read the entire year's syllabus to get ahead. I wanted to make sure I got a 2:1 and believed I could make a miraculous recovery and get a first. With help from Meredith, who was working as a receptionist in Chorlton, I started the preliminary work for producing and directing a modern film of the ancient Greek Tragedy, *Ajax*, written by Sophocles. It deals with the theme of madness and shows the noble warrior Ajax going mad then killing himself when he returns to sanity because of the humiliation he has felt. This was it, I was dealing with madness in my own way now. Nobody could stop me. I was sorted. I was together. I was going to get a first. I had secured funding from the Hellenistic Society and the Classics Department. Members of staff were giving advice, I had a producer, a cameraman, a place to hire equipment, storyboards written and had advertised, and set a date for, the auditions. My personal tutor was even helping me to choose the actors. Everything was in place.

Chapter 5 – Oh no, not again…

Just when my life seemed to have some meaning and I had at last found an identity that I was content with a catastrophe unfolded before (or rather *through*) my eyes. I was hit by a thunderbolt from Zeus.

In the same way that I'd failed to turn up at the Oxford University entrance exam three years previously, I failed on this occasion to turn up to my own audition. *I was a bit preoccupied… a little bit crazy… a little bit high… really high.* I had gone manic, too manic, once again – although how it all started is still a bit of a haze.

I remember walking through Mosside buying ethnic minority newspapers and thinking how I could save the world through the medium of film. I stayed up all night writing messages in books and on pamphlets that I had collected, also leaving my phone number to let people know who to call when the inevitable nuclear war broke out

News of the war was about to break the following day. At about 4am, I thought I'd call Snoop Doggy Dogg to ask for his help. There was an emergency number on the back of the CD cover of Doggystyle to contact his crew if anything went wrong. I rang the number and it didn't matter that I couldn't speak to anyone as my powers of telepathy had returned. Throughout the night of the 26 October, I was performing sexual rituals that are too disgusting to mention or recall. By 7.30am, I thought that the whole world had turned into the Red Light District in Amsterdam and that Chorlton in Manchester was the centre of world consciousness. I had never been so happy and intrigued in my life, not even during my first manic episode.

Meredith knew something was wrong and went to her boss to ask for time off. Well, I did need somebody to help me prevent nuclear war, didn't I? When she went to see her boss, I started to put my plan into action. The first people I could communicate with on a telepathic level were the homeless. To help get them off the streets and make them my recruits, I would skate round giving them bananas and books which I had left cryptic instructions in. I was so pleased to have saved the world from another nuclear war as a result of conversing with people like Dogg Pound. To confuse the enemy, I had bluetacked my *Usual Suspects* poster to someone's garage only a hundred yards away from the house. My mind was racing and my critical faculties were gone. I was completely unaware of this at the time. Instead, I was in heaven – the fleeting moments of hell hidden deep in my consciousness, the mania so powerful.

We stayed in during the afternoon and I put my boogie board on my back thinking I could fly anywhere I wanted to in the universe. I was also very proud that I could swim underwater to Australia in five seconds. While these thoughts were coursing through my mind, Meredith decided to take me to my mum's in Powys as she didn't know what to do. I had told her about my manic depression before and she'd said that it didn't bother her. Like Kev I think she thought the idea of it was cool, but she was about to discover first hand the traumas of what she'd let herself in for. She got more than she bargained for.

We went to my mum's by train from Piccadilly station. I was glad we took this route as I discovered time travel on the way which was most satisfying. I knew I had discovered it every time I clicked my fingers ... now ...now ... now ... I sat opposite a really nice old lady who was so senile that she seemed almost as loopy as me. I bought a great magazine on the greatest sportsmen in the world. It was refreshing to discover that I was the best at every sport in the world. Forget the cartoon *Sport Billy*, this was *Sport Jase*.... and this was real...I was real...

We arrived at Leominster and got straight into a taxi. I didn't want to be seen in public as my position in society was too important... It was too crucial. If I was going to fail in bringing about world peace then the world was doomed. I was the only person who had the potential – I was Jesus Christ, God on earth...

It was also my destiny to become the greatest film director on earth... People would come to the cinema and be influenced by my films... Their lives would change as a result and so would those of their friends and any other people who they ever came into contact with... No matter how slight the influence it was everlasting and continual... I could not fail. This was my destiny... My destiny was a destiny that even surpassed that of Aeneas founding Troy. Virgil's *Aeneid* was my favourite book and I was delighted to have surpassed the achievements of the hero...

When we arrived at my mum's Meredith explained that I was behaving strangely and that she was worried. My mum looked worried but that wasn't unusual as she always looked worried. Like most mums.

Mind you, wouldn't you be worried if you were the mother of God? That's a lot of responsibility, a lot of pressure to be under. Of course, I didn't mind them worrying... I knew that they wouldn't understand yet but would in due course although I wasn't sure when... but sometime soon ... sometime real soon, that much was certain ... Meredith soon went to bed as she was exhausted.

I stayed up talking to my mother while telepathically intertextualising programmes on television for everybody else in the world so as to instil world peace. I had slept with, and therefore conquered, my mother without her realising it by playing with her fire tools and holders, and was now king of the world. I was king of the castle, king of the mountains, king of the past, present and future, even king of Old Trafford. I was king of everything and everyone...

Before I went to bed I had to perform rituals. I did this by cleaning myself in the bathroom and rinsing my mouth out with soap and water. Indeed, just as in my first episode I had gone from believing I was dominant, king of all, to submissive, a mere subject, so too now I had suddenly become an abject slave to womankind. My mum and Meredith were the bosses now and to be a good slave I had to suck on a small teddy of Daffy Duck that I had covered in soap. I sucked for several minutes until I was led away by the

103

two goddesses. I was glad I had performed these rituals as I was now guaranteed a life of eternal slavery. I was going to become the next manager of Manchester United. We would win everything and, by playing sexy and exciting football, would be able to influence others and instil world peace... All it needed was for more women to take up the game and we were on our way...

However, that night as I lay in bed with Meredith, I realised for the first time during a manic episode that I was actually manic and that I was ill. I said: "I know I'm ill and I need help." I burst into tears and received comfort in the form of a cuddle. Now there were two people crying and things got worse. The next day a social worker came round and wanted to section me after I'd been reading the Classics and the Hellenistic Society handbook cross-legged and naked under a tree in the garden. It was a cold autumn day and my stepfather had ordered me to get in as my behaviour was extremely odd. I ran away from the social worker thinking she was evil... and most of all terrified that she was the enemy.

I ran into a pub and challenged a traveller at the bar to a competition. The two of us went into the games room and I bet him I could get the white as close to the pocket as possible without potting it. He accepted and I duly did this with the white stopping by the edge of the pocket. He bought me a pint and I drank it in one. On the way out I said that I didn't have any money and couldn't have bought him a pint if I'd lost. He said that was fine and pulled out a knife. "It's OK. I'd have stabbed you in that case, you cunt." As he laughed I laughed too and, thinking he would make a good extra in one of my imaginary movies, left the pub before things got too complicated. I didn't want to get distracted from my mission...

I walked down to the health centre and my stepdad got out of his car. He told me to get in the car and threatened to tell my dad about it and would even punch him if he didn't do anything. He said my mum shouldn't go through all this on her own and that my dad should help shoulder the burden.

However, at the time, I didn't really register what he was on about as there were far more interesting manic processes and formulations going on in my mind. When I got back to mum's there was a doctor and ambulance there. They said they were going to take me somewhere for a rest. Well, I was happy with that. I thought I deserved a rest – after all, it's not every day that you find out you're God, is it? I might even meet some people to cast in my film... I lay down in the ambulance as though I was on a luxury yacht cruising around the Caribbean.

About 45 minutes later we arrived at the Mid Wales mental institution, Talgarth. There was a big lounge, even bigger than the one in Coney Hill and certainly more colourful. The first person I saw was a Scottish patient heckling the staff. She turned me on because I thought she had telepathic powers like me. I also thought that she was into bondage. The nursing staff interviewed Meredith and my mum as I was shown around my new film studio... They both cried as they left, and I only realised something was wrong when I was prevented from leaving by five hospital staff who injected Haliperidol into my arse. (I did not discover until 2002 that I had an allergy to this and it was a lawyer who told me not a doctor.)

I spent over two months in that hospital in the Black Mountains in the middle of nowhere. It seemed like two years, however, because this time the depression hit me harder. In January, at my own request, I was transferred to Withington hospital in Manchester. This was the closest image of hell that I had ever seen. It resembled then, and resembles now as far as I know, something that Michel Foucault would have written about in *Madness and Civilization*: small wards, no colour, staff that treat patients like criminals or retards and certainly not the kind of place for any kind of rehabilitation. Perhaps I'd gone back to Manchester too quickly.

...

The consultant in Mid Wales wanted to put me on ECT, the horrific treatment Jack Nicholson went through *in One Flew Over The Cuckoo's Nest*. I knew as much about it as anyone else – very little – although being electrocuted didn't strike me as being particularly humane. I was told that it helped to shorten depression quicker than antidepressants on their own but could sometimes lead to short term memory loss and, in some rare cases, permanent memory loss or brain damage.

ECT is increasingly rare these days but the public should still be made aware of it. Perhaps the best medium is film which has the power to really get across how sick and disturbing it can be. *Fight Club*, for example, touched upon it, as has Birdie and Me Myself and Irene. Anyway, me? I declined the treatment as I kept thinking of when Chief put Jack Nicholson to sleep. I couldn't get that image out of my mind.

When I was offered ECT by Dr. Cooper in Mid Wales, I was frightened and humiliated. We discussed the matter in the weekly ward round.

"Is life worth living?" asked Dr.Cooper.

"Don't care."

"You don't care?"

"Don't know."

"Are you more depressed than the last time we met?"

"Yes."

"Do you have suicidal thoughts?"

"Sometimes."

"Do you think you might act upon them?"

"Yes."

"It looks like the antidepressants aren't working as fast as we'd hoped. We talked about the possibility of ECT treatment last time. Would you consider this an option?"

"How quickly does it work?"

"It works with the antidepressants and should double the speed of your recovery."

"What about the side effects? I've heard you can end up

brain dead."

"The treatment is a lot better nowadays. There is very little chance of that happening."

"Won't I lose my memory?"

"Short term memory loss is likely, but the chances of long term memory loss are very minimal."

"How minimal?"

"I don't know how much exactly."

"I heard it was one in fifty."

"No, I would think it would be less than that."

"The thought terrifies me."

"It's a scary thought but it has benefited thousands of patients. I'll give you some time to think it over. You can ask one of the nurses to contact me and we could start the treatment. Is there anything else you wish to discuss?"

"Don't know."

"Well, Jason (shaking hands), I hope you feel better soon."

"Thanks."

I felt like a python was slowly crushing me. All my will to live was being drained out of me. Nevertheless, I resisted taking the ECT treatment. There are a maximum of eight sessions over a period of four weeks and the anaesthetic stops you feeling any physical pain. Techniques have improved over recent years and my previous consultant and current psychologist both said that they would opt for ECT if they were given the option during the lowest ebb of an episode of bipolar effective disorder (technical term for manic depression). Well, I guess they know their stuff but they can see it from a more rational perspective than me. I've seen people straight after they've come out of the ECT treatment room and it's made me cry.

Andy, who taught me to play *Imagine* and *Jealous Guy* on the guitar in Mid Wales, was one of these. He kept repeating conversations that we had already had before. He had forgotten everyone's name on the ward and he was only middle-aged. It was soul-destroying to see such a talented man humiliated. He'd lost all his confidence and had turned into a fumbling wreck; this was a man who'd played solo guitar in front of 2000 people.

Most people who have ECT experience short-term memory loss and a few experience long-term memory loss forever. In 2001, the mental health charity, Mind, reported that there are 1300 "shock treatments" carried out each week in the United Kingdom. Two thirds of those who've received it would not choose to have it again, 40% of respondents reported permanent loss of past memories, 36% have difficulty concentrating, while three quarters of the total sample said they were not given any information about side effects.

Well, there you have it. Whether or not a patient should take ECT needs to be very carefully thought out. You have to look at cases individually and in-depth. You can't implement such powerful, arguably inhumane treatment, however scientific it is supposed to be, without looking at the state of mind of an individual person extremely carefully. Otherwise, you risk fucking up their life for good. I know if I was a doctor I wouldn't want the responsibility of someone's death on my shoulders whether during the treatment or afterwards through suicide. How would you explain it to their family? How would you explain it to their parents?

On the other hand, it would be naïve and defeatist to hold science back and most doctors believe that, when used with antidepressants, ECT halves the time of depression of a sufferer who only uses the antidepressants. In many cases, they believe it prevents suicide and is the most preferential form of treatment for somebody who is a suicide candidate. All I can say is that science is surprisingly ignorant when it comes to mental illness. There is no cure for it – only a series of attempts to try and stabilise patients as best as is possible. Manic depression is like the flu: it can come and go at any time – and it's hard to say why.

The same is true of the schizophrenic. One schizo in Mid Wales had the greatest mind I have ever come across – the wit of Paul Merton, the critical accuracy of Germaine Greer and the fascination of Shakespeare all rolled into one. His name is Magnus Robertson, and we wrote poetry together. He was totally paranoid and believed that spirits were following him around the hospital and invading his psyche. He was born in 1953 and was 45 when I was in hospital with him. He was always in and out of hospitals and, the last time I heard, lived in Neath with his mother. On 7 January, 1997, he gave me a poetry book. The note read:

For Jason, with warm and deep regards, never to be forgotten, Love Magnus. "When shall we three, meet again ...?

Whether he was referring to me, him and the book as a separate entity I can't remember, but this man's poetry was amazing. He even put my brother's intellect to shame and made me feel privileged to have met him. He wrote poetry in a luminous pen on his bedroom wall and we would hand our poems to everyone on the ward to try and cheer them all up, even the staff. As creative people, we also needed reassurance that our poetry was good and writing it was a great form of therapy for both of us.

I also kept in touch with a 60 year-old man I was in hospital with who lives near my mum. His name is Alan Greenwood. He has manic depression and, at his last count, had 18 hospitalisations to his name. He is unable to work, chain smokes roll ups, watches TV until the early hours of the morning and his flat is a health hazard. It's disgusting. Seeing the toilet would make you want to throw up. It's as close to the one in *Trainspotting* as I've ever seen. He's tried to kill himself several times and I believe seriously meant it. Thing is, he's too clumsy and too much of a mess to do it properly. He wanders around the pubs in the small, local community asking people to buy him drinks and is generally regarded, by people like my stepdad, as a pain in the arse. Despite all this, if you start talking with him, it's clear that he has a brilliant mind. His use of language is advanced and so is his critical thought and he has a powerful imagination. I've read short stories that he's written and they're fascinating. Rather subliminal, perverse and a little fucked up, but ingenious in parts. Alan, however, does not take care of

109

himself. He may have manic depression worse than I do but even if he hasn't, I'm not going to live like that – I'm not going to give up and bow down for anyone.

The longest I've ever stayed awake for is eight days during my second episode. I was just about to start work labouring at a building site in Manchester when Mark Doran, a friend, persuaded me to go to see the doctor instead. It was the right move as I was manic, already two hours late and so confused that I probably wouldn't have made it to the building site anyway. In any case, I could use my magical powers to lift bricks so why go to the site? Christ, I was so fucking magical that the magic worked itself through me rather than at my will. I didn't even need to consciously imagine it. How about that for magic? That would make me win the battle to be the slave for any mistress.

Sexual perversion and fantasy often takes over when I go manic. I'm not sure if this is common with other manic-depressives or whether it's peculiar to me. Too embarrassed to ask, I suppose... Something I'll discuss with my psychologist when she's ready. I keep mentioning it but she changes the conversation. Maybe she's conscious of avoiding transference, who knows? Maybe I've been and always will be a pervert. Don't think I've got the potential to become a rapist or a paedophile, but who knows? What is it in a man's psyche that constitutes this kind of behaviour? Show me the most revealing anthropological study so I can stop it happening to me and to others in the future. I know I could be a murderer if I was pushed to the end of my tether. I've been fortunate not to kill several people in fights I've had. That's why I stopped drinking. That's why I tried to change my life but still the mania came back and catapulted me into oblivion.

More research needs to be done on mental institutions, and more money given to them because they're pretty awful places. They're over-disciplined, regimented even, consist of too many untrained and uncaring staff, have too much bureaucracy and severely lack rehabilitation activities, humanity and any kind of release from depression, for example, comedy. Why can't they play comedy videos everyday, bring in clowns, entertainers and comedians? That's what my grandma always suggested and she'd been saying it for 60 years. It's because people don't generally give a shit about something unless it happens to them or somebody they are close to.

Mid Wales hospital had a TV area with several armchairs, a large dining area, a free pool table, a quiet room and a punch bag outside. The pool and punch bag were good forms of therapy and allowed me to escape from the other activities. However, the hospital was still militaristic in its make-up. Every mealtime, a patient would have to lay out all the cutlery or nobody would get served. The staff would order people around as if they were naughty children. I was only given my room after my father complained that I couldn't sleep because of snoring in the dormitory.

One patient wouldn't speak to me because she thought I was the devil. This was one of the few times I laughed when I was in that institution. I nearly got assaulted by one of the patients. She insulted me and called me stupid so I said: "At least I don't look like a whore." She picked up her mug of coffee and I dared her to smash it over my face. She looked like she was going to until she burst out crying and fled the room. When she returned, a few minutes later, I apologised to her after having been advised to show some humanity by one of the other patients. She was a middle-aged lawyer who had retired to become a writer and was normally quite pleasant. She said that she had never felt like doing anything violent like that in her life and that everything was getting on top of her.

I knew I had gone too far but there was a part of me that didn't give a fuck anymore. I was so depressed it was as though I had given up. I had gone through so much shit that my will was too weak, or so I thought. In fact, I was clinically depressed and the only way out of it is to wait. Time is the only healer. Drugs and environment can only do so much to lift you out of deep depression. When you experience it you feel that you're to blame for feeling like you do but that's not true. It's just something you have to endure.

I went back to Manchester to be with Meredith. My mum said it was too soon and that I wasn't ready. She said that I could only depress her, the mood I was in, and she was probably right. Thing is, I wanted desperately to get my life back on track and was even happy to accept the fact that Meredith now worked in the week so I would only really get to see her at the weekend.

Although I was severely depressed there was still some fight left in me. I was driven to Withington hospital, in Manchester, by a member of staff from Talgarth. I was handed over at 9pm. Being "handed over" was a term used by nurses when they changed shifts. It made me feel more like an unwanted dog than a human being.

The place was dark and barren. The ward was tiny compared to what I now look back on as the luxury of Mid Wales hospital. Why were they going to demolish Mid Wales when it was clearly a much more favourable environment than where I had ended up? Why had they demolished Coney Hill when it was paradise compared to the hell I was now faced with? How was I going to cope with this? I was depressed enough as it was. Now I had to face this fucking shit. I didn't know if I was up to it.

My first intention was to try and be positive as I still believed that I was a positive person. The first patient that I said hello to shouted at me to "fuck off". And that was after the staff had been so cold on my arrival. They had written my name up on the board in a green highlighter pen as though I was some kind of prisoner or, at the very best, some kind of experiment. Everybody was drawn up on a kind of ward diagram so that an eye could be kept on them from the office. They could be watched and controlled if anything got out of hand.

I was placed in a ward with four beds despite having pleaded for my own room before my arrival. At least there were only four people in the room, though. Sleeping was bound to be easier than in Talgarth and I prayed that there would be no fat old man snoring. While a new member of staff showed me around the ward, in a hurried manner, I noticed that the only form of activity was a four-foot pool table which was stuffed in the corner of the corridor. There was no room to play properly. A large woman said hello to me in a Manchester accent. I could tell that she was depressed and that it was a real effort on her part. I felt a spark of humanity reaching my soul when she asked if I had a cigarette. The spark soon faded, although she told me her name. It was Cecilia.

The handover was completed. I was subdued, felt very uncomfortable, and even frightened, as I was led along the corridor to my room. There was a teenager a bit younger than me already asleep. I liked his trainers. There was no bedding on my sheets and a window that wouldn't close next to my bed. The covering around my bed was like that in a hospital except that people could see in if they wanted to. I had no privacy. I heard the echoes of the member of staff who had dropped me off. He had told me to make the best of it and that I was over the worst. It was 10 minutes ago that he said this but it seemed so long. In fact, it seemed like years.

The nurse left me in the room and told me to leave any valuables I had in the office as the wardrobe doors were broken. The state of the people in there made me worry that all my clothes would be stolen and that I'd be walking around naked by the morning. When the nurse walked out an old man came over to me. He looked about 80. He said: "Give me a cigarette." I said that I only had a couple. "Give me a fucking cigarette." I gave him one and tried to leave the room immediately. As I walked out I heard him say: "I fought the Korean War for you and you won't even give me a cigarette. You fucking ungrateful little bastard, you'd better watch it. I'm going to fucking get you. You'd better watch your back."

I was distraught. This man was living opposite me – what could I do? If I hit him I'd be put on a six months' section, but I was so weak that I didn't feel I could win a fight with him anyway. I was also sure that if I told the staff they wouldn't give a shit and it would probably aggravate the situation. But I didn't like not standing up for myself as it made me feel a coward. As I left the room he said: "I want a cup of fucking tea when you get back and all. Make sure it's got two sugars." I left and went to the toilet almost in tears.

I walked along the corridor to the corner of the ward and lit a cigarette. Just as I was walking to another corner of the ward which the member of staff had not pointed out to me Cecilia told me that I couldn't smoke over there. It was one of the rules of the ward. The member of staff that had showed me around had not told me that. I sat down even more anguished, looking at her, the television and the floor. "Where are you from?" she asked. "I've got manic depression and I've come from Wales." I said.

She nodded her head and took a huge drag on a cigarette. I noticed that her hands were covered in cigarette stains and she looked like she hadn't exercised since birth. She looked liked she ate hundreds of donuts every day and had been wearing the same clothes for weeks. Was this my only form of rational contact? There again, speaking to a woman who was so fat and ugly made me question my prejudices. I was prejudiced against her because of her appearance, just as people were prejudiced against the mentally ill in society.

I guess other people feel the same way about extremely fat people as they do about the mentally ill. They're both in the minority and are therefore persecuted by the masses. These prejudices are typical of the foundations of racism in our society and need to be stamped out. Britain is now a multicultural society and people need to understand different cultures to function in an orderly fashion. It's an embarrassment to the nation that the British National Party has had so much support in places like Oldham and Bradford. We're in the new millennium. I mean, what the fuck is wrong with people? Are they fucking ignorant or what? The more different cultures mix and blend, the more educated and happier everybody should be. It's as simple as that. It doesn't take a moralist or a puritan to work this out – it's just common sense.

I had to get out of the shit-hole I was in. I knew I was ill but Withington hospital would make me worse. It couldn't be good for anybody staying in there. Time passed extra slowly in my new environment.

One of the staff approached guarding a sandwich trolley. "Only one sandwich each." she said to the black man who had told me to fuck off. "There's tea as well", said my new friend as she pointed to a huge teapot. The teapot looked almost as big as her in proportion. It must have had enough for 30 cups of tea in it. I drank the lukewarm tea in a few seconds and ate some egg sandwiches without chewing them properly.

Soon, I went to bed wearing a T-shirt, jumper and a pair of socks as I was freezing. The old man was talking to himself, cussing and swearing about being hard done by in life. I thought that he was some kind of schizophrenic. He was clearly not well and had an aggression problem. After trying not to hear him talk gibberish for two hours, I asked him if he wouldn't mind being quiet. He went mad and said: "Who do you think you are asking me to be quiet? You've only just got here and you think you own the fucking place. Where's my fucking tea anyway? I fought the fucking war for little brats like you, and this is how you treat me. You ought to be ashamed of yourself. I've killed people before, you know, in combat with my bayonet and I'm not scared of anyone." I said: "Look, I only asked you to be quiet, forget it."

"I'm going to fucking sort you out," he said walking over to my bed. I went to get out of my bed and he stopped me standing up by putting his hand firmly on my knee. "Don't think you're better than me you little prick." I'm 6' 4" and bulky but this mad, old, evil bastard was really scaring me. I was really weak and I left the room asking him to "just leave me alone". When I arrived in the ward I was confronted with a dirty, perverted, podgy man. He smelt awful and had yellow stained fingers from smoking too many roll ups. He tried to pinch Celia's arse so she attacked him, punching him and slapping him repeatedly. He cried for her to stop. Then he walked away hastily with his pyjama bottoms falling down and his own bare arse showing. She kicked him in the back and called him "a fucking pervert". She sounded quite scary with her Scottish accent, and looked it too, with her booming voice and eyes raging. "Don't come back in here tonight or I'll beat you up, you fucking pervert. He's a fucking pervert. Stay away from him", she advised me.

For five minutes, we sat there in silence smoking cigarettes. She had given me one of hers. The dirty man walked back in asking me for a cigarette and she chased him down the corridor. "He's a fucking pervert, a fucking pervert. A pervert." she repeated. One of the night staff came in and asked what the disturbance was. "He's a fucking pervert. He's a filthy old man. And he's ugly", she cursed. The member of staff walked off looking cross that a retard had had the audacity to disturb her. She was no detective, I thought. Why wasn't she doing her job, I thought, instead of reading the bloody tabloids? "You should all be in bed. Be quiet. And go to bed soon", she snarled.

I've often wandered around at night in hospital and discovered staff, who I've presumed should have been awake, sleeping. I used to feel a great antagonism towards mental health nurses as they held power over me unlike anyone else had ever done when I had been an adult. I used to think they thought the patients were unworthy beings. They were in charge and had nobody to boss them around. I was paranoid that the staff who didn't speak much thought that the patients on the ward weren't really people anyway and didn't warrant any special care or attention. The difficult thing about being mentally ill is that it's such a lonely experience. I also feared that the general staff consensus was that the patients were crazy and needed to sleep as they would be less of a nuisance then; that's the best remedy – sleep. They don't want to talk to anybody about their problems. Even if they did they would be incapable of being rational as they are mentally ill.

Meanwhile, back in the cesspit known as Withington, a girl aged about 15 popped out of the women's quarters into the lounge carrying a book and smoking a cigarette. It was now 12.30pm. "What are you doing?" I asked. "I'm writing a poem", she said. "I'd like to read it sometime", I replied. "Have you got a piece of paper?" She tore off a piece of paper. "Goodnight", butted in Celia. "And stay away from that old man in there – he's a fucking pervert", she said. "Goodnight", I replied. I wrote a rhyming poem in a couple of minutes. It was not very memorable and one of the thousands I'd lost or thrown away while being in, or coming out of, hospitals. At that time, though, it helped. "Can I read your poem?" I asked. "Sure", she said. "There's more in the back." I started reading through them and they weren't bad. "Can I look at your tapes?" she asked. "Yeah", I said.

We sat in silence. I read her poems as she smoked a cigarette, playing one of my hardcore dance tapes in the background. I said I liked the poems, and when she went to bed I went back to my sleeping quarters. The old man opposite was now asleep and I curled up in the chill of the night trying to forget everything that had happened to me – all the shit I was going through, had been through, and which was yet to come. That night was one of the lowest ebbs of my life. I knew I was going to have to get out of there if I was going to survive, going to save any self respect. I was losing dignity and the will to live fast. When my eyes were closed, I could still see the light of the moon through the flimsy curtains. My thighs felt as if they were covered in ice and my feet had terrible cramp. I was too depressed to do anything about it except to curl up even more. After a while, I got up and put my jeans and another jumper on but I was still freezing and the window wouldn't shut. A tear dripped down my eye as I said: "Fuck." As I curled back up in my sheets I started to cry. My only comfort was that Meredith would be there the next day. In the darkness that clouded over me I tried to imagine her as the light at the end of the tunnel.

Straight after finishing work Meredith would come to see me. At least there was something reliable in my life – something that had a little meaning. There was a sense of purpose and together we made a good team. We had come together under extraordinary circumstances but had grown to care for each other. It was a peculiar way to fall in love. We were devoted to each other and I was monogamous in a relationship for the first time in my life. We were thankful to each other for sorting each other's heads out and neither of us seemed to be able to function properly without the other.

She had inspired me, or certainly made it easier for me, to write my first screenplay in the summer of 1995 entitled: *A Can of Madness*. (Sound familiar?) It was about my first manic episode, although I had changed the names of the characters to avoid offending the people closest to me. Putting my own thoughts and behaviour through somebody else also acted as a form of therapy. It was the first thing of any real substance that I had written. I had written short stories about various fights that I had had and endless poems – my favourite of which were a collection on the theme of ecstasy entitled *E*. The collection describes taking ecstasy and its effect on my psyche and the chemical generation that I am part of.

When morning arrived, I noticed that my tapes had been stolen from the ward. They meant a lot to me and the staff showed no sympathy. They merely repeated hospital policy. "Any valuables that you have should be kept in your room." I told them that I had no lock for my cupboard and they said that they would "try and get a lock for me when it was not too busy". Well, in a hospital, especially this one, that was likely to mean never. Staff just forgot things like that – I knew from experience. My expectations of getting back the tapes were low and no member of staff ever came back to me on their possible whereabouts. I made several futile attempts to get somebody to look for them but nobody did.

There was no justice in there. Just a head fuck. You were just fobbed off all the time and if you persisted they just belittled you by saying there were more important things to attend to. They'd make you wait for ages. It seemed deliberate. After I gave up looking for my tapes, I gave my money to the staff and they put it in the safe. When convenient, I would have to ask permission to get access to it. Then I would have to sign and the member of staff would record how much money was left. Sometimes it was like Fort Knox trying to get in the staff room and then they would loathe you pestering them to get money out to buy cigarettes or sweets.

On the night I arrived, there was an act of gross misconduct by a member of staff. The cunt wouldn't let me take my lithium, I mean, he took it off me. I told him I needed it and that it was my lifeline but he said it was hospital policy that patients couldn't have any drugs on them. I told him that I understood that but said that I had not been given my lithium at medication time because my name was not on the meds board and they agreed I could take my own that evening. That fucking cocksucker. I spent a night without lithium because of him and he was supposed to be looking after me. The other staff told me that I would have to wait until the morning. I felt so pathetic: I couldn't even hold onto my pills. What a loser I was turning out to be.

The food in the hospital was appalling. There was a canteen along the corridor although usually the staff members that served the food were rude and impatient. It was another one of the demanding chores that an NHS mental nurse had to deal with. It was an example of them doing menial tasks instead of being able to concentrate on nursing. A typical comment you would hear was: "If you don't like it, then that's too bad. I'm sure someone else will have it." The only thing I can remember liking was sponge pudding with custard. The taste made me feel, for the merest part of a second, OK; like I felt when I was writing a poem. Time stood still for just a few fractions of a second. These moments were becoming fewer and fewer though, as I was starting to go deeper and deeper into depression when I arrived back in Manchester.

When Meredith arrived on my second afternoon there she looked exhausted. She hadn't eaten and her hair was dyed auburn brown. It didn't suit her and her clothes weren't as clean as they used to be. She was wearing too much make-up to try and cover up how physically and mentally exhausted she was. She'd lost that spark and she looked shattered. She didn't stay for long. She had to find the landlord because the heating in the flat wasn't working. Several months later, she told me that she used to cry herself to sleep because she was so cold. I hate that when people tell you things months after they happen. Why can't people be up front with each other? It would save a lot of pain in the long run. I mean, the more direct people are with each other the less their emotions are fucked around with.

Meredith was pleased that I was back. She'd wanted me to transfer to Withington Hospital for weeks but I hadn't been well enough. Now she thought I was better. It was a good job that I hadn't moved to Withington before as it was so nightmarish. I had no option but to discharge myself and did so the following day. I also cancelled an appointment I had arranged with a university friend the following day. It was with the guy I used to get drunk with, Roger. I didn't want him to see me in such a shit-pit. When I telephoned him and he didn't suggest an alternative time or place to meet I said: "C'ya" and put the phone down with regret. None of my friends had come to see me in Wales or in Withington, only Meredith and my family.

Going back to my flat was almost as big an ordeal as going to Withington. I went back to the place where I had discovered that the whole world would be in an orgy together, the place where Chorlton-cum-Hardy was the head of world consciousness. This was the place where I had to restore my sanity. What the fuck was going on? What the fucking hell was happening? Things went from worse to even worse. It was January 1997 and the depression took over. I began to sleep more and more. My only activity was watching cable TV late at night and the occasional shag with Meredith. I would sleep up to 16 hours at a time and at random times of the day. When Meredith got back from work, the flat was a mess and I was either in bed or had just got out of it. She came back for lunch every day and woke me up making me a sandwich, or we would share a salad.

She became more and more messy and more stressed every time I saw her. Back then, though, I didn't really notice or care; I just wanted to sleep. She asked her boss for a week's holiday. He had been very reasonable in the previous few months and she had told him about my illness but this time he said no.

A couple of weeks later we went to the travel agents looking for the dream holiday. We chose a week in Benidorm as opposed to a week in Bulgaria skiing as her ski kit didn't arrive from her mother's in time. She bunked off work and we went to Heathrow. I had had 10 cans of Stella by the time we boarded the plane and literally filled two of them with piss as we were taking off. My animal mentality had returned and became a metaphor for denying my illness. Something had to give sooner or later.

This was not a romantic start and was similar to how things were when we first started seeing each other. We spent three nights getting pissed up in a tacky bar where a woman would extract bottles of wine and candles from her fanny. We didn't see any of the sights. I was drinking incessantly. I would drink at least 15 pints of strong lager in one, and each one through two thin straws as they didn't have the thicker straws that I had become accustomed to back in Manchester. I had to have a witness for each one. We were hung over in the day and only managed to spend a couple of hours on the beach.

On the fourth night it was Meredith's birthday. We went out for a nice Chinese meal and then I started drinking more than usual. We befriended two Scottish heroin addicts and somehow got separated. Meredith had stormed out because we had had an argument. I was too pissed to remember what it was about. She was probably jealous of me gawping at the girl who did the magic tricks. I left one club and made my way to another. As I ran up the stairs to the exit I slipped on something and went flying. As my jaw hit the floor, I must have passed out straight away.

The time was 7.50am. The place was Alicante Hospital. The reason I was there was because I had broken my jaw.

This symbolised a moment in my life when things had to change. I started writing my first novel. It started off being a positive book about an alcoholic with a mental illness who was trying to lift himself out of depression while recovering from a broken jaw in a Spanish hospital. He had a girlfriend who loved him but then he would fantasise about being a paedophile. After writing a couple of pages about the latter, I ceased writing and wondered what the fuck I was on about. The depression had really got a hold of me this time. I'd lost my own identity for real and I wondered if I would ever be able to get it back.

The night before, I had threatened to jump off a walkway onto the beach. I also remember threatening to jump off the balcony of our apartment on our first night there. It was on the eighth floor. Meredith didn't need that shit. I didn't know if I really gave a fuck about anything or if it was a cry for help, a cry for somebody to lift me out of my depression.

The fact that I had broken my jaw turned out to be a blessing in disguise. It knocked some sense into me. It forced me to put my life into perspective before any serious suicide attempt took control of my mind. Meredith went home at the end of the week and I stayed an extra week for an operation that proved to be successful. The hospital and staff were very professional and I even learnt some Spanish. I couldn't open my mouth for six weeks, though. At least this stopped me getting pissed. I wasn't stupid enough to drink through straws and breathe through my nose. I wouldn't be able to puke up my own vomit and could swallow it and die. Jimi Hendrix and Sid Vicious would have been proud of me if I'd done that, but I wasn't that stupid. I wasn't as stupid anymore.

Before I'd gone on holiday Dr. Cooper had put me on Sulpiride. The pills seemed to start working soon after the metal was released from my mouth. Six weeks free from drinking had sobered me up and lifted my mood as well. I could now face life again, but first I had to face coming to terms with madness. I had experienced two manic episodes. It was no one-off and it was likely I was going to have others. There was still hope though, as Dr. Cooper told me, as I had not been maintained on Lithium and for 90% of people who have the illness it controls their mood swings. This could prevent an episode. My girlfriend had stood by me and I was determined to go back to university later in the year and finish my degree.

It was only April so I decided to get a job. I knew it would give me some much-needed confidence and I could also pay off my £1,200 overdraft. I joined several temping agencies and got a job through one of them as a security guard at Manchester airport, preventing protestors from sabotaging building work.

I met someone at a bus stop on my first morning to work. He later proved to be one of my best friends. Tom Robertson understood what it was like to be a bit crazy and his positive attitude and constant encouragement to, from and during work sanitised me and helped me deal with the biggest dilemma of the illness. Relying on Tom for spiritual and philosophical support enabled me to come to terms with going mad. The transition back into society became more bearable. My conversations with him also cleared the path in my relationship with Meredith which had been very rocky up until that point.

We worked 12-hour shifts, from either seven in the morning to seven in the evening or vice versa, seven days in a row. In between changing shifts we would alternate between three and four days off. I worked from the start of April until the beginning of June. Life was looking up. Meredith got a promotion – which included a good pay rise – to a marketing position at work, and even set up a website for her boss's company. I bought her a new outfit to celebrate. It was a professional looking designer aqua blue jacket and skirt. We had the occasional row and she would sometimes shout at me. I never raised my voice, though, and if I felt really frustrated I would call my old school friend, Panji.

He played basketball for Manchester Giants. He deserved it as he had practised so hard before and after school from the age of 14 onwards. Panji liked to party and was usually available if I wanted to get out of the house. He was finishing a degree in Mechanical Engineering at Salford University and was disillusioned with basketball. He would come and pick me up and we would go for a few pints and talk about what we were doing and wonder what other people we used to go to school with were doing. We would go to the sports bar, Cheerleaders, and other bars in Deansgate, or cruise around student hangouts.

The Panji I knew had always been a very quiet and determined individual. He drank too much but managed to lead an extremely active life. I admired him for that and liked listening to stories about what he and his team-mates got up to when they went out at night. I remember drinking polish vodka with him on his birthday. Panji introduced me to the best player on the team. His name was Mark Robinson. The guy just blanked me. I couldn't believe it. If that was what a bit of fame did to him then fuck him, man. If I ever had a bit of fame, which I always wanted, I wouldn't treat anyone like that.

When it was time to come out, I felt as if I was one of those 12 year-old boys being hit on the backside – the most painful place apart from the nuts and face – by one of Panji's flying tennis balls. Meredith wanted to go back to London and leave me, knowing that I had to stay in Manchester for another year and finish my degree. She said that she wanted "her mummy". We had been living together for eighteen months and she had enjoyed the first six. My illness had taken its toll and she had no fight left in her. Having discussed things in detail and cried throughout I thought it best to grant her wish. I made the most painful phone call that I had ever made. I rang up the landlord, an amicable man called Joe, and gave him a month's notice. The following month I have never cried so much in my life. I was a pitiful wreck whose heart had been broken. I didn't know that it was possible for a man to feel so weak. She was crying almost as much as me but it was she who had deserted me just when things were turning round. She had given up. Run out of steam. She'd run out of the juice, man.

We stayed together for the next few months with me

spending most of it in London with her parents. We did the things that normal people do. We visited art galleries, went out and socialised and even did some of the tourist things like visiting Madame Tussauds and going on a Big Bus London bus tour.

Chapter 6 – Back to life (the second transition)

In September 1997, I moved into some quiet university halls on the outskirts of Chorlton. This was just the kind of environment I wanted to be in to focus on my final year, and the exact opposite of what I'd wanted in my first year. Within a few weeks of starting the first year a group of us had wanted to leave halls and get our own flat. Thing is, the halls wouldn't give us our money back until they rented our rooms and since they couldn't guarantee this we all stayed put.

My new digs were near a huge green, with the local pub bordering a canal. The flat was very smart and a cleaner came round once a week. The cleaner even did the washing up which was pretty essential with six blokes living in a flat. It was a multicultural flat. My male flatmates were from India, Portugal, France, Malaysia and Ireland. It was a new home and a place where I could concentrate on my work. There was a little green outside the kitchen window and I could see people going to get their mail from my bedroom window. I would play football whenever I saw people kicking around – it was always a nice break from studying.

I made a conscious effort not to tell people of my illness. Ironically, of course, I always ended up letting the cat out of the bag. I was embarrassed by it and didn't want to be asked too many demanding questions in case my head exploded. Basically, I felt that I could never be my real self, especially when meeting people. People would ask me what I wanted to do when I graduated and I told them that I wanted to be a writer. They would ask if I had written anything or ask me what I was going to write about. I would tell them that I had written and would continue to write about drama. Eventually I would write comedy. They would try and make me be more specific. I would tell them that I wrote empirical texts and conclude their interrogations with profound remarks stating that I had had an interesting or crazy life that was too complicated and too personal to explain to somebody that I had just met. I couldn't open up to complete strangers. I didn't want them to judge me for what I had become: a retard. I was somebody who passed in and out of madness and who was unable to control when he did. Just as Oscar Wilde had been persecuted for being gay, I didn't want to be maltreated for being mentally ill. I knew I had a problem and writing about it would be the most cathartic way of dealing with it.

On 5 October, 1997, it was my Nan's eightieth birthday party. I bought her a picture of Van Gogh's *Café Terrace on the Place Du Forum*. It was one of two hundred canvasses he painted in 1888 and this man, like me, was a mad genius. I stayed with Meredith in the luxury suite at the hotel where my mum worked as the receptionist. We had some champagne the night before the party and pretended that things were OK. For that night things actually were ok although, as a whole, our relationship was resting on thin ice. At the party, Meredith looked stunning, mature and sophisticated, as she always did if she made an effort.

The party itself was a bizarre affair. There were about 20 people there of whom I only knew half a dozen or so. So this was the rest of my living family tree? They appeared so small-minded, simple and content, living in the past. These, then, were the roots whence I had sprung. They were not, however, the side of my family that had given me my mental illness, as this was the sane side, my mum's side – the *caring* side. My dad's side was the one with the mental problem. They were the crazy ones. In fact, it's widely accepted that if a family has manic depression in their genes there is a 27% chance of a member catching it. Well, I always knew I was special.

I remember closely watching Meredith interact at my Nan's party. It was to be the last time that we would see each other for a year. We were to grow apart and lead lives in different directions from then on. How can somebody you have spent so much time with, and been so close to, suddenly disappear out of your life like that? Thing is, it happens everyday to thousands of people all over the country.

Meredith and I tried our utmost to remain amicable towards each other and stay friends, but it proved to be impossible. The human condition rarely allows people to be friends once they have been lovers. It is too weak. Love is either painful or a delight, and ex-lovers are unable to remain friends, in most cases, as the emotions that run through them are too strong and lead to jealousy, resentment and anger.

I guess the ending of my relationship took a course similar to that of many others. It slowly fizzled out. She had visited my new digs the week before the party, which was my first weekend there. Some of my flatmates remarked how good-looking she was and I was proud to show her off, but that was the last time she came. She asked if she could come up the week after the party, but the truth is I didn't want her there. I couldn't forgive her for leaving and although I still wanted her in some ways, I wanted a new life. Above all, I suppose, I wanted to see if I could cope without her. I told her that she couldn't come up that weekend and she pretended not to be upset. If she had pleaded, on the other hand, pleaded like I did to her to stay with me I would have let her. But she would never do that. She would never resort to begging like I had. She was too good, too strong for that. She was too well-brought up. She couldn't humiliate herself as I had done. She had given enough up already, looking after an invalid.

Meanwhile, I had asked another girl out to the cinema and she had accepted. This could be the start of something new, I thought. It could be the start of a new relationship where things could be right from the start. If it didn't work out long-term then at least I might get some sex during the week. In the event, nothing materialised with the girl I went to the cinema with – I think I scared her a bit. I mean, she started shaking when I put my arm round her in the cinema. Anyway, I didn't give a fuck really. It really helped me stop thinking about Meredith – as to my great annoyance and frustration I was thinking about her nearly all the time. It's hard when someone is such a part of your life and then you become separated, especially when it isn't your decision.

...

Over the next few weeks, we were both coming up with excuses and the phone calls to each other became less and less frequent and more and more detached. We fell out on the phone in January 1997 after I asked her if she had a boyfriend and she said: "It's none of your business." I told her that I had had a girlfriend since and she told me that she did have a boyfriend and hung up. Her response was to write me a nasty letter blaming me for her troubled life. It was so melodramatic it would have been more appropriate in a Shakespearean comedy. I think of the ass in *A Midsummer Night's Dream* when he gets his oats. His lover doesn't know what's going on just like Meredith. She had blamed everything on my illness and now hated me – it was crystal clear, the evidence was right there in front of me. I didn't need that shit. So that was it. That was fucking it. We were finished. Fucking finished, for good. I burnt her letter and put that episode of my life behind me as best as I could and started my final year at university for the second time.

In halls, I had become an avid student for the first time since I was 17 and drank heavily only once or twice a week. The main reason for the reduction in alcohol consumption was my love of tae kwon do. The instructor, about my age, was a charismatic African and his sense of humour and positivism, combined with my own fascination, was enough to get me hooked. It restored me into the physical world and did a lot for my self-confidence. It also helped control my aggression which had been a problem since I started drinking when I was 14.

I showed my screenplay to two of my lecturers who admired me for having the stature to put my experiences onto the printed page. I remember the head of department, after I had told him that most of my script was autobiographical, saying: "I hope your life really wasn't like that." I brushed his remark off with a deep sigh and some extra tae kwon do training.

My personal tutor was encouraged by the way I could accept criticism of my work in an unpretentious manner. My marks improved from medium to high 2:1s, to low firsts and

129

eventually to high firsts. I made applications for postgraduate study in writing, theatre and film. I entered my screenplay into the Manchester University Film Competition. To my bewilderment, they claimed that they never received my entry. I went to the University Film Society and discovered that the students there had the home number of Danny Boyle, the director of *Trainspotting*. He had been the patron of the Film Society for two years and they had been too scared to phone him even once. They refused to give me his number as he was making some film in Bali (*The Beach*) and my creative mind was left wandering around again. My final year studies were keeping me more than occupied thanks to all the essays that needed to be submitted for coursework.

Whenever sane, I found it difficult to avoid playing on the fact that I was a loony, especially when people got to know me better. It was my way of saying: "If you fuck with me, I'm gonna fuck you up." I still had that Snoop Doggy Dogg mentality in me and although I was white, I was, in the words of Ice Cube: "The wrong nigger to fuck with." The halls consisted mostly of foreign students which was both refreshing and annoying. All in all, it helped me to socialise on a superficial level. This was good for two reasons: one, I didn't feel so much of an outcast, and two, I could revert back to my studies without too much distraction.

On New Year's Eve, I had my best fuck for a long time. She was a 33 year-old Irish stunner. She was extremely slim, blonde, pretty, looked sophisticated and laughed a lot. I had gone out on the piss with my Irish flatmate, Mark, and his brother, and at the beginning of the evening had said, in a Larry Fishburne (*King of New York*) manner, that: "I'm gonna go down town, find me a girl and get my nob polished." It worked.

We latched on to three Irish women prowling outside a public house in central Manchester. One of them was really good looking, the other two were not. That was OK as I didn't have a great deal of competition that night. In fact, I didn't seem to very often. I set about putting my plan into action. I ignored the good-looking one but made enough innuendo and gave her just enough attention to keep her interested. I kept cool, so I could reel her in when I wanted.

When the New Year approached, she called for us to join her friends who were dancing. I knew she was up for it and New Year's Eve led to a snog, a good fuck and an interesting couple of months. It was unfortunate, though, that she turned out to be a bitch. And I don't mean a bitch. I mean a fucking ho. You know, a prick tease and all that kind of shit. First, things went great. Lust is natural. After I'd fucked her, she remarked how relaxed a person I was. I spent the next few days and nights drinking with her and her friends and then fucking her in their hotel room. After five days of horny fucking, with her mates spending a lot of time out of the room leaving us to it, she went back to Dublin but invited me over whenever I wanted.

Half term was coming up and I had worked hard so I decided to go and stay with her the following week. When I arrived in Dublin, she kept me waiting in a pub for two hours as she was with her mum having her nails manicured. I mean, what kind of shit was that? I didn't make an issue out of it, though, as I desperately needed to empty my bollocks. They felt like fucking watermelons man. I mean, I didn't have elephantitis of the nuts or anything, but I had nowhere to stay and I wanted to fuck some pussy and have my balls sucked.

We eventually got back to her flat after getting rid of her mate and I realised what a spoilt bitch she was. Daddy had bought her a brand new pad in a trendy suburb of Dublin. She was manageress at a travel agent's and went to work during the day. I read and answered exam questions on the great Roman orator Cicero and went to University College Dublin to check out their film studies department. I had an in-depth conversation with one of their lecturers and he convinced me that I should apply. I fucked Debbie and came over her nine times during one episode of Grandstand. I was quite proud of that achievement and it was nice to watch a bit of Football Focus while I was doing it. There was a lot of shagging during the week but the relationship had nothing else to it. It consisted of her insulting me, apologising, cooking a nice

131

meal, me watching her get drunk and trying not to drink much myself. Hardly the cultural side of Dublin. I met her sister who was even more vacuous than her. There was not a jot of intellectual capacity to them, only a belief that their daddy was better than everybody else's because his BMW had cost £80,000. They were totally fucked up and unlikeable, but when you think through your dick, you think through your dick ...

I left Dublin and spoke to Debbie (yes, she has a name although it clearly isn't an aristocratic one) a few times in the weeks that followed. She had arranged to fly over for Valentine's weekend. I mean, talk about being a hypocrite – what's a tart like that doing flying over for Valentine's weekend? What the fuck? What the fuck was going on? By this time, I was studying harder and getting closer to having a six-pack by taking tae kwon do more and more seriously. I met her at the airport and we stayed at the Copthorne Hotel next to Old Trafford football ground. She was paying. I could get used to this, I thought. It wasn't long, though, before I was made to look stupid. We were only into our second drink at the bar and she was chatting up the barman. He was only about 18. What the fuck was going on? If any bloke gave me shit I'd kick fuck out of them, but when a woman gave me shit I kept quiet and became paralysed. Better to do that than lose my temper, I thought.

I reluctantly took Debbie's bags up to the hotel room as she flirted with the barman. I remember asking her if she'd had any abortions. She admitted that she'd had two and said that it was none of my business when I asked her how she had felt. It seemed that any attempt I made to get closer to her rebounded off a wall that had already been strategically set in place. We eventually got to the hotel room and I remember the sex wasn't as good as it had been the last time. I had bought her a Valentine's card, as I thought girls always liked that kind of thing even if they said they didn't, some aromatherapy oils and handcuffs to try to add a bit of kinkiness to the proceedings. She replied that she didn't want a card, as she guzzled the chocolate that accompanied it, and

132

said that if she put me in handcuffs she would leave me tied to the bed and fuck off to the bar. I was sick of her cruel humour and knew that there was a good chance that she meant what she said. It would be something that Debbie could tell her friend who would be arriving on a later flight with her boyfriend from Dublin. The weekend was a frustrating one.

We went to a nightclub but they wouldn't let me in, apparently because my shoes weren't smart enough. I had to go all the way back to my flat in a taxi to get some smart shoes because the stupid cow I was with insisted that she didn't want to go anywhere else. The last time I saw her was at the airport and when she guessed that I had had a shit weekend, she said: "Don't worry I've only been messing wid ya." I had shown my sensitive and jealous side and she was not interested in it. She just wanted to have a good laugh by humiliating me. My head was fucked enough already without being trampled on by a callous bitch like that. That was the last time we saw each other. I rang her a few times after that due to lust and confusion; I was grateful that she never called me back.

Tae kwon do became more and more an inspiration and a way to channel my aggression. It helped relieve the tiresome hours spent studying and acted as an escape from anything that was bothering me. By Easter 1998, I was training everyday, sparring privately with my teacher and doing advanced yoga classes. I was as fit as a fiddle and agile as an anteater's tongue. I had a few close friends and my self-confidence had returned. I hadn't missed a lecture at university and had handed all my work in on time, usually ahead of schedule. I was a scholar most of the time and managed to channel my aggression effectively for the first time in my life.

I was totally absorbed in tae kwon do and other martial arts such as jujitsu, judo, ninjitsu, karate and kung fu. When things became too stressful, I would go for a few games of pool or snooker and have the occasional drinking binge. I was so proud of my figure that I would limit my drinking for the first time ever and burn off the fat the next morning or afternoon if I ever had a hangover. The return to the physical world helped my health and work. I was also conscious of complying with my medication everyday and for once my lithium levels were normal. Every couple of weeks I might forget, in which case I'd take an extra dose. Sometimes, though, I simply didn't need to.

I had a few loose relationships with women. I slept with this Austrian bird and would kick her out because she kept me awake. The most unforgettable was a pissed-up venture with a girl who lived next door and who was studying Russian. She wanted to go out, but once I'd sobered up I didn't want to go out with her. After a meaningless one-night stand we never spoke to each other again apart from when I would say the occasional: "All right." She was too embarrassed because I was a "good catch", as she put it, and although I felt guilty about being picky I had my standards. I knew I was prejudiced but I just couldn't help it. I had another fling with a girl I met on the internet. I sent her a picture of my cock in the post and after a five-hour telephone conversation decided to stay with her for a weekend in Scunthorpe without even knowing what she looked like. It was a pleasant surprise as she was very pretty. She was 20 and had a two year-old kid. We didn't see each other again as the situation was too bad. She must have thought that I was some kind of psychopath ... If she only knew … Ha, ha, ha.

I also met a woman through an advert in the Manchester Evening News. I travelled to Crewe to meet her. Again, this was a blind date. She was thirty-eight and had four kids. What was it with me and single mums? Maybe I didn't want kids of my own as I was told that my illness was a genetic condition and I didn't want my kids to go through what I had gone through. I thought that I could bring up somebody else's kids. Yes, that was it. And if we split up it wouldn't matter. It wouldn't matter if I lost custody as they weren't really mine and it would save me money too. Think of all the money I could save on nappies and shit like that, or schooling and food.

I watched *Golden Eye* at the cinema with the blond, single mum and she was good-looking for her age. We made out in her car as she didn't want me to meet her kids yet. She said she'd call me a few days later. After a while she didn't so I called and asked to see her. She said that she didn't want to see me again as she thought I wanted something that was too serious. Fuck, I was only being a gentleman. I didn't give a fuck about this wrinkled slut bag. I mean, treat a woman nicely and she wants you to treat her like a slut; treat her like a slut and she wants you to treat her better. I never understood women. What the fuck went on in their heads? You think you know what they're thinking and everything's OK and then they always surprise you. They fuck up men's heads, man. Well, that's the attraction I suppose. We're all masochists at heart. Just like we all need loving once in a while.

Soon after I last saw Meredith in October 1997, I started to write to sexy advertisements in naughty magazines. It helped me get over her. Thinking of women as sex objects instead of lovers made me more rational. Most of the ads I responded to were time-wasting women who were prostitutes in disguise. Others wanted naked photos of an erect penis so I obliged after borrowing my Portuguese flatmate's camera and taking photos of myself. I had some good responses, the most amusing of which was seeing a woman I had formed a no-strings relationship with in *Escort* magazine. "I didn't realise that you had become a celebrity", I said.

The Sunday Sport proved to be the most successful. It led to some interesting encounters which turned me into more and more of a misogynist. Things were really starting to take off when I stumbled into another relationship with an Irish girl. This one was very pretty, tall, brunette, 24, lived in halls and, what's more, had bigger tits than the Irish slut from Dublin. Basically, my flatmate Mark had told me that one of the best looking girls on campus fancied me but that he couldn't tell me who.

I guessed which girl it was and made my move. Her name

was Katherine O'Donnell. I saw her bored out of her mind with a bunch of fuck-wits in the bar on campus and decided to teach her how to play pool. We had some swift pints and went back to my flat. I had five pints of Caffreys in five swigs in twenty minutes as I was pissed off for leaving Scunthorpe a night earlier than expected. We went to my room and downstairs to pinch a bottle of my Portuguese flatmate's wine. She started snogging me and so began two weeks of almost constant, hard-core sex. She gave me all the compliments under the sun; told me that she had fancied me for ages, that she had never met anyone like me, that I was the best fuck she had ever had, that she was falling in love with me, that she loved being in my arms and loved spending time with me, and that I was the most intelligent person she'd ever met. I'd never met a girl that was so infatuated with me so quickly.

The only problem was that she had a boyfriend. He was a big fucker and had never lost a fight. That wasn't too much of a problem, though, as he lived in Belfast and I knew I was a crazier fucker than him – and a better man. Christ, I had to be with all the compliments she was giving me. I was also at my physical peak and felt confident that I could knock out four clones of her boyfriend at the same time, *and* on my own. Nobody could fuck with me, I was invincible. I was a fucking mean machine. We debated at length whether she should go back to Belfast or not for Easter, and eventually she did go back and stay with her friends. She couldn't stay with her family as her dad wasn't speaking to her because he disapproved of her going out with a Protestant. I was pleased with this situation in one respect as it made my position of keeping her a little stronger. Mind you, if her dad refused to speak to her because she had a boyfriend with a different religion, wouldn't he be prejudiced against a manic-depressive as well? I tried not to think about that.

Anyway, when she went away, I concentrated on studying as my finals were looming and I didn't want to underachieve. She was going to see her boyfriend but she convinced me that I was the special one. Things weren't going to change – they were going to stay the same. After all, our relationship wasn't just one of lust. She had been going out with her boyfriend for three years and I was the only other person she had slept with in that time. She didn't want to upset him but she intended to stay in Manchester and get a job as a teacher when she qualified for her PGCE in June 1997. I was planning to do an MA in Screenwriting at Manchester University at the time, which could have included a writer from Granada Studios as mentor, so I saw the possibility of a long-term relationship with her. Things were going to plan. I was coming of age and my life had cemented after all the crumbling in the past. I was not going to end up writing for some shitty magazine like Concrete World; I was destined for the top. Soon, I would be on top of the world.

Katherine came back from Northern Ireland a week later and we went out and got drunk the evening she got back. We ended up fucking in the woods in the dark and it took us a couple of hours to find our way home. Our short cut didn't work and there was also a slight problem – we discovered, in the morning, that the condom had split. As she wasn't on the pill, I had to take her down the clinic so that she could take the morning after pill. Afterwards, she was throwing up in a bad way and said that she didn't want me to see her being sick. Then I discovered that she needed time to think as she was not sure if she wanted to carry on seeing me. What the fuck was going on here? Yet another woman fucking with my head? Oh no, not again. I even lent her my screenplay as I thought that would convince her that I was a great writer and to try and impress upon her that she was privileged to find me.

I turned to Mark for support. I had told him about my manic depression after a game of snooker one evening. He was easy to talk to. He had told me that he had warned Katherine not to get involved with me because he cared about me as a friend and didn't want to see her fuck my head up. I found out then that he had told her about my manic depression before even I did. Fuck me, he thought he was such a fucking counsellor that he could control my

137

relationship before it had even started. What the fuck was going on? I felt like kicking his teeth in but he was so easy to talk to that it would have been unjust.

His problem was that he told everyone everything. He was the sort of mate who would fuck your bird behind your back and then, if you found out, blame it on her and try to return to the friendship you had had before with him. I found out that he did this a year later to one of his best friends. And what's more, he did it to one of his Irish mates.

The night in the woods was the last time I fucked Katherine. We spent the next morning getting her the morning after pill at the clinic and she dumped me soon after that. We fell out soon enough at a party. She was pissed out of her mind flirting with a few of the blokes there. Another tart – why couldn't I find a decent bird? Couldn't I find one that wasn't a slut? That's all I wanted. My mum would always tell me that I was too desperate and that girls can tell that. "It scares them away", she would say. "When you least expect it, that's when you'll find one. When you don't go looking for it." She was right. It took me a long time to figure that out. When you frown, you use 60 muscles; when you smile, you only use 16. I guess girls can sense that.

Our break-up now seems quite comical. I was fed up with her flirting at the party and when she sat on Mark's lap and started flirting with him it was the last straw. My pulse was beating pretty hard and in my sober state I poured a glass of tap water and threw it in her face without uttering a word. I left the flat immediately and returned to mine, satisfied with the morsel of retribution I had won, although I was angry that I had been made such a fool of. My ego had taken a knock and I couldn't handle it. At least everyone else now knew that she was a tart. More importantly, they knew that I wouldn't let anyone fuck with me.

My anger turned to Mark. This was the wanker who I had been pouring my heart out to half an hour before. I had only left my studies to go to the party and try to win Katherine back. Her friend had phoned the flat and he had told me that she was round there. I thought he was my best friend apart

138

from Tom. Then I realised he was everyone's best friend – at least he pretended to be. He was not a genuine person; one of those fake people in life who are always out to impress others. Their own life is so shit that they project themselves onto other people. Mark was a loser. I mean, he was 30 and was in his first year at the Polytechnic studying an Engineering degree. He didn't have the required A-level grades like most people I knew so had taken a foundation year instead. His best job had been as a security guard. Once he told me: "Once a security guard, always a security guard – I hoped that wasn't going to be me." When he had moved to London aged 18 his parents had paid for his single ticket from Ireland and didn't want him to come back. They wanted to get rid of him because he was such a fucking pain in the arse. At many different times of my life, I would have kicked the living shit out of him and cracked his skull open. The fucking Irish tosser.

As I went to sleep that night, I wondered what the reaction at the party would have been. I was woken up at two in the morning. It was Katherine on the phone. She started hurling shit at me like women do when they're angry, and once I told her a few truths she forced me to apologise. It was the only way I was going to get any sleep. So that was it: another head buried in the sand and another girl waiting for her fucking prom. I went back to sit-ups, and counted to myself: 1, 2, 3 and 4 kicks, side kicks, flying kicks, punches, all low, middle and high. I went back to blasting out House of Pain on my stereo and making my six-pack even more defined. Soon, there didn't seem to be an ounce of fat on my body. I was ready for battle, ready for my finals – already two years overdue (as my dad would always remind me) because of my fucking illness. I mean, what the fuck did he know? He told me not to go back to university, as he didn't think I could do it anyway. He told me to get a job. He didn't think I had the strength of character to go through all the shit and see it through. Well I did, so fuck him. Fuck him, man. I did have the strength of character and it was nearly over. Then I could get on with different shit.

As my memories of Meredith, Debbie and Katherine became more of a blur and my finals approached, I reflected on university life and what I was going to do after it had finished. Since January 1998, I had spent time in chat rooms having cyber sex and trying to invite myself to stay with rich women all over the world. I wanted to be a gigolo. Unfortunately, I couldn't scan my photo properly and that put an end to that. I was charming enough on the net and had to make do with cyber sex. I was ripped off by several escort agencies, spending a few hundred quid in total to sign on, and not getting any work. Then I noticed an ad wanting someone to become a live-in slave with Mistress Debbie in Leeds. She wanted help writing for a magazine which one of her Mistress friends edited. I wrote her an abject letter and took some raunchy photos. She sent me a printed response saying that I was one of her possibles. I hoped that she would invite me for an interview or even a day's trial. This didn't seem an odd thing to do at the time as the classical literature I was reading was far more liberal towards sex than the puritanical attitude in Britain and the world in general. I guess I allowed fantasy to clash with reality. Or maybe I was just being a pervert. My mind was also a bit racy but this was to be expected with the pressure of the exams.

Sometimes I would feel a bit high, but whenever I did I would try to relax. I also had recurring migraines which were signs of stress. The fantasy was also a pleasant break from everything. My tae kwon do lessons had stopped and, although I did wrestling, boxing and jujitsu with some of my friends, I was often training on my own. My teacher didn't want to fight me in combat as he feared for his safety because I was "too much of a psycho". I wrote again to the Mistress in more detail and the next reply was hand written in greater length. This excited me and I wondered what might happen ...

By now, I had begun my finals. The first paper was "Cicero and the year 63BC". In my view, he is the greatest man who has ever lived. He was a complete all rounder, brilliant orator, lawyer, politician, public relations expert, consul, philosopher and humanist. His poetry and historical works are criticised throughout history and it was unfortunate for him that Mark Antony arranged for his disposal, exhibiting his head and writing hands in the Forum. Then there was "Ancient literary criticism". This was a look at the origins of deconstructing texts, beginning with Homer, Plato and Aristotle and discussing the effect they had had on subsequent writers such as Longinus. The lecturer, Professor Michael Haslam, had spent 20 years teaching in California and was the head of the classics department. He made the course easy to understand from the start. I had already studied Greek comedy in the first semester with Professor Bain, who was an expert on writing about Black Magic and Necromancy in the ancient world. Aristophanes' comedy was the most memorable text. It parodied Socrates and his sophistry in an entertaining and ironic manner. That left only two exams to go.

I was mentally drained but also excited when the penultimate exam approached. The course was "National identity and the Roman past". It was a disappointment throughout because the lecturer never made clear what she was trying to accomplish. The course had no real structure and was too general a topic. In the exam, I made some grandiose comments almost trying to correct the whole course.

The final exam was "Latin love poetry". I wrote two essays on Catullus and one on Ovid. The essay about Ovid went too far. I was making literary allusions, quoting the text and saying that he was taking over the world. Shit like that. I got pissed immediately after the exam and passed out early in the evening.

The little boy whose teacher, when he was six, told his parents he was far more intelligent than anyone else in his class and was definitely university material, could finish what had always been expected of him and get on with his life. It was time for a change, a new beginning, and a new chapter.

Chapter 7 – End of uni, third time loony

After another drinking session the following day, I travelled to the Lake District to meet up with my Gran and brother for a few days. Now, if there are two people you shouldn't be with when you're going manic it's these two. Their characters and peculiar relationship made it difficult for my mind to rest. Nevertheless, spending time with them was "exhilarating" to say the least – my Gran with her senile dementia and my brother, a walking literary encyclopaedia.

They were both eccentric – a couple of poles short of a scaffold – and enjoyable to be with at times, but spending too much time with them could easily make me manic. However, I felt stronger now that I was about to graduate and felt I owed it to them to spend some time with them both, despite their incessant bickering. I hoped, in short, I would have a good time. I knew we would drift into our own little worlds and look back nostalgically to a time when life was better and people were kinder. I longed to see the countryside that they had so often talked about when I was growing up.

I went to the Lakes that year on a positive note. They travelled there together several times a year but this was the first occasion that I had taken up their invitation. We stayed in a lovely country house and saw some wonderful scenery. We also had some crazy conversations that didn't seem so crazy at that time. For the first time for many years, five minutes of conversation with them both at the same time didn't give me a migraine. It was remarkable. We talked for hours about history, politics, nature and I really enjoyed listening to my Gran's stories. Because she was so happy, I even think she told me a couple that I hadn't heard before.

The day I got back to Manchester, after my little break, the halls were really quiet as most people had left. I couldn't get to sleep and stayed up watching TV until six in the morning, thinking how I was going to take over the world. I went to my room and masturbated on and off until nine in the morning. I also reorganised my room while rubbing Vaseline all over my body. After all, it was time to prepare for an important rugby match (not that I had arranged to play one for years) and ready myself for appearing in the Guinness book of records for being the most intelligent person in the world: Jesus Christ (in fact, why Christ when you can be God?)

I went down to the kitchen when I heard Mark had got up and started talking gibberish to him. He knew that I wasn't well; in particular because I was quite convinced the chess pieces I was playing with were flying saucers. He asked for my mum's number. He phoned her and said that he would take me to the doctor's. That's good, I thought. I wouldn't mind fucking the doctor. Mark told me to get ready and have a wash and shower and kept calling me to get out. Otherwise, I would have been in there washing myself all day. We walked to the doctor's. I was acting like a complete lunatic, dodging traffic, leapfrogging over bins and other objects and greeting people I had never met. Fortunately, I didn't hurt myself. Steadfast and determined, Mark led me to the doctor's.

"Jase, stay on the road, you're gonna hurt yourself. I don't want you to get run over. I'm glad you decided to come. You did the right thing, you know. Come on, stop messing around, you're gonna be late for your appointment."

"Did you like playing rugby?"

"No, I was too much of a wimp. They put me on the wing. I was pretty fast when I got the ball if I could catch the goddamn thing."

"Lets get a rugby ball and have a match."

"We'll do that another time. Let's get to the doctor's now and get you sorted. At least your mum knows, that's the main thing. I told her I'd look after you so come on, Jay, if you can't get over here for me do it for your mum. All right. That's a good lad. We'll be there in a minute."

Jason chicken runs in front of a car and smiles at the driver. The owner beeps his horn.

"For Christ's sake, Jase, that was close. Stay close to me. That's it. From now on, you're staying close to me."

"I'm immortal anyway. Cars can't hurt me. But thanks

mate."

"Yeah, whatever."

When we arrived at the surgery, Mark convinced me to open up. One jumbled sentence of thinking that the whole world was a brothel and Dr. Black put me in a safe house for a few days. I can't remember if they gave me anything to calm me down – if they did, it wasn't enough. It was too late. I was out of my fucking tree. In the safe house there were two other people having a breakdown and a member of staff. One woman had taken a Lithium overdose. I fucked her when she was asleep by putting different coloured pencils outside her door. This could not have been done without my magic powers.

The other woman was 79 and told me that she had a 15 year-old boyfriend. *That's OK, I didn't mind a wrinkled pussy and her walking stick turned me on anyway.* The member of staff showed me to my room and I went to work... I immediately started performing my manic rituals... First, I licked up all the dirt on the floor. This took over an hour and was quite dangerous as I was constantly chewing blue tack with drawing pins in my mouth. The next stage was to undress and tie all the bed sheets and spare blankets around my cock. This made it ache like a chest would ache if it had to do a 24 hour dumbbell session. When you're manic you can absorb more pain than when in a sober state, so I carried on making links ...

I turned the bed on its side along with the wardrobe and chest of drawers. I thought that my room was bugged so I was turning myself into a huge speaker to detect the bug and keep the thoughts of God away from Satan. The staff member knocked on my door and, when he persuaded me that it was OK for him to come in, lost his temper. He asked me what I was doing and told me to get dressed in the bathroom. I went to the bathroom to get dressed while he started to return the room back to normal. He told me to calm down and suggested I get a drink from the kitchen as my psychologist Kath Porceddu would soon be arriving to see me. That was a nice surprise. I had been seeing her for about six months now

144

and hadn't fucked her yet. Hers was another pussy that was soon to be decoded. Things seem so much easier when you're manic as your imagination seems to become your reality. You don't actually have to do anything to believe that you have accomplished it.

Kath arrived and in due course she told me that I would be transferred to Withington Hospital the next morning, as soon as a bed became available. To start off with, I hadn't wanted to go there but now I was so high I saw it as my duty to make my presence felt and restore happiness on earth. It was time to stop human suffering and make everyone immortal. I was in a celebratory mood. She had undergone seven years' study and training before she had her own practice, far more than the counsellor I had seen when I left Coney Hill, and it showed. She was perceptive, intelligent, logical, understanding and sympathetic. She also knew I was God but kept it to herself. That was very important and a nice touch, I thought. When she had left, I relaxed in my new surroundings and performed the usual manic acts: I fantasised about worshipping the women that I saw, and watched England lose 2-1 to Romania in the World Cup (but was terribly confused as I thought I was controlling the game... so why didn't England win?)

I filled the sink with water and drank as much as I could in one gulp counting numbers in my head. After all, numbers always had significance and made the world go round: they determined how much money people had in their bank; they determined geographical distances ... when people would see each other ... I spent two hours in the bathroom. Most of the time I was doing a handstand and cycling. This was the first time I had ever been able to do a handstand unassisted. Well, as the saying goes, leave the best things to last, and by God, I did.

I allowed the Spice Girls to come down through the air vent and shower with me. Geri was first and then they all joined in. This was far more powerful than Eminem thinking about impregnating them a few years later, although I do think he's a great rapper. I had actually fucked all of them

145

while doing a prolonged handstand and smiling inanely. That was the ultimate hard-core fuck. As a result of my actions, I was soon going to be a TV celebrity, perhaps the best way to get my message across and start saving the world.

After my five orgasms, one for each of the girls, I finished off my salute to myself by moving the metal lockers with my feet and kicking them close together so there were no gaps. This took an amazing amount of balance and strength and was something that nobody in their right mind would attempt as the whole bathroom floor was soaking from the shower that had been running for ages. I pushed one of the lockers too hard and it crashed making an enormous racket. It just missed my feet and would have severely fucked me up if it had landed on me.

I was pleased with the way the ceremony had gone but then heard the same staff member from before yelling for me to come out. I got out and he asked me what the mess was. I didn't say anything. He asked me if I was OK and, when I nodded, he told me to go to bed. I knew he had to clear up as it was a servant of God's duty to do such things, and I went to bed. Not surprisingly, I was wide-awake for the rest of the night.

The first thing I remember about my second stay at Withington was gluing pictures of black women to my bedroom wall. To enact world peace I had to be seen in public with a black woman to reduce racism, reminiscent of the film *Bulworth*. I was telling all this to my black friend Andy, who was visiting me at the time. However, although he was laughing and seemed at ease with me, this was the last time he would visit. That was OK, even though we were close friends. The main thing was that I'd sent him on a mission to train as a junior school teacher: he had to stop little kids playing with action men and teach them how to roll spliffs instead; then they could get into Bob Marley and everything would be all right.

The following days and weeks will always be a blur. My mum and dad came to visit a couple of times but I have no recollection of this. Mark told them where I was and up they came. It was good of them to come together, put their differences aside, and support me. They realised they had made mistakes in the past and had come to see their son who was ill. Did they feel guilty? Did they want forgiveness? Well, any Christian would forgive them. Sometimes I did and sometimes I was still angry – about the past and all the arguments, and how it had altered my psyche and arguably led to my illness. As time passed, though, I forgave because I couldn't be sure that my condition was down to them anyway. The most frustrating thing was that I'd never be able to turn the clocks back and find out what would have happened to my health if I'd had parents that got on. That said, I realised that I was fortunate that I had the love of my parents, friends and family as some of the patients didn't have any visitors. Some families simply give up on members of their family who have a mental illness; they can't carry the extra burden. Thank God I've never felt that isolated. Even if I get upset or angry with them, I know that when push comes to shove, they'll be there to support me. That helps keep the morale up, especially during episodes or at times when I'm too introspective.

After a couple of weeks, the high subsided. In its place, depression had set in so I called my Grandmother for help. She told me to hang on in there and told me about when she had walked out of a mental hospital with her head held high. She was never ashamed and never gave a rat's arse what anyone else thought about anything. I also rang my Nan whose advice was limited as she wasn't the sharpest knife in the drawer. She advised me to eat what I could – fruit if possible – and to drink plenty of water as that's what it said in a programme on television. What the fuck? Still, I was so low that to hear the voice of anyone who cared was a comfort.

I remember Tom and his girlfriend, Perry, coming to visit me. He was my best friend left in Manchester; Panji had retired from professional basketball and had got a job in Southampton as a mechanical engineering contractor. Tom and Perry were really positive people and, after talking with

147

them, I realised that this episode had been a lot quicker than the other ones. There were also justifiable reasons for relapsing. My lithium level had been recorded as too low in March. It was only 0.3 and it needed to be between 0.5 and 0.8. This was due to occasional binge drinking and sometimes forgetting to take it. My level was normal when I was in hospital but being too low over previous months could have triggered a manic episode. Basically, the need to manage my illness more effectively faded as the depression got worse.

My mum and dad came up for my graduation and both told me how proud they were of what I'd achieved, especially after what I'd been through. I was given a 2:2 first of all, but this was later upgraded to a 2:1 because a letter from my head consultant, Dr.Thomas, confirmed that I was as high as a kite when I sat my last two examinations.

Graduation day was far better than staying in hospital for the day but a huge anti-climax. I hate looking at the photos now because it's obvious, if you look closely, that my eyes are bigger than normal. They're pumped full of drugs, man. What kind of a fucking sick celebration is that? Perverse? Fucked up? Unfortunate? Just like my eighteenth...

Everyone else gets to celebrate their graduation properly. I was a walking zombie and nervous wreck during mine and drank orange juice at the social gathering afterwards when everyone else was getting pissed. All I could say to people was that I had had a breakdown. Yes, I had had them before, and I was appealing for a higher grade because I wasn't well when I sat my examinations. No wonder I haven't seen any of them since. Who would want to invite a maniac to a reunion? There again, it was probably the last time they would meet anyway. I mean, I was out of control. I was in and out of my mind from day to day.

There are different stress causing factors for each episode and one contributory factor for my third must have been the nature of my dissertation. It was an exploration of madness in Greek tragedy. Starting with Foucault's *Madness and Civilisation*, I attempted to define the madman and describe his plight across the ages. I made allusions to certain plays, notably Sophocles' Ajax, and Euripides's Bacchae and Heracles, and found prejudices throughout. You didn't have to be a rocket scientist to work out that madness was the ultimate humiliation enacted by the gods upon humans. Such punishment was dealt out as a result of *hubris* and usually resulted in suicide. It was fucking intense. Imagine a mother and daughter parading around with a lion's head, after they had ripped it limb from limb when mad, only to realise that it was in fact the head of their son or even brother. Discussing the treatment of mad people in ancient and modern times was too much for me to cope with at that period in my life. I wasn't prepared for it. I was unable to eat the apple and spit out the pips. I had choked on my own vomit. I had wallowed in my own shit. I would have been better off doing a dissertation on the more stable Cicero. I could have been more creative and maybe even recreated my own Ciceronian speech. I had come top of the class for doing that before.

Writing about madness when it was too close to me had done me more harm than good. Let's take a simple analogy: reading about snooker can make you more of a snooker player if you study where to hit the cue ball for different shots and alter your stance. It will certainly make you think about snooker more. The same is true with madness. Read about it and you are more influenced by what you read. If you're susceptible to it you could end up more anxious, with higher blood pressure, and forget to manage yourself properly. Before you know it you're back in the bin and your opponent has potted the black. You're three frames to nil down and not paying attention. You don't even know if you're up for another game. You're too depressed ... and your opponent is Ronnie O' Sullivan and he's on top of his game. He's already got the confidence as he's world champion and he's showing no mercy. You're one game from being whitewashed and he's just got a 147. In a nutshell, you're fucked.

Withington was still a shit-hole. A 20 year-old girl who had two kids and was getting a divorce from a husband who knocked her about had a crush on me. I had to get out of there, man. A 30 year-old I had a crush on had already left. Once, she actually came back to visit and gave me a cuddle, but after I called her at home and asked her out she declined because she was in love with somebody. I never called or saw her again.

One of the characters in hospital was a massive black bloke. A manic like me, he was a black belt in tae kwon do and had joined the army when he was 17. When I was high, I kept thinking he was 10 years old and even thought he looked like the black guy who had kicked me in the head when I was 14 before another bloke had smashed my nose and a gang had kicked the shit out of me. I would tell him this a lot when I was high and it was the only time that he ever looked serious.

The place was so bad and my mum felt so sorry for me that she dragged me out of there after three or four weeks. I recuperated by staying in all day and watching MTV. My mum would go to work in the afternoons and as I could sleep in till 3pm, sometimes I wouldn't see her until 6.30. I'd spend the rest of the afternoon with my Alsatian dog, Ben, by the fire.

One night, though, Michael gave up the pretence of being the perfect stepdad and I did not forgive him until February 2002 when my mum told me that he was sorry. He came home pissed one Saturday night and threatened to leave my mum if I didn't move out straight away. I couldn't believe it. All those pints he bought me at Christmas and attempts at bonding were just an act. I felt betrayed. The Thursday after the ultimatum, with my pride getting the better of me, I moved back to Manchester in a terrible state. If I'd had time to think I would never have moved back there. I would have spent a few months recovering in Wales and then probably joined the rat race and moved to London. Meet Jason Pegler, star of the rugby team and chess captain. I could have any job I wanted.

Chapter 8 – Gina

I went to stay with my dad for a few days which I hadn't done in three years. He opened up to me for the first time since I was 17 and assured me that he loved me – despite the fact that he hadn't invited me to his marriage to Claire a few months earlier, which continued to play with my mind. Above all, though, I felt under great pressure – from society, my parents and most of all myself – to perform and get a job.

On my last evening in Manchester I'd spent the night with a pretty Bajan Mancunian called Gina. In the morning, my dad had picked me up: he was really good at that kind of thing: being practical; the painter and decorator putting up shelves, etc. In fact, he was so good that he could have had his own TV series. He knew both trades through and through.

Anyway, Gina and I stayed in touch and she invited me to stay with her for a week, or at least until I found my own flat. She was also a manic-depressive but seemed to be able to handle it much better than me. She was 29, 5' 9", slim, large breasts and had a kind nature. Not as intelligent as Meredith but more motherly and easier to talk to. We forged quite a close relationship.

I moved into a house just round the corner from her and we had sex all the time. We lived in a Black and Asian neighbourhood called Whalley Range, next to Mosside. Her brother, MC Buzbee, was famous on the local scene. He was with a bloke called Justin Robertson in a group called Lionrock and wrote some wicked lyrics. I saw him sing live and he was a brilliant performer. He was also a brilliant dancer. He was unlucky not to have made it big. His best friend as a teenager was Jason Orange from Take That. Gina sang on a couple of his albums and there used to be breakdancers on stage. They had danced in front of 5,000 people at some special events. They were a talented musical family. Her mum was lead singer for the African group,

Abasinde, and the first time I saw her she was singing solo onstage at the Leeds carnival in front of 15,000 people.

Gina had a 2:1 in Fashion from Liverpool Polytechnic. That was a pretty good effort considering she came from the ghetto. As we saw more and more of each other, however, race became an issue. I would meet her friends who were polite and then, behind my back, call me a 'honkie'. Most of them were Jamaican. Jejune ones at that. She kept on saying she wanted to be just friends. Two or three times a week I would cry because of this.

The episode I had suffered was still taking its toll. Most of her friends were unemployed and had schizophrenia. This became irritating when I eventually got myself back together. Within a month of returning to Manchester I had found work with temping agencies. My first job was as a mailman within UMIST (University of Manchester Institute of Science & Technology) and it was bizarre. All these students saw me probably thinking that I was uneducated and I already had the degree they were striving for.

Next came a few temporary, but full-time, data inputting jobs. Then, in December 1998, I started at Barclays Bank as a Workflow Processing Operative. I was to work there for six months. Almost everyone there had a degree but couldn't find anything better. I applied for graduate jobs and scored outstanding marks at an HSBC test day that I had been invited to. I went for a final interview in Sheffield and missed out as I had no computer experience and wasn't prepared to become IT-obsessed until I got the job. That was my first big interview and I'd blown it. I remained positive, though, as I had forced my way out of depression by going to work.

I saw my psychologist regularly in order to prevent further relapses and, although I was embarrassed at earning a meagre amount, at least felt my dignity returning. I took my Lithium regularly and stopped drinking entirely. I played squash every week, sometimes twice, with Tom. One of my flatmates was a social worker and he would counsel me if I was stressed out as he knew about manic depression. The

152

other was a boring dip-shit with a PhD in Microbiology. He would only say "all right". Getting a conversation out of him was like chatting to a stiff. There was no response no matter how hard you tried. I became more and more ambitious and saw no quick promotion so got a slightly better job at Barclaycall as a "Sales and Service Advisor". I was proud of myself as I'd passed a telephone interview and two further interviews. I had also started to write again. I started a second screenplay about my second episode and my first children's story about a little bear that Gina, to my great surprise, had bought me for my birthday.

My brother kept advising me to go to London, as did Dominic who had now won a few financial journalism awards. I knew I was destined for greater things and didn't like my new job. What's more, Gina was annoying me. She was argumentative and our relationship was up and down. We were either both very happy, or one of us craved for attention. I felt like a used yo-yo that couldn't find anybody good enough to do some decent tricks on it.

Gina and I went to Paris and Tunisia together. We went up the Eiffel Tower at night and it was a truly beautiful setting, but as I stood there I knew that something was missing in my heart. In Tunisia we went riding on the camels and smoked nicotine-free tobacco through the huge water bongs. We watched and tried belly dancing and made friends with two local journalists. One of them tried chatting Gina up behind my back and to my frustration I never had the opportunity to knock him out because I never saw him again.

Gina also flirted with two different blokes at two different clubs. I had to push the first one off the dance floor to make him understand he was flirting with my woman. I was so pissed off with the way that she looked at the second one that I went up to the sexiest bird on the dance floor and started dancing right in her face. That was enough for Gina to stop and kick-off with me. Man, I didn't want a relationship like that. Her main problem, apart from jealousy, was that she was unable to rid herself of the fear of going out with a white man.

Part of her attraction to these men on holiday was due to my physical condition. I was impotent. For the first time in my life, apart from a few drunken one-night stands, I couldn't get it up. I had a problem with my libido because of the Sulpiride. Although at least it stopped another episode: in February 1998, I felt high and it brought me down. Gina was very understanding and after a few months my libido was functioning as normal again. Manic depression had taken hold of her and she would put on and lose weight in an unnatural manner. It was the pills. They helped us but symbolised that we were not well. Every night we took the Lithium together frustrated that we weren't normal anymore. The illness made us limited in the activities we could do. I had little or no energy after work and never wanted to go out. I couldn't face going to the pub or anything; I didn't want to see other people having a good time. It's difficult to join in when you're sober but eventually I realised I didn't want to associate with a bunch of beer drinking twats anyway.

Her brother moved in with her in March 1999 and this became a great stress on me, her and our relationship. He made her flat messy and sponged off her. Her priorities were mixed up. She would lend other people money and then ask me to lend her some. I saw that as irresponsible and hated it. I mean, half the people she lent money to never intended to give it her back anyway. She was easy going with people, which was a nice quality. But sometimes she was too easy going and that made it easy for people to take advantage of her.

Like her best friend Debbie, who had spent the first half of 1999 in hospital with schizophrenia, Gina was not diagnosed until her mid-twenties. This shows how mental illness can turn anyone's life upside down. Debbie had had a good job at the BBC in London as a make-up artist until she got sick; she then spent four years struggling through a part-time college course in fashion textiles but managed to make troop winning carnival costumes with Gina. They won the Mosside carnival designs three years in a row and were very talented but lacked the health, and therefore drive, to do anything about it.

I often thought of a maxim from Robert De Niro's *A Bronx Tale* when I thought of how their lives were going: "The saddest thing in the world is wasted talent."

However, the saddest thing for me regarding Gina was that she had an angry streak in her that she couldn't control. Her aggressive tendencies erupted once when she'd tied me up. She was reluctant to do so but I kept insisting. She tied my hands tightly behind my back and also my ankles together and sat on top of me. "Do as I tell you. Do as I fucking tell you or I'll hit you", she shouted as she slapped and punched me in the face. I started crying straight away and she untied me looking confused. Her problems stemmed from her stepdad, Burt. He was a motherfucker. Sometimes I pitied him because he was schizophrenic. Other times I wanted to kill him. Once, he touched Gina up when I was seeing her and I only let it go because he was living with her mum and any damage I did to him would be taken out on her. He used to beat the shit out of her. It made me really angry. I couldn't help them as much as I wanted to.

Burt spent three months in prison in 1998 for attacking a woman in Aldi. They'd had an argument about who was first in the queue and he'd gone ballistic. He dragged her into the street and kicked the fuck out of her. He was also a dodgy and lazy bastard. I remember him telling me about a security job he had had. He told me that he used to sleep most of the time and that people would pay him to steal bricks and timber from the place he was supposed to be guarding. I wanted to take Gina out of the ghetto but I never had the strength. In the words of *Naughty by Nature*: "For those of you who've never been to the ghetto, stay the fuck out of the ghetto."

Sean nearly got a gun to kill Burt but Gina persuaded him not to. Sean had two mixed race children who were two and four and Gina used to baby sit them. Gina would scare me by saying during sex with her that she wanted a baby. She wasn't on the pill and I used to pull out of her. She had an abortion with a previous boyfriend and I made sure I didn't get her up the duff as I knew she would want to have a child with me. Looking back, I was a complete muppet not to have had Gina on the pill. My life would have been well fucked up. The offspring would have had a good chance of being manic-depressives and would also be confused as to whether they were black or white. They would also be confused about which culture they should identify with and what role models they should adopt. I would have had to buy them the Public Image Limited song, *Rise*, where John Lydon sings: "I could be wrong, I could be right. I could be black, I could be white".

I wanted Gina's parents to show some kind of commitment for our "future together". Really though, I just wanted some kind of financial reassurance if everything fucked up. When I met her dad, who was going back to live in Barbados and was selling his house, I tried to persuade him to give Gina some money so I didn't have to spend my savings to move us both to London. Why should I have to pay the bill? I'd be fucked if we split up. There'd be no way she could pay me back. She couldn't get a job and if she did she couldn't control her spending. He was no help and neither was her mum. I knew then that there was no way I was going to move in with her. I just didn't have the balls to come out and say it.

I had admitted to my psychologist that I was overly vigilant, obsessive even, with money but it was one of the things that gave me stability. Knowing that I had a bit of money in the bank made it worth drinking water when I saw everyone else drinking a pint. It made it worth settling for Supersaver food instead of the more expensive brands. I was behind others in my career as I had been ill and this was a way of catching up with them financially. I wasn't prepared to sacrifice myself when there could be so many problems in the move to London. Receiving benefit could take a long time. Living in London was far more expensive. Getting free bus passes in London might not be easy.

One night we had a horrible argument because Gina was jealous that I had looked at another girl. It had really upset her because it was on the same day that I met her dad, but at least it gave me the perfect reason for eventually splitting up

156

with her (although I had to repeat it a thousand times as she was so upset). We were lying in bed going to sleep. I had work the next morning. She started punching me really hard all over my body. This happened a few times and each time I calmly pleaded with her to stop and tried going back to sleep. It was nearly midnight and, when I thought she had calmed down, she started kicking and punching the shit out of me. I grabbed her and pushed her up against the sliding wardrobe. One hand was on her throat and my other punched the glass of the wardrobe. I told her that what had happened was the last straw and we were finished. I told her how I had witnessed domestic violence when I was younger and I was not going to lower myself to that level for her or any other woman.

I would move to London without Gina. I felt bad the way I left her, but all along I had doubts about moving in with her. The last time I moved in with a girl she had fucked off and left me. Gina was too dependent on me. *I wanted an equal relationship where my woman had a career. I didn't want to be supporting a kid on a shitty job in a shitty part of Brixton for the rest of life and spending my spare time visiting a manic-depressive wife in hospital or being in hospital myself.*

The more I encouraged Gina about her fashion career, the more disillusioned she got. She had won several competitions with her designs and, a few years earlier, had even been featured in the Manchester Evening News as the most promising new fashion designer in Manchester. She had a magical quality but I couldn't seem to bring it out in her and I knew that she would be happier with a black man. I only hope that she finds one and she is treated well by him. She helped me out, man. She was a good friend to me when I needed one and I don't know what I would have done without her.

...

I moved to London in July 1999 and enrolled on a Fast Track Postgraduate Journalism course. It was a start and I

157

moved in with Dom until I found myself some shared accommodation. Gina and I were still going out but I was starting to be attracted to other girls. The girls in London looked smarter. They looked like they had more class. I couldn't believe I was being so shallow. They looked more together and career-minded but still wouldn't have the sensitivity or talent of Gina. And we had been through a lot together. Gina still planned to move to London but get her own flat. I didn't think she'd go it alone as she had a lot of friends in Manchester.

Gina was the sort of person who attracted others. She was jovial, kind, friendly and a motherly figure. She was a caring person and we would often hide from people when they called at her house so we could be on our own. I couldn't believe she was prepared to move to London and leave everything just so she could be in the same city as me. I didn't think things were going to work out between us but I could never tell her that. I didn't want to upset her as I cared about her too much. She was like a sister in a way. She was my best friend. How can you upset your best friend? I felt a coward for the way I behaved but I was a sensitive person. We had both gone through enough pain already. Why should we suffer more when I could prevent the suffering? Couldn't we pretend that everything was all right? Couldn't we get ourselves sorted and bounce back at the same time? Couldn't we show these cockneys a thing or two? Show them how charming and tough the people up north really were? Couldn't we be an example of bridging the North/South divide? I was back to my roots in the south and sufficiently psyched by Dom and my brother to cope with any obstacle that stood in the way. I remember when I told my mum that I was moving to London she started crying. That was pathetic. What kind of a fucking response was that? I love my mum but that was a weak response. Hadn't I proved I could make a new start? Hadn't I proved already that I could battle through adversity? She loved me so much that she worried I would get ill if I left the medical back-up and familiar surroundings in Manchester.

The night I told Gina I was going to cancel our deposit and move to London on my own she was devastated. I had never seen anyone so upset in my life. She begged me to change my mind and said she would do anything. I said I was sorry. We didn't have enough money but I wanted out of the relationship. To this day, I don't know what all the real reasons were and that's why I was never able to explain to her why when she asked. I guess I had a Ferris Bueller philosophy within me: "Life moves pretty fast. If you don't stop and look around once in a while, you could miss it." As much as I cared for Gina or loved her or whatever it was, I thought the grass might be greener somewhere else and I wanted to search for it. I wanted a happier life, a change and a relationship without arguments. I wanted to relax and live and behave how I wanted with my future, but I was too scared to let go of her. I was not man enough to let her go and get on with her life.

I found a flat in Vauxhall right next to college. The landlord was called Felix Dilke and he lived there too. He was a really affable and polite intellectual with an aristocratic background. Mind you, he was a little bit odd and a little bit crazy. In fact, he reminded me of my brother. He had graduated from Cambridge University in mathematics and worked as an IT consultant. He was erudite and pleased to chat with me about anything that I wished to discuss. He proved the ideal flatmate for the transition from Manchester to London. He didn't drink either which was a real bonus.

I spoke to Gina at length most nights on the phone. We would have romantic chats and say we missed each other, and we did. She came down a few times and soon became jealous of Felix (she would understandably have been jealous of anyone given the circumstances). He often used the Internet which would annoy us if we were trying to get through. My enthusiasm for the relationship was waning and it was a great relief when Gina said she would stay in Manchester. My course was 17 weeks and we could plan what happened after that.

London was exciting and Gina seemed slow in

comparison. People in London worked long hours and socialised a lot whereas she would skip college and sleep during the afternoons to avoid getting stressed. If Gina had been well with fewer problems, I sometimes thought we could have been happy, but there was always an "if". And there was the race thing. When it really boiled down to it my family turned out to be a bit racist which really pissed me off. At that time (though he has changed now) my brother didn't want me to marry a black girl. My dad thought I had "enough problems without having mixed race children". My mum thought "it was not fair for two of us to be together when we both had the same illness as it would be too painful". But this was what brought us together. We would lie to people saying we met in the pub. After all, how many couples meet in a mental hospital? More than would admit to it that's for sure. We learned from each other how to cope with being mad and anxious from day to day, from minute to minute and second to second. Sometimes it was too intense.

One day I acted on my impulses and became a bastard who stopped being monogamous. I deserved having my foot shot like that kid who Joe Pesci's character Tommy shot and eventually killed in *Goodfellas*. Just as Gina didn't deserve being cheated on, the waiter didn't deserve the fate that Tommy dished out for him. I'd talked to girls without saying I had a girlfriend before but that was all until I got some work experience at a top shelf fetish magazine The Forum. I arranged for myself to interview a dominatrix in Brighton. When I arrived, she was dressed in her rubber gear holding a crop and it made me feel pretty horny. To avoid a good thrashing I told her to put some clothes on and bought her a pint of Kronenbourg. I was so nervous that I had one too.

It was the first time I'd touched alcohol since I'd finished my finals in June 1998. The drought had lasted until September 1999 and then the monsoon arrived. We got pissed and went out for a meal. The publication was tight and would only pay for my rail fare. When we got back, I made advances and she was horny. She invited me into her torture room and although I wanted to go I stayed in the lounge and kissed her neck. I eventually gave the interview the next morning after spending the night with her and, after one more interview with the owner of a fetish shop, discovered that I was fired for being unprofessional. This happened in the most theatrical manner. The deputy editor, who turned out to be a complete bitch, screamed at me in the office in front of everyone and told me never to go back there. Then she stormed out. I couldn't understand it. I knew journalists who fucked their clients when the opportunity arose and they got away with it. What the fuck was going on? It wasn't the best start to a career, I suppose. I think I pissed her off because she wanted me for herself. Or maybe I had usurped her authority; whatever, I didn't really give a fuck.

Sometimes there's so much office politics around it's confusing as to what the fuck is going on. I had more work experience the following week at a health magazine called ZM. It proved to be more successful. I refrained from jumping in at the deep-end here and had my first articles published – three short pieces of copy totalling about 500 words that I wrote the first morning I was there. Then I filled up the magazine with things like 100 different ways of describing having sex. This was tabloid journalism but I soon moved onto a more interesting magazine. Every Friday for the next few months, I worked for *Total Film* magazine. The features editor said that I could be the journalist he'd been looking for after he'd liked a few film reviews I did. However, it turned sour when he saw my proposed double spread on the film *Scum* as too much of a sociological study when all his readers really wanted was to read a witty review.

The journalism course was shit although I did make a good friend out of the class, and that was the only positive thing that could be taken from it really. It taught me about copyright and libel and put me off journalism as a 9-5 career forever. I was glad that I would never have to go through it again. Law, current affairs, newspaper journalism and shorthand could send anyone to sleep, especially when taught by the NCTJ and at Lambeth college. Shit teaching and shit organisation. There was good food in the bed and breakfast place opposite, though, and for the first time in my life I became overweight.

I kept making excuses not to see Gina as I preferred going out on the pull. Between September and December 1999 I slept with over a dozen women – making love to one – and that was not Gina. They were from all over the place. There was a good looking, 30 year-old blond tart from Belfast who I pulled at the Plug in Brixton. We saw each other once after which proved to be less fun. There were two birds from Turkey who I happened to pull in the same night. I was going to go home with one but she didn't wait for me to collect my jacket so I took her friend back to my house instead. I gave her my number in the morning and she asked me if it was for her or her friend. I mean, fucking hell. I felt sorry for her so said it was for her. She never called me but I didn't mind as she was just another notch on the bedpost.

In my life I'd fucked well over 50 women. I was back to being a womaniser again and finding it easier every time I went out. One time, I ended up with a French girl who I brought back from a party in the West End. She was a good looker. There was another girl from Dublin who I pulled in the Swan in Stockwell. She ran a pub in Leicester Square. We only met twice, though. She said that I was too young. I didn't really care. I only wanted to get laid. There was also a one-night stand with a girl from Holland who I met in the Dog Star in Brixton. Not to forget the Austrian whore who I met at the same venue. There was a South African rowing champion who was built like a bloke. That was a one-night stand. There was a slim black girl from Kenya whose dad, a psychologist in San Francisco, specialised in looking after Vietnam War veterans. Later, I got off with her Portuguese friend. There was the Scottish dominatrix who I forged an arrangement with and three women I chatted up on trains. One was a pretty blonde from Manchester who lived in Swiss Cottage, a middle-aged businesswoman from Blackburn and an IT Consultant from Cheshire. There was also a hooker, a Brazilian and an American on holiday at Christmas and numerous others.

All in all, things were getting pretty hectic. Binge drinking made me lose my inhibitions and led to more sex. Gina became more distant as I became more deceitful. She didn't know what was going on and I didn't have the strength to tell her. In November I went up to Manchester for five days and took Gina to the doctor's. She was getting high – talking more quickly than usual and extremely excited and passionate. Sounds OK, but if you've seen mania before and if you've had it, it's easier to recognise. *The GP was a bitch. Gina was reluctant to increase her medication as it made her put on weight and she didn't want to get depressed. The doctor threatened to try and place her on a section if she "refused to take the prescribed medication".*

All Gina needed was a bit of coaxing to go on it, a few well chosen words, and a bit of sympathy and she would have done what we advised. She was nowhere near the hospitalisation stage. Look how bad our society is. There was no sympathy, or understanding, just an abuse of power. I bit my tongue to stop myself strangling the bitch to death. Who the fuck did she think she was? That was no way to treat a human being. If a neighbour saw you treating a dog like that they'd call the RSPCA. She was out of order and was a fucking disgrace to the medical profession and the rest of us.

I knew of several incidents where doctors had been unsympathetic and unprofessional. The most obvious one was when Doctor Copestake in Powys told me to stop taking Lithium because there was no sign of any in my blood. (The bloody idiot also told me to stop taking it as I probably didn't need it anymore – he knew my medical history and he told me this!) He should have told me to increase the dosage and cut down on the booze. Then I would have listened to him. I just needed somebody official to confide in but he didn't have the time. The fact that I phoned him from a phone box in Manchester and told him how scared I was of having a relapse didn't change this man's mind. He just didn't give a shit when it came down to it. I'd lost faith in the medical system but was begging this "lovely man", as my mum called him, to take an interest in my life and make me responsible for my own health. Instead of telling me how important it was for me to take my medication he saw me as a lost cause and gave up on me. If I was a doctor I'd never do that to a patient. Thanks to Dr. Copestake I stopped taking Lithium and was in hospital within eight months. I had previously been well for three years.

People are reluctant to criticise the centre point of our communities. That would be a disgrace. Well, I don't mind. Doctors may be overworked, their departments underfunded and they may have too much paperwork and too many patients to see, but some of them have spent so much time studying that they can only act with people on a superficial level. Somebody who is mentally ill needs more than that. They need a doctor who is good at people management, and there aren't many around.

The stigma doesn't help. Doctors work their arses off and see lots of mentally ill patients blagging off the DSS. Well, fuck me it could happen to anyone just as it happened to me. Any one of us could get manic depression just like that and we'd be fucked. The illness takes over your life. If it wants to it destroys you for good. It moves in and out of you at will and there's no escape. It's like clinging onto a ship in a storm. No matter how hard you hold on, if the storm is too strong, you go overboard. You'd just better hope there's something to hold onto and the storm stops before you drown. Doctors are usually middle class people from stable backgrounds so it can sometimes be difficult for them to empathise with lower class and unemployed nutters. It ain't easy ...

Gina took the medication and insisted that we went to church with Debbie on the Sunday. I hadn't travelled 200 miles to go to fucking church but went as I felt guilty about being a bastard. Sean's friend Mark came as well. Within five minutes of the Mosside service it was clear that they were Evangelists. My worst suspicions were confirmed when I noticed that in their magazine they asked for massive donations from their members to build huge buildings for worshipping their gods. Mark and I left while Gina refused to leave. I had a deep conversation with him and he said I needed to be with her through this religious phase. For whatever reason, I agreed and we went back to pick her up. My fears worsened as she described the service as a "bloody amazing" experience.

I tried to get her to leave but the head of the service started to preach shit at me. "You're not a believer are you?" "Whatever you believe is up to you", I replied. "You're not a believer are you ... and you're going to hell ...you're going to hell." As I walked off, I heard him talking to Gina telling her not to have sex with me before marriage. So that's why she was reluctant to have sex with me when I was there. That was the last straw.

I jumped onto the first car I saw outside the church, balanced myself on the windscreen and smashed it to the fuck with one perfectly timed kick. I jumped off the car saying something to the effect of: "He's a fucking con man not a Christian – that will fucking show him." I sprinted off and got into a taxi. Gina went back and told the preacher what had happened. I couldn't believe it. She shouldn't have done that. She had her priorities mixed up. Her loyalties should have been with me. What the fuck? Our relationship was becoming a farce.

Thirty minutes later she arrived home and I had already packed. I got a later train as we made up for a couple of hours. Every time I spoke to Gina after that, that fucking Mark seemed to be there. He became an interfering prick although at least he was a good shoulder for Gina to cry on in the weeks that followed. Mind you, he'd just been in the bin too, was 32 and had never had a proper job. He was also a protestor when I had been a security guard at the airport. His girlfriend had dumped him because he was "a loser", as she put it. Instead of providing for her, he wrote poems, was obsessed with green issues, and ran off to Ireland to work as a part time shipbuilder. He'd promised to decorate his girlfriend's flat for two years and never paid any rent. She was sick of his broken promises. He wasn't a reliable man, not like my dad. If my dad was going to do some decorating then he'd do it. There was no tiptoeing around with him and as I got older I respected him more and more. I had met so many people in my life that had promised things and never delivered them. Waiting for others to get their shit together usually wasted a lot of time.

Come to think of it, Mark's best friend, Gina's brother, was 30 and had never had a job either. Furthermore, he did not have a flat, could not support his two kids and could not even sort out his mum's fucking boyfriend. Gina was surrounded by people who were worse than she was. I had promised to make things up and spend Christmas with her at my mum's when I received a very tempting offer.

Felix invited to pay for me to go on a 10 day holiday to Miami over Christmas. That was the most generous offer I'd ever had. The only condition was that I was to drive him around a bit to see his business partner. I sought advice from people at college, Dom and my new friend Mark, my parents and my brother. They thought I should go. Even my mum didn't mind and this would be my first Christmas without her. I was drawn between upsetting Gina and doing what I wanted to. My dad's advice was the most telling: "Don't let anyone hold you back, you're too young", he said. "What about Gina?" I asked. "You've already told me it's going to end sooner or later so what's the problem?" Gina was really upset and said she hated Felix because of what he'd done. I knew she didn't really hate him – his generosity had just speeded up the inevitable, that was all (I realised afterwards, in fact, that he had saved me a lot of pain.) When she was saying how upset she was and I was apologising to her, Mark, who I didn't even know was round her flat at the time, grabbed the phone. He wouldn't let me speak to her and hung up when I got angry. That motherfucker. If I ever see him again I'll bite his fucking nose off. Interfering motherfucker. Can't get his own life sorted so he'll fuck up somebody else's. In the event, Gina and I talked soon afterwards and arranged to spend New Year together.

Chapter 9 – A ray of sunshine

On 16 December we had an end of term party at the Circle Bar where Dom lived; that night, however, something happened that would change the course of my life – for the foreseeable future, at least. Hopefully, it will change my life forever. After a shed load of Stella and a few shots of Absinthe, a group of us headed off for Leicester Square and ended up in a cheesy nightclub called Equinox. By that point, I'd sobered up a bit and made for the dance floor which was covered in foam. All my college buddies were buzzing around a girl who didn't like me anymore because she'd taken me out a month before but I had ended up in bed with someone else instead. I went round the dance floor on my own. As the music blared out and the lights spun round and round, the alcohol cleared my system and I entered a dream world. I looked at a couple of girls and they smiled at me, pointing to their friend.

I turned to where they were pointing and was faced with this gorgeous little figure; she was majestic looking with longish dark hair, and probably not English. She was beautiful and had the prettiest smile I had ever seen. Her face was covered with her hair as she nodded her head up and down and gently shook it from side to side in time with the music. It was poetic. Time stood still for a moment. Time stood still for a few moments longer. It stood still for longer than ever before.

Funnily enough, I didn't feel the usual "will I get anywhere here?" as I was transfixed by her wonderful smile and small graceful movements. Her knees and feet were rocking and her hands were swaying around in perfect rhythm. She wore a warm blue/greyish jumper and black trousers. She looked good enough to eat. I just wanted to pick her up and cuddle her right there and then. We made eye contact a few times and eventually – I didn't like rejection, especially from such a cute girl – I made my move.

We smiled as we danced next to one another. I was trying to use all my charm and I craved that it would pay off. I consciously made an effort not to touch her yet. I didn't want to spoil the beautiful, Stoical scene. I wanted to tease her a little. I wanted to make her think that I was a bit special – make her think that I was as special as I thought she was. I wanted her to believe that I was capable of satisfying her needs and making her happy. This dancing went on for a few songs and I felt like a winner. I felt like life had a meaning, like love was the greatest thing.

It was a fresh attraction, but would this one turn out to be one of the great ones? Was she the great one? Time stood still for what seemed like an eternity. I moved my left hand (now, it seems like it took forever) and placed it gently on her waist. When she gave a smile I noticed even more how beautiful she was and strengthened my grip a little. Her eyes were the most beautiful things I'd ever seen. They were like two brown gems, which was great, because all I'd wanted all my life, as Van Morrison once sang, was a "brown-eyed girl". These gems were like a type of stone that nobody had ever seen before. And they were for my eyes only. I didn't want to let her go so after a few more intimacies, which included rubbing my hand on her waist, I plucked up the courage to put my other hand on her waist. She smiled again. I was in paradise. It was like the whole world had been lifted off my shoulders. I felt like Christian must have when he was accepted into heaven; like Sisyphus pushing his rock over the hill, or Tantalus having a drink. We danced and teased and smiled and cuddled, glad to have found someone that made us feel good. She was quite short and that was nice and that also very fitting as my Nan had always told me that a tall man should have a short girlfriend. Like her and my granddad.

Women admire a man who can show this sensitive side rather than all that macho shit and the baggage that accompanies it. If you don't believe me, ask them. Fortunately for me, I've got both but sometimes it can get me into trouble as I don't use them at the right time. I can be so sensitive and then, suddenly, a paroxysm of suppressed violence. That can be quite upsetting for a woman (you know how sentimental they are). On the other hand, they don't want a wimp so get down the fucking gym and pump some iron – cause if some wanker tries to rape your girlfriend, they don't want the coppers to sort it out (or do they?) – they want you to go and get some revenge (or do they want you to cuddle them?) They want you to protect them as well. You have to be able to adapt to the circumstances. Just as in Ovid's *Ars Amatoria,* The Art Of Love, which is his guide to pulling, you have to be on the ball or you'll lose that ho to another bro.

The more you think you know a woman the more frustrating trying to figure them out gets.

Back in Equinox, things were going well. I was reading the signs as well as I used to read those flash cards my mum would wave in front of me when I was two years old. That must have aided my hyper intelligence, although a lot of it probably came from my genes too. The beautiful girl with the beautiful brown eyes was having a good time. There was a connection between us that was strengthening. We became more intimate and my pulse started increasing as I thought what it would be like to kiss the girl with the wonderful smile. I took my time and after some squeezes on the waist and lots of hugging kissed her on the right cheek. At first, she smiled. Then she responded by closing her eyes and putting her lips together.

We kissed for the first time. It was great. All the anxiety in my life turned to ecstasy from the moment we started kissing. We hugged and I stroked her back and her hair. I made sure I kept my hands moving as I wanted to arouse her and also made sure I didn't scare her as she was a great catch. I never knew how innocent she would turn out to be. I would never have guessed that this was not the sort of girl who slept around or not the kind of girl who kissed a lot of boys on the dance floor. I hoped that she was special but had had such a torrid time with women that I didn't really know. Did she really mean it when she kissed me or was I just another snog?

The kiss lasted for several minutes and it was controlled. Not one of those really sloppy ones. It was the most natural thing in the world. I was scared to end it as I didn't want that feeling to go away – ever.

You never know when or where you're going to meet the love of your life. I mean, Tom had pulled in a supermarket once. Imagine that. Even in Equinox which was notorious as a pulling joint and where there were plenty of fish in the sea there could be a magical one. One that was better than the rest. The problem was that I had so many defence mechanisms to avoid getting hurt that I would find it very difficult to trust a woman again. I didn't want to get hurt by another bitch.

I stopped the kiss and smiled at her. She maintained that perfect smile and her eyes were even more beautiful. I knew she wasn't English. Perhaps she was from the Mediterranean. It was romantic thinking about it. We danced closely and it was comforting to see her friends smiling at us. It was a relief and a surprise to see that I seemed welcome in their circle. There were half a dozen of them and I was sure as I glanced round that I had made the right choice. Now, I didn't want to blow it, I wanted to progress.

We kissed and danced and turned around for another 10 minutes or so when I decided it was now or never. I invited her for a drink and led her off the dance floor holding her hand. She didn't say anything but seemed happy to accompany me. I asked her if she wanted a drink and she looked confused. I kissed her again more passionately and shouted in her ear so she could hear over the bass. She spoke for the first time: "Que." I paused for a moment. She didn't speak in English. No wonder she was so pretty, I thought. I'm not letting this one get away. "What is your name?" …. I couldn't hear her, so asked again: "What is your name?"… "Sonia", she said in a beautiful Mediterranean accent. "Where are you from?" "I am from ... in ... of Spain." Fuck me, I had pulled a Spanish bird. No wonder she was so beautiful. I'd never seen a girl so naturally pretty.

We kissed romantically and I led her to the bar and bought

us two cokes. Time to freshen up and get to know her better, I thought. I asked her if she wanted to come home with me. She didn't want to do that. I asked her one more time and told her that I was a nice guy, that I really liked her, just wanted to get to know her and have some coffee. She still said no, but seemed to be interested in talking some more and having coffee. I repeated that I was a nice guy and that she was safe with me and after a few minutes of persuasion and romantic kissing, we made for the door.

I'd passed the next hurdle. She had allowed me back to her house for coffee. I managed to get my jacket quickly from the coat supervisor and I saw some of my college colleagues on the way out. Some of them smiled. We made a quick exit, careful not to get bogged down in idle chat and settled to getting ripped off by a Leicester Square taxi driver. I didn't care how much it was going to cost – I was in there, man, with a really sexy bird. We arrived back at her home in High Street Kensington and she made me some coffee.

The night was getting better. We were alone in the lounge and now I was sober I felt even more attracted to her. That's a rarity – as most guys know girls usually look worse sober than they do when you've had a few drinks. We talked a little about where we were from and what we did. She was from Burgos, which was a small city in the north of Spain, and had worked as a receptionist in a hotel in South Kensington since September. I told her that I'd dabbled with journalism and about my fascination with writing. The lounge became a place to explore each other's bodies as she told me that we couldn't go in the bedroom because she shared it with three other girls. That gave us a chance to experiment with the small space available in the lounge and she bought a quilt and pillows out from her room. I even managed to make some curtains out of a blanket.

We caressed and hugged each other and had an extremely romantic time. I had never been so gentle with a woman. It was if we were in tune with each other on a metaphysical level as well as a physical one. She was divine and I was privileged to be with her. I would never forget this night and it was the best possible start in forging anything more lasting should the opportunity arise. Of course, there were a lot of obstacles in the way as there always are in life but on that night we were locked as one and happy not to go looking for the key to loneliness.

I left at about seven in the morning and went to college after only an hour's sleep. I had a great night and, once I got her number, told her that I'd give her a ring. She thought I was referring to the ring on her finger and took it off giving it to me. That was the cutest thing I'd ever seen and I kissed her and told her to put the ring back on, explaining that I would phone her later in the day.

Hardly anyone was at college, just three girls and me. Everyone else was too hung over from the night before. I told the birds there that I'd been with this beautiful Spanish girl, intimating that she was prettier than they were which she was. As I left, I saw one of my classmates who I played football with and told him I'd pulled a Spanish bird. "I love Spanish birds", he said. This would turn out to be the response of all my friends. I met Sonia Fernandez Bascones on Thursday evening and persuaded her to come South of the river and meet me at Stockwell tube.

She was radiating innate beauty. We went for a pint and I thought it was cute that she drank pints and not halves. We had Guinness. After two pints and pleasantries that actually interested me, I realised that she was more intelligent, intriguing and adventurous than I had ever hoped for. She had two degrees in Economics and had spent the previous year in Denver, USA as an au pair. She'd even won a cruise for two around Europe, live on Spanish TV. This didn't make me jealous as she had taken her younger brother.

Sonia also had an older brother who was married. It seemed as if an entire new world was opening before me and that there was now light at the end of the tunnel, as if I could hear the song *Tender* by Blur in my ears whenever I was with her or thought about her. I was so happy that I took her out to my favourite Indian restaurant and paid for us. For those who knew me, this was a great feat "cause I was tighter than a gnat's chuff" when it came to money (have to be if you never know if you're going to be well enough to have a lasting career, if your life is so disordered that you can't create any order out of it). Meeting her, I was careful not to tell her anything about my illness. Not even when she played me *Lithium* by Nirvana. In fact, I was really worried about telling her of my depression.

I had come to terms with the mania. Although it grabs you by the bollocks and swings you round in all sorts of directions, it is an enlightening, although admittedly horrible, experience. I would no longer pretend to my friends that it was a magical experience, one to cherish or one that merited solitude on a desert island. It wouldn't help prevent a nuclear war if manic geniuses were allowed to go without medication, they'd just become more of a mess. They couldn't save the world, they only thought they could.

As I got older, I was becoming more scientific in my way of thinking. I had to if I wanted to avoid another relapse. I wasn't sure if I could go through it again: the depression. Fuck me, the depression man. There's no way to describe it except that I wouldn't wish it on my worst enemy, and believe me I've had lots of enemies (I've still got a few, come to think of it). I had managed to come to terms with rejoining society. And although, after each episode, I felt a lot further behind everyone else as regards my social standing and my career prospects, I trained hard and caught up as best as I could. I may have been lapped but, as in Olympic track cycling, I could gain extra points on the sprinting laps and get double if I was placed on the last lap. I was the toughest competitor on the track and there's no way I was going to give up.

I've including one of my raps that I have written and performed to show how I feel sometimes. Events in my life have meant I've had to change and evolve as a person, and that is something that can happen to anyone.

I'm MC Jase you'd better watch yourself
I'm MC Jase and I'm full of stealth
This is MC Jase

You'd better watch your health
Cause I'm feeling hyper and I'm fucking crazy
Listening to this rap gonna make you hazy
Lying in bed at 1.30
I'm only 25 but I feel like 30
Can't go to sleep 'cause my head's too strong
Been through too much shit for far too long
I don't give a fuck if you think I'm wrong
It's no fucking use for me to have a bong
Just messes with my head and spaces me out
There's no point in that I have no doubt
Fucking with a bitch is no good for me
Glad I have a girlfriend that looks after me
Cause I'm trippin all the time
Can't even earn a dime
'Cause my head's fucked up since I was 17
I went really manic you know what I mean
I was in the bin for 6 fucking months
Being controlled by a bunch of cunts
No one gives a shit unless it happens to you
Not even any members of ya nigga crew
So next time your gonna pull the trigga
Think of what I say and grow bigger
... Causing more shit's just part of a cycle at the end of the day ...
You gotta get out ... Get the fuck out ...
And shout. Shout what it's all about ...
Before you're another dead nigger or in the penitentiary
For fuck sake's homies, it's the twenty-first century.

I'd battled through suicidal periods in my life when each time I thought I couldn't. Oh, I was soon to find out that my life had been so different to that of this innocent and beautiful Spanish girl.

After going to the restaurant with Sonia, we went back to my house and Felix introduced himself in his formal, friendly and welcoming manner. After a few minutes, Sonia and I went to my room and had a great evening. We spent a cosy night together inside. I was getting more and more into her as the minutes went by but was terrified of getting into a relationship that I feared could eventually crumble. The only girl I had moved in with had left me, which was a shock and had made me feel bitter towards women. Also, I didn't want a jealous type like Gina again. I was also aware that whenever I finished a relationship I was prone to dive into another one. I thought I could eradicate all the bad from the previous one and just take the good into the new one. Therefore, I could make the new one work.

The next day Sonia didn't have to go to work until three o'clock so we went to Clapham Junction. She looked so cute dressed in black trousers and a pink cardigan and brown leather jacket. I was going to be sad not to see her for the next couple of weeks but I was so excited about checking out Florida. I got some friendly looking Christmas cards from a charity shop and wrote one out to Sonia. I wasn't sure how she felt about that but she smiled and we went into Battersea theatre for a coffee. We were in there talking, kissing and cuddling for a couple of hours. I wondered what it would be like to know her better and to become a part of her life. I knew I'd want to see her again when I came back from Miami, and I promised to send her a postcard.

That night, Felix had left a note saying that he had felt stressed out and was sleeping round his sister's. He said that he would recover by the next day and looked forward to the holiday. He was like that. He'd work really hard as an IT consultant and hammer away at the computer for most of the evening. After a few weeks he would burn out, sometimes take a day off, recharge and then return to normal. He's a bit of a geek really and rather posh but was always well mannered. He's got a kind heart and is one of the most genuine people that I've ever met. He's been good to me and sometimes I almost see him as another big brother. He happily shares his intellectual opinions and massive knowledge of literature. We became good friends. I helped him calm him down when he had been overdoing it. He's extremely intelligent, and a technological genius. He tried setting up his own business with a friend in 2000 but this didn't work out. However, he persevered and then forged a different partnership with another friend and now works from home. They're setting up a business in Atlanta, Georgia. His great-grandfather was a prominent Victorian politician by the name of Sir Charles Dilke.

We were both really looking forward to going to Miami. I sat by the window as we took off and flicked through a guide to Florida, which my brother had lent me. He hated lending out his books; it was as if I was taking part of his soul from him. He had lost faith in people and preferred objects instead. Harvey is four years older than me and when I was nine I thought he was so cool hanging around in a skinhead gang and listening to Two Tone. He's basically a genius and is probably the most eccentric person most people would ever meet; anybody can see that. One time, in the late nineties, he was featured in the Daily Star for being an eccentric with the most peculiar looking car in the world, covered in pictures of thinkers, royalty and philosophical quotes. He has such a vivid imagination and sometimes voices his inner thoughts through his teddy bears (a few years later I would pick up on this habit myself, although take it up a step or two).

I used to worry, as did my mum and dad, that he was a schizophrenic but the more I observed him the more I realised that he was OK. He's just in his own little world, unique. He's visited psychiatrists but he probably knows more about psychiatry than all of them put together. My first consultant saw him and said: "You're always slightly manic." When my brother asked what that meant in practical terms, the doctor said: "That means that you will be generally happier than most other people." My brother smiled and thanked him for the interesting conversation.

For my brother, everything is often a game as he doesn't believe in the real world. He believes in the metaphysical world, a world of parallel universes. For example, it doesn't matter that I'm writing a memoir as somebody else is writing it at the same time in another solar system. He's a walking encyclopaedia of quotations and literary facts and can make any intellectual I've ever met feel stupid when he is on form. Sometimes he can be so engaged in philosophical thought that he is unable to do the simplest things – he can't find his way around familiar routes, loses things constantly – but I suppose everyone's got their faults. Even my brother.

On a social and intellectual level Harvey's got an answer to everything. It's futile arguing with him unless you like arguing because he will never give in. He will outwit you, convince you that his argument is right, or otherwise will go off in tangents so that you lose sight of what he was talking about in the first place. He lives, as he admits, "to be deliberately provocative". His goal is to stand aside from the norm and become as educated as is humanly possible. For him, "only in the imagination is one truly free". He can be a good example of how to live your life when in a positive mood. I mean, sometimes he can really inspire me – more than anyone else in the world.

From the summer of the millennium year he had a Scottish girlfriend. She really mellowed him out. She gave his life structure, meaning, and purpose and got him to trust people again. She gave him life again in the real world and I will always be grateful to her for that. Her name was Angela. As time went on, the relationship became a real rollercoaster. But that's another story.

...

Felix and I arrived at the airport close to midnight and took a taxi to our hotel in South Miami. The state is less than 100 years old but seemed far more high-tech than London. Felix went to sleep and I checked out the bar in the impressive hotel. Everyone looked like models. They all looked chilled out apart from the ones who had done too much coke. Even the 75 year-old man sat in the corner, and smoking the biggest cigar I've ever seen, was surrounded by a gaggle of top-notch totty. People were singing karaoke and there was a rapport amongst the locals that I hadn't witnessed in England. The camp barman was really friendly and answered my questions about the places where I might like to hang out during my stay.

Although there were two of us on holiday we had two very different holidays. I would hang out with Felix during the day: we would go shopping, to restaurants, visit the Everglades, watch Miami Heat play basketball, go to South Beach, sunbathe and meet his business partner Richard. On Christmas Day, we went jet-skiing. I was a natural like I was at skiing. I could get into this jet-skiing. Hell, I might even move out to Miami and buy one. Then I could go jet-skiing every day.

Each night, Felix would go to sleep by midnight and I would hit the town. I made friends with a couple of up and coming actors, one of whom showed me he'd worked with De Niro and Al Pacino. I drank heavily, mostly Budweiser and Jaegermeister. I drove around pissed out of my mind in the flash sports car Felix had hired. I went to nightclubs, strip clubs, toured for hookers, pulled a hooker and a Brazilian babe. I had some coke and stayed up until six in the morning most nights. Felix would sunbathe in the morning and by late morning I would be sobering up by the swimming pool drinking Sprite. We would then drive off to Denies, Dunkin' Donuts and other joints for breakfast.

One evening, I got lost trying to pick up Felix and hit 130mph on the way back. I was buzzing. On the way, I pulled up at a bar and the locals insisted on getting me pissed. One of them let me follow his car back to the hotel. His name was Eddie Bauer. He was from Austria and his brother had won a few downhill races. He was also a black belt in tae kwon do and in several other martial arts so we connected with that macho lark and also on a spiritual level.

I went back to the bar with Felix on Christmas Day and we went jet-skiing. It was my first time and hitting 65mph on the water was an adrenaline rush. It made me want to come out to Miami again and have some fun. We went to a Christmas party that night with the locals from a bar in Hollywood, and my drinking heights reached the old levels. After umpteen bottles of Budweiser we went to a bar to celebrate Christmas, and getting a witness for each one, I drank 12 pints of Guinness in one, and two cocktails. Every drink was downed through a thick straw. One American woman I showed looked unimpressed and calmly said that she had never seen anyone drink like that. This sent alarm bells ringing in my ears but I loved the sound of them and just walked off and carried on dancing to the hip-hop.

The night I had the coke I could have had my head blown off. This bloke had just got out of prison, for selling the rock, and I was asking him what his five favourite rap movies were. I was a writer and was certified as crazy back home so I had the right to ask these questions. The old man with the cigar was there. His name was Joe and he bought the hotel that Felix and I were staying in for his son as a birthday present. He asked me to give a friend of his from New York a lift back to the hotel at 8am, and I got away just in time.

At 7.30am on Christmas morning I was driving through a small suburb of Miami called Hollywood. I was hung over and had been awake all night. I stopped off to get some coffee. I really needed some as I'd been falling asleep at the wheel on several occasions. The cafe didn't open till eight so I walked onto the beach. The sun was rising and it was the most beautiful landscape that I had ever seen. It was like a wonderful painting, so surreal but yet so full of life. I thought of my life up until that moment and decided it was time to take a chance. Time to move out to Miami, write and work, and hit the real Hollywood later on. I looked out over the ocean and felt stronger than I had ever felt before. I felt a *novus homo* (new man), as Cicero would have felt when he first gained entrance to the senate. He had risen above his own class and I would do the same.

When I'd had a few coffees, and still in ecstasy from the sunrise, I got talking to the only other customer in the bar. I couldn't believe it. He had manic depression. Fate had brought us together. He was a local and asked me my name, saying that he would remember it if I spelled out my surname for him. "P...E...G...L...E...R." My destiny would soon come to fruition. On Boxing Day, Eddie drove Felix and me around and gave us a comprehensive tour of Miami. He knew

179

its history inside out. He took photographs of us outside Madonna's, and Stephen Spielberg's houses, among others. Shit, I didn't have my screenplays on me. I told Eddie that I was going to move out to Miami for good and he said I could stay with him until I got settled. I could work for him cash in hand for $200 a day, expenses paid, helping him to organise concerts in the US and Australia. Well, fuck me that was a good offer. Might never get an opportunity like this again. I would have enough spare time and be inspired enough to write.

Thing is, with all the glamour, Miami could be a dodgy place. It was the sort of place you needed to keep your wits about you otherwise you were fucked. The incident with the hooker exemplified this. I saw this big fat mamma on the street tarted up and she started chatting me up. A guy I walked out of the club with had pointed me in her direction. I gave her $20 and within 15 seconds she'd blagged 50 out of me because I was so pissed up. We went behind a tree right next to the main road and she wouldn't let me touch her up much. She told me to lean against the tree and went straight for my trousers unzipping them. She sucked me off for about a minute with a condom over my cock and it was droopy. I mean, I needed a bit of a warm up – I was fucked. She suddenly walked off. I told her it was getting hard. She walked off saying she had work to do. I called her a fucking bitch and asked for my money back.

Within a few seconds she was back on the main road with three or four of her colleagues. I kept calling her a fucking whore, telling her I wanted my money back. I would never hit a woman so I just walked off in a rage. I saw the guy who had advised me to go over there and he had no sympathy at all. As he saw it, I had asked him for hookers and he had told me where they were. The rest of it was my fault.

People in Miami are also very cliquey. They are vain, sometimes shallow, and money (even more so than in most other places) equals reputation and status. Going into one small club someone offered to get me in for $50. I said it was OK. I really wanted to get into the club next door. I tried to

180

get in the small club in a bad mood and the camp doorman refused to let me in saying that I was rude. I couldn't believe it. I walked back 10 minutes later and asked more politely and he let me in with a smile.

After a few drinks and some funky dancing, I left the club and asked him if he knew of anywhere else as I couldn't get in the club that Madonna had performed in the night before. He walked me over to the other club (I thought he was going to hold my hand), past a queue of 100 people and told the door men of the hip-hop night that I was his friend, "Jason", from England and could they do him a favour and let me in straight away, waiving the entrance fee. He told me to have a good time and I walked in. I couldn't believe it. Shows how far you can get with good manners. I felt that I had unwittingly kissed a gay man's arse and although that bothered me for a few moments I soon forgot about it when I got inside.

All the women had breast implants and model-like figures. They had expensive make-up and wore designer clothes. One woman was eyeing me up a lot and asked me to wait just a minute. She was with some dodgy-looking black guys at the corner of the bar. After a few minutes, I tapped her on the shoulder and her immediate response was: "I'm not going to speak to you anymore." I mean, what the fuck, I hadn't even spoken to her yet. I bowled off and thought how she had missed out. She had missed the opportunity to meet the great Jason Pegler. Within two weeks, I had become as vain as the locals. Well, you need to be vain if you hang out in America, especially in Palm Springs, where I was planning on working with Eddie. I also planned to do some business with a friend of my brother's who was now a good friend of mine, Sean. He was from California and lived in London. His parents lived in the Bahamas and were planning to build a holiday resort and wanted me to keep an eye on it.

I had let my hair down and would prepare for my NCTJ examinations in the first week of February 2000. One more adventure, however, when leaving Miami was pulling an American broad at the airport. She had gone to the same

181

school as basketball legend Michael Jordan and was state manager of a leading cosmetics company. She was on the same flight and we talked and had a few drinks. Felix left for his relatives' farm straight from Gatwick and the horny slut I'd got off with on the plane realised she'd arrived in England a day early. She came back to my house and we fucked a few times despite the heating not working. She left the next day.

I had to break it up with Gina as I'd felt closer to Sonia even though I'd only known her one night. I'd told my psychologist the week before of the inevitably of the relationship with Gina ending, and she'd told me to come clean. She'd advised me not to go to Miami as I hadn't driven for several years. That, combined with other stressors such as exams looming for my journalism course and the recurrence of the binge drinking, could make me ill. Well, I'd only met her a couple of times and I'd put all my faith in a psychologist in Manchester only to get ill again. What was the use? I was worrying too much about getting ill all the time, becoming a hypochondriac. I wanted some fun. I'd been in a relationship with a possessive woman and not gone on holiday as everyone else had when they'd finished their degree. I'd been in the bin. The last time I'd been abroad I'd broken my jaw. I needed to let my skinhead grow and have a good time. And the holiday was free. For fuck's sake, nobody in their right mind would turn that down, certainly not a manic-depressive who was feeling better than usual.

The American girl had answered the phone before she left and it was Gina. She was really upset and became suspicious. I was still too afraid to upset her so said that it was just a friend. Gina was coming to London for the New Year and I said I'd phone her later. I told her I didn't think it was a good idea that we spent the New Year together and told her that it was over. She was devastated and I felt like the cruellest man on earth. She said that she was coming to London to see me and I said I'd meet her but that she couldn't stay with me. She turned up at my house when I'd asked her to call me first. I let her in and she begged to stay with me, saying that she would do anything. It was horrible to see someone I had been so close to and cared so much about, as if she was my sister rather than ex-lover, looking so distraught and weak.

She wanted to stay with me just one more time and hug. I kept telling her that it was over and tried to get her out of the flat. I couldn't push her out without hurting her as she was so strong. I managed to persuade her to go out for a pint and ran away to get back into my flat. She forced her way in. I would say she was pathetic, but I was the pathetic one for being a two-timing motherfucker and a gutless turd. Still, after all the racism I had suffered, being taken for granted and constantly being dumped by her for the first five months we went out, my behaviour had its own internal logic.

Gina was so upset that I'd tried to stop her getting in the flat and must have known that I'd been unfaithful, as I wouldn't answer her whenever she quizzed me on it, and she eventually left. When she did, she was calling me every name under the sun and we were both crying on the street. I felt relief and a great sense of remorse. How could I have fucked up someone's head like that? Her head was already fucked up enough as it was and she had manic depression, after all. But so did I. As selfish as it was, I had to look after myself or I was going to relapse and go through the shit mill again. And next time, I might get minced too fine. I might be minced so fine that my identity is lost forever. I might even end my life once and for all during a bout of depression.

I was longing to see Sonia. The events in Miami had been extremely stressful and I needed a girl I liked to save me from my recklessness. She received the postcard I had sent her the same day I phoned. It was a comfort to hear her voice. And it sounded even sexier but still kind. It was the sexiest voice I had ever heard. I was exhausted and slept for the next 24 hours. Sonia invited me out to spend the New Year with her and her friends, but I didn't want to get too close too soon and, anyway, I was planning to move to Miami.

My brother urged me to spend the millennium New Year with him and Sean. They were going to a champagne reception overlooking the firework display across the Thames. Instead, I spent it with Dom's mate, Doug, at the

Circle Bar in Stockwell, pissed out of my mind. I was in the pub from ten at night until five in the morning, drinking Stella. Next day, I phoned Sonia and we resumed our intriguing relationship. She looked stunning as usual, like a wonderful oil painting with that endearing smile. I wanted get to know her better and to go to Miami. Why not have the best of both worlds, I thought? She could even come with me if she wanted an open relationship. I didn't mind. I was a writer. I was willing to experience anything. I'd been well for 16 months so why not live it up.

I hadn't really wanted to celebrate the New Year. Whatever I did, it wouldn't have lived up to my holiday in Miami. The New Year had always been an anticlimax for me. I'd spent several with Dom pissed up, or drugged up, with us both slagging off the world in existential, fatalistic or nihilistic terms. *Why did people always get so worked up about the New Year? Nothing ever changed. The resolutions were always forgotten within a week and shit life resumed soon afterwards. People went back to work, even more in debt, with no holidays to look forward to for a while and with accentuated drink and drug problems.*

The millennium just escalated those problems. Fuck this new beginning shit. Anyway, it wasn't even the millennium until the following year. That's what the Australians thought anyway. What a waste of money all those fireworks were. Why didn't they give the money to the homeless, or to the third world? They could cancel third world debt. They could use it to help people to help themselves. Educate the underprivileged, the disadvantaged ... Yes the uneducated, the backward people, the freaks, gay groups, mentally ill, organisations like Mind and the World Health Organisation. If I went out and joined the party and pretended that everything was OK I would be accepting that I was happy with the way that everything was going on. I would therefore not have the strength of character to fucking change anything. There was also a huge gulf between ideology and reality. I knew that very few artists ever got to change people's perceptions and be remembered for doing so. I

184

didn't want to give in. I never wanted to become one of the herd, one of the cattle, one of those muppets that conformed to what society wanted. Work from nine to five, later if it was worth it, go to expensive restaurants and drink to relieve stress in the short term. Constantly postpone problems and forget about the state of society rather than facing it, dealing with it and trying to speak out against what really matters: justice, humanity, redemption, civil rights, understanding people, making the world a happy place for everyone, giving people a fair go. Especially the mentally ill – that's how I could help so that's what I did.

Thing is, how could I change anything when I couldn't even remember if I took my pills or not, half the time? Not that I wasn't responsible or conscientious, I just couldn't remember the physical act. Sometimes, I could see myself taking pills during a night the previous week. I could imagine myself looking at them, pushing them out of the packets and even putting them in my hand, but not placing them in my mouth and the physical act of swallowing them. I guess my subconscious just blanked that part of it out as it refused to admit that there was, in fact, everything wrong with me. It was only society that told me I was wrong; I was really OK.

Above all, the task is so mundane: putting pills in your mouth. It seems futile because you don't feel an immediate effect; in fact, any effect is hard to identify and, also, what's the point in taking them if you'll probably only get ill again, anyway? The Lithium might not be working, and if it does work the doctors don't even know why. Mental illness is too complicated a phenomenon for the medical profession to understand. Even if the brightest psychiatrists and psychologists work together they won't have a fucking clue how to control it. They can monitor its behaviour on individuals as biologists dissect frogs and learn things from that, but that's all. Even new psychological theories have their limits. It depends on how strong the individual is, how much effort they can put into it and, sometimes, on sheer luck. Some people have manic depression a lot more severely than others so it will always be difficult to quantify how well

185

proactive therapy is working.

As I started revising for my exams I managed to cut down on the drink and saw Sonia more and more frequently. We got on really well and she helped calm me down. I'd always got nervous before exams as I'd never really done as well as I thought I ought to. Think it just stresses some people out too much, gets their pulse racing. I'd quit shorthand by Christmas and revised thoroughly for the others. They were all over in early February and, before looking for a job, I took some wallpaper down for Felix. This seemed a good distraction from reality. My exam results were very disappointing but I knew I didn't really need them to get a job in journalism. I could talk the talk and walk the walk. I set myself up with an interview at Shares magazine and they offered me some work experience with a good chance of gaining employment if I impressed them. That sounded good as I could get the perks that come with financial journalism. There would be private functions, free drinks and meals, and the like. I liked the idea of being spoilt a bit.

I also did some voluntary work with homeless people in day centres at Victoria and suddenly realised that I had found my vocation. I could help people at grass roots level and actually see people getting better. Journalism was too indirect a way of influencing people, and I couldn't write what I wanted to. Things weren't right with my head. I'd spent all this time setting myself up for a career in journalism and then eventually realised that I'd never really wanted to do it anyway. It was too cutthroat, and most journalists seemed to be rather nosy.

I had an interview as a receptionist at one of the homeless centres. I'd spent a few mornings there serving coffee, doing the dishes, collecting ashtrays and wiping tables. It was a drop-in centre that cooked fried breakfasts (meals were only a few pence), and provided somewhere for people to socialise with others for an hour or two. It must have been good for them as they would spend so much time on their own sleeping or begging outside tube stations. On my first day there, I remember chatting to a posh woman whose husband was an ambassador for somewhere or other. She pointed to one of the clients and told me that he had manic depression. She then started to tell me what a terrible illness it was and that she would hate to be left alone with him as the illness made his behaviour unpredictable. I just stood there flabbergasted. I was going into this career intending to keep my illness a secret. I didn't know if I could keep it a secret for a day, let alone throughout my career. Should I keep it a secret or would it be better to be upfront about it from the start? If I was upfront it would certainly explain all the gaps on my CV.

The job I really wanted was a sleep-in warden at a brand new homeless complex. It housed 40 homeless people and was a place of rehabilitation. They had to pay rent of £3 a week, and for that, got free medical attention, and alcoholic and drug advice. They had to be in the hostel at a certain time or they would be locked out. The hostel was quite lenient and officers would try to find the clients – who signed in and out of the building – permanent accommodation. I stayed over one night for a trial and impressed one of the staff so much that she said she was going to recommend me for the job. A great strain had been lifted from my mind as I had at last discovered what I wanted to do for my working life, and I was one of the fortunate ones. I was going to enjoy my profession and could offer people some comfort. A lot of the homeless are mentally ill so I would be able to identify with them. I would, of course, be careful to keep any rapport I struck up with clients purely professional.

Chapter 10 – Kicked in the head

On 17 March, 2000, I got pissed with Mark and was assaulted by Doorman 419 outside Clapham Grand night club. This really shook me up. I called the police and told them: "I've got manic depression and my head's fucked," but they still took ages to turn up. I felt I had a right to say this as it was true. That bouncer could have fucking killed me. As I was walking off, he did a 360 degree karate kick right into my throat. I was shaken up. He was on the third step when I was on the street. He laughed after he'd done it, saying "Yes." It was a Bruce Lee-style kick and the best I'd ever seen. The police refused to let me and Mark make a statement – we were too drunk, I suppose – and I ended up spending the night round Mark's. He wanted to do the bouncers over with a baseball bat but I wasn't like that anymore.

I told him I wanted the wanker brought to justice. I discovered I wouldn't get much money if it went through court – it would be a head fuck anyway – so instead I went through CICA (Criminal Injuries Compensation Authority) with the help of victim support. This would take a long time but I was prepared to wait. The problem was that the police caught me pissing in the street when they drove up. They seemed to think that we were so pissed we asked for it. I had to prove that this was not the case.

The whole incident was unjust. You can't go round bullying people like that. Doormen are meant to have good communication skills, but the two we came across that night had no communication skills whatsoever. They were just thugs.

It's clear in my mind that this incident triggered a manic episode that proved to be the worst yet. Without the incident, I could have spotted it sooner and taken some pills, avoided hospitalisation and that dreaded suicidal feeling.

The following week my brother came down and he said that I was behaving oddly. For him to say that meant I must have been really fucked. I remember playing squash with him on four different courts for three hours and I wasn't even tired. When I served I would hit the back wall first and I enjoyed humiliating my brother as it was the first time that he had ever played. When we got back to the flat I fried and ate 24 eggs – the amount only someone like Mr. Strong would eat – and washed my hair with a cold can of Heinz tomato soup. My brother said: *"You've just poured a cold can of soup over your head. Do you realise this? Do you behave like this when Felix is around? My response was: "Me and Felix are good mates." Before I knew it, my brother had gone to see Dom in Clapham and I was rearranging Felix's flat...*

To this day, I'm amazed that my brother never thought of phoning a doctor or even calling my mum or dad and telling them what was happening. Didn't he realise that I was getting ill? Why was his answer to this question to say that he thought I was like that all the time and that Felix just put up with it? I think he was so upset that he didn't know what to do.

Anyway, back at the ranch. In a confused paradise, I basically rearranged all of Felix's books, while putting anything that was black in the bath and throwing anything that was white down the stairs; among other things, I also fixed the cat a fried breakfast and threw all my CDs around the flat (because I thought they were flying saucers that acted as boomerangs). I was also becoming more and more confused as my thoughts became racier. I thought the flat was turning into Noah's ark and I was Noah so I set about my business ... I left the bath water running, made a bridge down the stairs, throwing everything I could find down it, completely trashed my room and started painting Felix's carpet blue. Dom phoned at about seven and said I really did have "serious psychological problems" if I couldn't find him and Harv in the pub.

So, I left my ark and ventured into another world. It was absolutely terrifying, like being spiked with one billion black microdots at the same time. I was so fucking high it felt like acid was crystallising in my blood and I was overdosing a million times. It took me two hours to walk what would normally have taken me less than ten minutes. I kept stopping everywhere thinking that everything was significant. Problem was, I had no fucking idea in what way the things were significant or why they were. That's what freaked me out so much.

I got to Stockwell tube and knew I would be making a crucial mistake on behalf of mankind if I didn't drink three cans of Sprite at the crossroads. I spoke to this Jamaican guy for an hour. He was displaying posters on the floor. He was quite friendly but didn't want any of my Sprites. The only part of the conversation that I remember is that he said he rode a bike in Jamaica for 12 years. I said that he must have been exhausted. How did he do that without having a break? No wonder black men were such good athletes and nearly always won the 100 metres in the Olympics. We parted on good terms and it took me another two hours to get to a pub in Clapham Common. Thing is, I was in the wrong pub. So I ordered two pints of San Miguel, one for me and one for Sonia who was not even there – although she was looking for me at the time. She was worried that she couldn't get in touch with me as when she had rung Felix he had told her that I had totally messed up his flat.

The San Miguel was really strong. It felt as if I was drinking 200 bottles of Jack Daniels. Apparently, people were trying to get me thrown out of the bar because I kept on going up to everyone and talking gibberish. A sympathetic barwoman saved my bacon. I told her I was really scared, more evidence that you can be conscious that mania is a bad experience even when you are manic (*so all you doctors out there, try and pay more fucking attention to manic depressives who say they feel funny – you never know, you might save them a year's misery and even stop them committing suicide*). She called me a cab but the Ethiopian cab driver hadn't heard of the bar where my brother and Dom were waiting. Anyway, by now it would have been closed so I got him to drop me off at the only place I could get in, and the only place that I could feel safe. This was Rileys' American Pool and Snooker Club on the Wandsworth Road. I was a member there and although I was running out of cash in my wallet, had my visa card.

Once inside, I chose the pro's table and started inventing new games. I thought I was at the Crucible Theatre in Sheffield and that I was the best player in the world. *I placed10 chairs on top of each other, played with a bare chest because I thought I was in the Brunel Rooms in Swindon ... played on both tables ... and then on the floor ...* I hadn't eaten all day so went out to order the food. I walked out bare-chested and it must have been obvious that I wasn't well ... The French barman walked into the room and asked me what was going on. I said that I was "playing snooker". I said it was OK as "I've got money." He told me quite forcefully to leave and I did so as at the very back of my mind I felt humiliated. I also felt very weak and scared of everything – myself, my thoughts and any form of social contact. Scared of everything that you could possibly imagine. I thought I'd walk back and see Felix. He'd make me feel better. I could trust him maybe ... After all, I'd tidied his flat for him ...

It took a long time to get back to Stockwell tube and I bought my first packet of fags for four years. I chose Embassy No 1 because Adam Rimmer used to smoke them. He had telepathic powers so I thought I'd tune into him and see how he was getting on ... I stopped at Stockwell tube and chose to hang out with the beggars instead of going back to the public school world of Felix. They welcomed me, giving me swigs of their Tenants, Special Brew and Skol Super Strength. I told them of Crucial Brew in Manchester. It was 10%. We talked in great length about blagging, crime, and the strengths and quantities of the cider they would consume. They shared their spliffs with me – the first I'd had in years – and even their fag butts. They were nice people, a little bit scary, a little bit mad, but genuine. I told them about manic depression and they joked about it. This was what I wanted at the time because I was unable to confront my problem. I was too scared, too weak and incapable of doing so. The mania was controlling my mind too much for me to do anything about it. Dionysus was in my head for as long as he wanted to

191

punish me, and any attempt to stop him would be futile.

The police called me over and told me that there had been calls from "members of the public who had been worried about me". In hindsight, I think this was bullshit. They were just trying to stop me hanging around the station, or with the "wrong crowd". I told one of them that I wanted to be a police officer but I couldn't as I had manic depression. A police officer that gave a shit would have got me medical attention, but not these wankers. They just pressurised me into going home.

I asked them for a lift and told them I was scared. One of them just put his hand on my shoulder and told me to go away. Now that was bad policing and this is a clear example of an incident where the Metropolitan Police did not meet up to its responsibility. I realised I had no key to get in at home and when I knocked at the door Felix wouldn't come down. He told me from the kitchen window on the first floor that he would not let me in as I'd ruined his flat. I begged him to let me in as I was scared, and he refused. When I asked him what I was supposed to do he said that it wasn't his problem. Fucking hell, that was one of the worst moments of my life.

I spent hours wandering round Battersea trying to get to Sonia's. I gave someone a fiver so they could get me a taxi and they just fucked off with it. That was all the money that I had on me. I was too ill to think about going to a cashpoint. I tried about 100 times to ring my mum through the operator, but the number didn't work – it wasn't registered. I got one of the numbers the wrong way round and it never occurred to me to mention my stepdad's surname when ringing the operator, as I was too distraught. I waited at Battersea station for ages but there were no trains. I just sat on the platform crying, freezing and wearing a cap that I had found on the track. I don't know what would have happened if a train had come. Don't think I'd have jumped in front of it. Probably would have thought about jumping over it ... or got on it and got even more lost. I constantly thought about Sonia. She cared and she could help. I didn't want to burden her with my mental illness but I had no other option. I phoned her and she was crying, saying that she had met Dom and my brother and had been trying to find me all night but just didn't know where I was. This really touched me – somebody, at last, loved me in a different way. She was true to me and at that moment I became joined to her, gave her my soul. I cried like a baby. I told her I'd get a taxi to her house. I'd been there before a few times but had forgotten where it was. I didn't know where anything was at the time ... *That can be the scariest thing about being manic. It's like being the only member of a universe. Fucking shits you up, man.* She just said to remember High Street Kensington tube and Flat 2 F. She would come out and pay as I had no money. It took me an hour to find a taxi, and I arrived at her house at three in the morning. When I arrived, I told the taxi driver I had no money and he looked well up for a fight. He was a massive black geezer. I told him my girlfriend was paying and when she did I felt relieved but was still fucking scared. Scared that she would leave me, that I wasn't well, and most of all, terrified of the mania that had taken over my psyche. Fuck, I wouldn't commit hubris again. Now I knew my station. I was mortal ... then immortal ... then mortal ... then immortal ... Mania was swinging my balls round again and would continue to do so until the depression finally took over about 10 weeks later. *Someone cared who was not one of my family or one of my friends. Someone new.*

When I arrived at Sonia's I was filthy. I was wearing white jeans that were covered in mud. She immediately threw them away, undressed me and ran me a bath. She washed me from head to toe. I was as timid as I was when my key worker had washed me for the first time in Coney Hill. I was incapable of doing it myself. Sonia arranged for us to sleep in the lounge as she still shared a room with three other girls. I thought the four of them were witches who practised necromancy and fronted this by living as dominatrices. Sonia was the head dominatrix and I was blessed to be in the company of such a goddess ... Let alone having her take such good care of me ... I hadn't slept for two days and looked weak and thin. I tried to relax but would do handstands in the sheets and invent new sexual positions. I went to the bathroom and performed the ultimate sacrifice that I knew my goddess would be pleased with. I had a shower and washed my hair and body with dozens of different types of shampoos. With this action, I was cleansing the world of pollution, infidelity and everything else that a politician might have used to gain votes.

I threw Sonia's black leather shoe out of the window, which acted as a metaphorical tightening of a leash around my neck. Now she owned me and I would never be able to escape. That was fine by me because I never wanted to. It was what I had dreamed of all my life. This was belonging to an individual, at last ... but it was scary ... We would be together forever ... and that was great ... but was I doing the right thing ...? I had to complete the ceremony by having a feast. I went into the kitchen and felt extremely naughty looking through all these mistresses' food while they were asleep. I felt as if they were controlling my actions just as Dionysus controlled Pentheus. I was being lured into a world that no other man would have the privilege to see. Dionysus had persuaded Pentheus to dress up as a transvestite to witness Bacchanal Chanting first hand. I, however, was more privileged. I was an abject slave to a mistress. What could be better than that? It was better than scoring a hat trick in a 3-2 win for Manchester United against Liverpool in the FA Cup final.

When I got into Sonia's flat I felt as if I had just escaped from hell. Thing is, I was still in hell when I arrived and would be for several months afterwards. The next morning she took me to my GP who couldn't pinpoint the problem. We waited on two separate occasions for several hours at St. Thomas' Hospital and spoke to a duty psychologist. They couldn't decipher the problem, crack the code. I was too good an actor. I could convince them that I was sane and would start being manic again as soon as we parted company. I was scared of losing my high, scared of being controlled by people who would never know exactly what I was going through. They could never empathise. They just wanted to stick me in a cage, man. Destroy my life again.

All this had taken its toll on Sonia, especially as she had never experienced this kind of thing before. The only way I could become an inpatient was by setting off the fire alarm in the hospital, screaming, shouting and crying that my head was completely fucked. There were no beds in St. Thomas' so they sent me with Sonia and a nurse to Chelsea Charter Clinic in a taxi. This was on the first of April and it wasn't any April fool joke, man.

Sonia soon left as she needed some sleep. She had sacrificed a lot over the previous few days, including missing her second day at a new job because she was looking after me. She told her new boss about the problem straight away, which made it easier for her in the long-term. She needed to rest and at least now had some peace of mind as I was in the right place. They could give me the right drugs and make me better. Sonia had proven that she cared enough to fight and bring our relationship closer together. And this fact became something that meant more and more to me as time went on.

On arriving in Chelsea, I was interviewed by a female doctor. *I thought I was on something like Record Breakers and that Roy Castle was interviewing the man who had changed the world for the better...I was pleased to be interviewed and answered each question politely, coherently, intelligently and in detail. I was proud of my achievement ... Soon I would be awarded for my life struggle, which had cured the world of its imperfection. I looked forward to spending the rest of my life in ecstasy with Sonia. It was nice to be immortal and even nicer to make other people immortal ... It felt great being a saint and that night I had a proper sleep, with the Droperidol that they had given me, for the time since I was assaulted only two weeks before. I dreamt of my kingdom and my forthcoming accolades ... the speeches I would make ... and how I would be modest about the everlasting fame that was due ... Happy that I had found the partner that would share the special honours with me ... And we both deserved it because of the old adage: "What goes*

195

around, comes around." We deserved it because of all the suffering we'd endured.

My first consultation in the clinic was with my head of security (in reality, another patient). Paul, from Brixton, told me what it was like in the ward, what the discipline was like, what the food was like, when we had to go to sleep, etc. He laughed at my directness and charisma and I knew he would be good at his job. He had a fourth dan in karate and wasn't scared of anyone.

I walked into the hospital lounge where somebody was sat watching TV. (Shaking of hands.)

"All right, mate", I said.

"All right", said Paul.

"What you watching on TV?"

"The news."

"I'll be on there soon when I stop the nuclear war that's coming."

"I think I'll join ya."

"What's it like round here?"

"It's all right. The grub's good. They let you have a smoke. You know what I mean? Gotta leave here at 12 though which is shit. You got a telly in your room?"

"No."

"You wanna ask them. They'll get you one. Then you can see yourself on the telly. Saving the world wasn't it?"

"That's right. Where are you from?"

"Brixton."

"You can look after yourself then?" I asked. Paul nodded his head, smiling. I offered him a cigarette.

"Cheers mate."

"I'm Jase. What's your name?"

"Paul."

"What are the staff like?"

"All right, apart from the wanker that's on tonight."

"That big bloke in the corridor?"

"Yeah. I'd like to give him some of my knuckles."

"With fists the size of yours I reckon he'd be in trouble." Paul laughs.

"You're all right you are. Funny. I like that."

"How did you get that bruise?" I pointed at the blood on Paul's knuckles.

"Training."

"Training in what?"

Paul stretches and yawns. "I'm going to sleep. You all right?"

"Yes, thanks."

"See you tomorrow. Try and get some sleep you nutter."

"Would do but I gotta stop the war. Night."

Paul leaves the room laughing.

I still had my own room, and although I was still manic I didn't feel as confident in my new surroundings as I did when I painted my landlord's carpet blue.

I had several visitors in hospital. Sonia came almost every day. My brother's friend Shaun, Dom, Mark, and his friend Carolyn who also had manic depression *(there are other victims that live outside hospital walls, you know)*, and mum and dad. Brad phoned (we eventually became close again, as we had been so many years before) and Felix came which was very forgiving of him. Ed from college came as well. He was now working as a news journalist. He was also an inspiring writer and lent me his brother's laptop so that I could enter the BBC talent Sitcom competition 2000. This meant a great deal to me. Ed had been through a torrid time. His brother had killed himself the previous year during a severe bout of schizophrenia. He had also had to deal with the death of his mother from cancer in 1999.

Ed had been through so much shit that I felt a close affinity with him. He was also the first bisexual friend that I had and, as my friendship with him developed, I empathised more and more in my life and writing with gay issues and minority groups. This fed my appetite for sociological studies. He became a very good friend, and the first writer I had met who I could talk to about the art of writing without wanting to slit their throat. He was also extremely intelligent and it was refreshing to have intellectual and artistic conversations with somebody who was never pretentious.

Anyway. My friends put up with me talking a load of gibberish while I was manic. They said that I wouldn't let them speak and that I had grandiose thoughts. I told my brother that I was going to play rugby for England so he bought me a rugby ball, and I rang up Wasps rugby club for a trial. They didn't reply. I even left a message for Gloucester Rugby club telling them who they should pick for their next team. It was a combination of all the best players that I had played with. Half of them didn't even play rugby anymore.

I wasn't very popular on the ward. My mania, intellectualising and vanity were too much for people to handle. I was smoking 40 Embassy tabs a day and the only time people were nice to me was when they were blagging one. Fucking using bastards. I would bore people by telling them I would be a famous writer. I would handle my illness and everyone else's by writing about the experiences we'd all had.

My arrogance even surpassed Tim's, and he was the most popular person on the ward. Tim was 31, wealthy, trendy, an artist and a manic-depressive on ECT. Our personalities clashed when we were in the group, but when we were alone we got on really well. Sometimes, I would go into his room and check out his CD collection. We would listen to Moby and various dance tunes. I would try and bring him out of his depression but he usually preferred not to talk about it. He told me that the consultant I was under, Dr.Tannock, had been his consultant for five years and was the best doctor he had ever had. Tim had been court-marshalled in the army when he was 26, for beating up his sergeant. His paintings were brilliant and he had sold some for a few thousand pounds each. At first glance, they looked beautiful but the closer you looked, the eerier they became. What brought us together was our medication. He was changing from seven years of Sodium Valporate to Lithium and I was changing from seven years of Lithium on to Sodium Valporate. With this in mind, we gave each other advice on how to cope with the medication. It was as if we were swapping lives. Sometimes, he would get anxious and need solitude. That was OK with me. I respected his privacy and was glad that I wasn't on ECT for two reasons. Firstly, it made me feel better because it hadn't been suggested for me, and secondly, I was terrified at the thought of it. I imagined it as an electrical rewiring of the brain. This felt unnatural even though it was popular with consultants.

When I'm manic I can come across as being insensitive. This isn't intentional, though, it's really a subconscious cry for help. A rare time I was shown kindness in hospital was when several patients were watching the film *American Pie* on video in the sitting room. I was bawling my eyes out saying that the film was cruel as it took the mickey out of people. It reminded me of the girls in junior school calling me moonie addict and the boys parading around chanting that they hated Manchester United. I had forgotten until then how much those two childhood experiences had affected my fears in adulthood. Katie, who was on the ward to cure her heroine addiction, hugged me for most of the film in an attempt to stop me crying. She kept saying that it was OK. "Don't cry, because we care about you. We're all together here. We've got to help each other." I kept saying that the world was a nasty place and that "it's not fair that people hurt each other. It's not fair."

One bloke, Trevor, a mercenary after being in the army, was telling me that "everyone cared about me" and they didn't want me to suffer. They wanted me to get better just like I wanted them to get better. He'd spent eight years in prison for doing an armed robbery on Natwest Bank. He kept his mouth shut, though, and got £20,000 when he got out. What the fuck did he know? His head was mashed. He tried to overdose on pills twice a week and kept having to go to A&E to have his stomach pumped. All he needed was a bird to love him. Every time he saw Sonia he would kiss her twice on the cheek as if he were Spanish. This was the closest to having a bird he ever got when I knew him. Mind you, I only knew him when we were in hospital together. I tried not to be the jealous type as my mum always told me that a girl would wind me up if she knew that I got jealous. There was one

199

time, though, when I had to put my foot down and show that Sonia was my bird and nobody else's. This happened on the arrival of a new neighbour.

Sonia and I were sat together one night on the patio, which consisted of a dozen chairs and was surrounded by an enclosed fence so nobody could escape or jump off and kill themselves. Quite a handsome young man dressed in baggy clothes came outside and asked if he could sit next to us. A nurse followed him but sat by the entrance of the patio and lit a cigarette. Sonia and I were holding hands and kissing each other. He asked me who I was. I was still manic so I told him I was Snoop Doggy Dogg.

He asked Sonia if he could kiss her. She said he could kiss her on the cheek as a friend. That's how the Spanish kiss so I didn't mind. He kissed her on the cheek and then went to kiss her on the mouth saying that she was his girlfriend. I stood up and shouted "Come on then, motherfucker, you're dead." Several hospital staff came out from nowhere, grabbed hold of him and dragged him away just as I was about to kick fuck out of him. I never saw him again. He must have been transferred to the secure unit in Brixton. That's a bad place, full of convicted Rastas. I unwittingly sent Paul there. One afternoon, he was teaching me some karate and when I punched him my knuckles were bleeding. When a member of staff asked me why I was bleeding I told them, and he was transferred a couple of hours later. You normally got a few days' notice, but not Paul. The staff didn't want that kind of stuff going on. I didn't mind it though – it made the stay more bearable.

In the canteen, I would eat on my own as nobody wanted to sit next to me. They all wanted to sit by Tim. The food was better than in any other loony bin as it was a private hospital, but the environment was just the same. Staff bossed everyone around and didn't really give a shit. Then there was the monotony of chain smoking, cups of tea, medication time, watching television, people screaming and people crying. I felt more like a name and number than a human being. Mum and dad would come up together and that really helped. Sonia would leave me alone to be with them. One day, I upset my mum by saying that I wanted to see dad alone. It was the best day I had ever spent with him. We walked round Chelsea and along the Embankment, talked about how I was going to try and conquer my illness, and sport and life in general. It brought my dad and me closer together. If only it had happened years before, then perhaps the gulf between us and our suffering would have been a lot less. Still, I didn't regret anything. It was a special day.

Sonia and I would take walks around Battersea Park at weekends and cuddle, kiss and flirt beneath the trees. We got closer and closer as the weeks went by. She was starting to mean the world to me. Whatever I was doing, whether eating or brushing my teeth, I would be dreaming about her all the time. She was becoming more important to my existence than even myself. This was comforting and, in the psychological model of transactional analysis, I was the child and she was the adult. I was unable to cope with my own problems so she coped with them for me. I was very confused at times: seeing her as a mother figure, as a goddess, as an angel as well as a girlfriend. I looked up to her and couldn't believe how strong she was: rushing to see me everyday after work, not having eaten and still with a smile on her face. She never got angry and never got flustered, always 100% what any man could wish of his girlfriend. Then one day I really fucked up.

Now, it wasn't really my fault as I was still manic and wasn't sure what I was doing. Even so, it was one of the biggest regrets of my life, and I wish I could turn the clock back and eradicate it from our past. There was a black girl in hospital suffering from anorexia. Her name was Patricia and she was 17. She knocked on my door one evening, crying, saying that a patient had stopped her getting out of her room and had tried to rape her. She didn't want to tell the staff as she was too scared. I was going to tell the staff when she said that the man hadn't molested her but just physically stopped her leaving the room for a few seconds. I made her promise to tell her dad everything that had happened. She said she didn't know how to so I said I'd write her a poem explaining

201

how to tell him. She asked to have a bath in my room. I said it was OK as I felt responsible for her welfare. She had nobody to help her: her dad was a reggae DJ. *I had an understanding with him (even though we'd never met) just as I had with MC Buzbee. By tuning into each other telepathically we could make the world a better place ... After all, I was God ... and I was wearing the black and gold signet ring of Jesus ... He lived further down the ward ...*

He was a man with manic depression who worshipped me ... He knew that I was special the first moment he laid eyes on me ... I would tell him what to do for the rest of his life. I would tell him how he would serve God. After Patricia had had a bath and dressed herself in private, I read her the poem. She took it and sat down on my bed. I was nervous. I was responsible for her safety, her guardian angel. It was my duty as the white God to look after her while the black God, her father, was away ... She also needed initiating as a healer. Once I showed her how to heal she could heal others. She kissed me on the lips and our mouths were closed for a single moment when the night staff stormed into the room.

Patrick, who was a big black geezer and intimidated every patient in there, said: "He had his dick out." I was fucking angry. A female Irish nurse, who was Patrick's superior, accompanied him. I told her that what he said was bullshit and she must have known it was as she entered the room the same time as him. How could I have got my dick back in, in two seconds? I wasn't even thinking of having sex ... I was God. I didn't need to have sex ... I had a girlfriend ... Patricia left straight away and I told them that I would be making a written complaint. I made the complaint but there was no reply by the director, which there should have been by law.

I told Sonia what happened straight away and she was extremely hurt. What must she have thought? *"How could he be like that when I've taken such good care of him? What a bastard. I love him and he treats me like that. Who the fuck does he think he is? Does he really love me or is he just using me for sex? How ill is he? Did he know what he was doing or not? I don't understand what's going on and I don't want to*

202

see him tomorrow. I want to see my friends instead. He's upset me too much. He's broken my heart."

I don't know why I did what I did. I know that I was very confused and manic and was having grandiose thoughts. I knew I wasn't well and wasn't in a normal state of mind when it happened. Nevertheless, afterwards I felt guilty. How could I keep going in and out of mania like that? It was a really weird sensation. Thing is, with mania, it stays with you like an electric shock. One minute you've got it and the next it paralyses you. You might not be conscious of it but you have it. To quantify my state of mind at the time would require complex psychological analysis, and it may never be solved. It was obvious I was unwell and I will always regret what happened. I just hoped that Sonia could forgive my mania and me. Exactly what made me do it I still don't fucking know. It wasn't me. It was something fucking with my head. Dionysus or someone, but I could never see them.

The next day was the first time I hadn't seen Sonia since I'd been in hospital. I spent the day crying and telling all the patients what had happened. They knew I wasn't well and knew that I loved her and said that our relationship would be OK. They said that she loved me and would forgive me, as it wasn't the way that I would behave if I was well, especially as we looked like we were so close. One of them, Pete, a Millwall fan who was caught with 36 E's after falling off his motorbike, said that he would talk to her for me. He spoke to Sonia in detail saying that she was the only thing I ever talked about. Their chat seemed to stitch things up a bit and a few days later Sean very kindly invited Sonia and I out for an American meal. Sonia hardly said a word and would only eat salad. I realised how much I had upset her and I felt like the devil. It broke both of our hearts and I yearned for them to heal and beat as one again.

With some women, the "treat 'em mean and keep 'em keen" approach works. But with Sonia this wasn't the case. We had a genuine goal and tried hard to make things work. Still, if you're nice to a partner, and let them, they can take you for granted, however much they love you. Likewise, if you sometimes wait until you show your affection they can melt in your hands. Good thing with us was that we melted in each other's hands when we saw each other, as we were in love. We worked hard to overcome problems that got in our way. We could discuss problems without shouting and tried hard to be as rational as possible and make up when the other was sulking or angry. Add that to love at first sight and that's true love.

On 15 May, I was transferred to St. Thomas' hospital, and my high mood mutated into depression. The depression was aggravated by one incident. Tim had hanged himself in his room the previous week. The night he killed himself I'd been playing CDs with him in his room, trying to cheer us both up. At about 11.30pm, I had knocked at his door.

"Hope you don't mind me coming, I felt like listening to some music."

Tim was holding his forehead and looking worried.

"No, it's all right, come in."

"How's about some Fat Boy Slim?"

"All right ... Not too loud, though."

"How you feeling?"

"Fucking shit."

"Like me. ECT treatment going all right?"

"Don't wanna talk about it."

"Sorry."

"It's all right." (Lying down on the side of the bed with his eyes closed.)

"Good tune this. (Sitting back in the chair and crossing my legs.)

"Yeah." (Both sitting, eyes closed, listening to *Talking About My Baby* by Fat Boy Slim. I put it on repeat and we sat there motionless listening to the song twice.)

"I'd better go now. Cheers Tim." (Nods his head, scratches his forehead sharply, looking distressed and shuts the door.)

Fuck, I must have been the last person to see him alive. I kept going over that thought in my mind. Tim was dead. Poor Tim. Could I have done anything that would have prevented his suicide? Was it my fault in anyway for not preventing it? As tragic as it was, I knew it was not much to do with me. He had done what he had to do on his own accord. I had to look after myself man, especially after this. That was it for Tim. His life was over, finished; it had ended just like that. Those fucking bastards didn't look out for him. They could have saved him if they cared, but they didn't.

Tim had had seven of his eight ECT treatments. Maybe they had caused his suicide. They sure as hell didn't fucking prevent it. I mean, the treatment hadn't worked in time. The whole ward was crying and the management brought in extra staff. Now the staff cared but it was too fucking late. Tim was dead. The most popular guy on the ward had done himself in.

I blamed Patrick for intimidating everyone in there. This disciplinarian was a bully and epitomised everything that Tim despised in the army. His attempt to exert control over everyone may well have sent Tim over the edge. Although I was very upset by what happened, I couldn't believe the way that everyone was acting. All the patients were wallowing in self-pity. They were feeling sorry for themselves rather than for Tim. What about his family? How would they have reacted? Wouldn't they have been more affected? Of course they fucking would. I didn't show a lot of emotion. I was asking questions, and had to be told to stop talking as I was upsetting everyone. I wanted to work out why this happened. This wasn't one of those fake suicide attempts after which I had seen so many bandages and bruises. Tim really meant it and did it. Fair play to him – he had got out of the stinking shit hole and would live forever. If he wasn't alive in the afterlife then at least he would live in the memories of all the patients and staff in the hospital, especially with his dramatic exit.

I wondered if I would be next. He was the only person who I had met, that I knew, who had taken Sodium Valporate and Lithium, like me. Was I going to kill myself next? It was about this time that my depression was starting to sink in. Could I be as brave as Tim? Was my predicament anything like his at all? Or was his far more serious? Did he have any option? What made him give up? What was the final straw? All these questions plagued my mind in a room with half a dozen patients crying.

I remember the way I found out. His parents were informed first, and everyone was summoned to the lounge. I knew something was wrong and the first thing I said was: "Where's Tim?" The female patients burst out crying and a male patient, Chris, who had also been in the army, said "We don't know yet, Jay." He held my hand. Katie was talking out loud: "Why don't they fucking tell us? I know he's dead. I know it. He was fine before. He was on one-on-one. They were checking him every 15 minutes. Then they took him off it. And he's killed himself. Fucking bastards, it's their fault. They fucking killed him." I sat down on the side of the chair and said "shit", as the tears rolled from my eyes. It was the staff's duty to inform the parents first, but people knew as they wouldn't let anyone near Tim's room. Tim's death seemed to bring out all the suffering we felt and reminded me of the one million suicides that take place in the world each year.

The director announced, in a sincere fashion, what everyone feared. This was the same man who hadn't responded to my complaint about Patrick. That seemed so trivial now. But was it? I know Tim hated him as well. He was the one who should have been keeping an eye on him. The staff offered extra support. Thing is, most of them weren't trained for it. How could the patients have faith in the staff when most of them felt they were treated like naughty children rather than adults with mental health problems?

The only ones who had shown any compassion before had been an Australian nurse called Greg, who had spent 17 years as an engineer, and a Scottish nurse called Pamela. The rest of them weren't very nice at all – more concerned about puffing cigarettes and reading the newspaper than healing the mind of a loony. I had a chat with my doctor the same day. She was from South Africa and had compassion. She cared about the people she saw and believed she could help them psychologically as well as medically. Her approach was the complete opposite of Dr. Tannock's, who was 100% rational.

On the morning of Tim's death some of the patients stayed in their rooms and lounge and mourned while others went to art group to write poems in his memory. These would be presented to his parents as a tribute at some later date. Tim's drawings and paintings were on display. One of them was a picture of birds flying over a beautiful sea and blue sky. They looked so free. I looked at the date and saw that it had been drawn only two days before. I remember having to tell a depressed, but quite sophisticated, middle-aged woman called Jean, who was very close to Tim, what had happened. She was devastated and was escorted to her room by a member of staff. The art group was the only creative activity in the hospital apart from a few groups such as "Managing your illness", "Understanding your illness" and "Relaxation". *I'd been painting an ashtray in the colours of the Spanish flag for Sonia for a few weeks. It had "Sonia Te Quiero" written on the one side and "Jason Te Quiero" on the other. It looked cool and I was delighted to discover that Jason and Sonia were practically anagrams. The "I" and "J" can look extremely similar, especially in art. That made my sentiments and gift even more romantic.*

I felt morally obliged not to kill myself as it would be too selfish. I loved Sonia and my family too much and could never hurt them like that. The day was for Tim and I wrote a poem from my heart saying the positive things about meeting him. A dozen of us took it in turns to read our poems, and the therapist wrote a new poem with one line from each on the blackboard. He was a kind man, a Buddhist who believed his work was important to those he was helping, and it was clear that he enjoyed what he was doing. He had excellent people management skills and was very patient with me when I was manic. I was flattered, once, when he said that I was "really quite amazing".

Later in the morning there was a discussion group on how patients were going to deal with Tim's death. I didn't go because I'd overheard that some people would not welcome me. They didn't want a classicist philosophising about his own anthropological theories in an attempt to make the world a better place. They just wanted to feel their own pity and pull themselves together. Some of them may have wanted a bit more – to find out the root of the problem or blame others – but none of them really had the intelligence to achieve this. They needed someone with a bit of balls. That's why Tim and I didn't get on in a group. He knew that I was the only other person there who had balls. When we were alone, though, we got on great.

Sad thing was I felt closer to him than anyone else in there. I used to wink at him when everyone was at lunch kissing his arse. He used to smile back. The last thing he ever said to me was random: "Do you like Kajagoogoo?" I said "Yeah, they're all right", and he smiled. I didn't like them but I knew that was the answer he was looking for. There was an affinity between the two of us and, for me, that was the saddest thing about him going. I still grieve for his family and resent the hospital, as I see it, for being unable to prevent, and even contributing to, his death.

The memories of Tim surfaced for two reasons. I was worried that I would end up the same, and the woman I had told of his death was transferred to St. Thomas' and insisted on talking about it with me. I was so depressed about everything that talking about his death felt absurd rather than comforting or upsetting. I was becoming devoid of any feeling apart from being low. The resources at St. Thomas' and the staff were worse than at Chelsea. I spoke to Brad on the phone a few times and Al Greenwood, my 60 year-old friend from Wales. I would sit and smoke, staring at Big Ben. I had a great view from my bedroom window although I never appreciated it while I was there. I just thought of Parliament and the Government and how fucked up the treatment of the mentally ill was.

Big Ben certainly reminds me of one event during my stay at St. Thomas'. Right near the beginning when Sonia took me to hospital to get me help, we had sat in the cafe at night looking at the clock and I had imagined myself as the first headline on the BBC's Nine O'Clock news for being

208

responsible for curing manic depression. It was "all in the mind", as George Harrison said in the Yellow Submarine.

During my time at the hospital, I would often set out on day trips. Sometimes, I would wander around the Millennium Eye among all the tourists although I'd feel more depressed and paranoid as time went by, and return to the ward. There were a couple of excursions I forced myself to go on. A member of staff took two of us to the Tate Modern. The other patient was an annoying Australian woman who'd gone manic and spent all her money shopping in Milan. She would even talk about how great it was to be manic …Well, I didn't agree with that. Didn't this woman get depressed or anything? I couldn't believe that she treated the illness as if it was some kind of joke.

Two staff escorted several of us to the Aquarium. I wanted to see the Dali and Picasso out of my love for Sonia. People went to the Aquarium as it was better than being alone on the uncarpeted ward. Sonia still visited and we had some nice cuddles on my bed. In Chelsea, we had been caught about to make love by the staff so were more careful in St. Thomas', especially as I was sharing a room. The patient I shared the room with was called Patrick. He was an Irish alcoholic. Fortunately he was never there. Then he ran away. He didn't return so Sonia and I at least had some privacy.

I stayed at Sonia's flat for a weekend, and went to Gloucester to stay with my dad. He was very supportive and the bond between us was strengthening. He knew I was in a terrible state and listened to me when I told him that the depression would get worse. They were reluctant to put me on antidepressants as they could make me high if I wasn't low enough.

…

I will never forgive the hospital for the way they discharged me on 12 June, 2000. A hospital nurse basically discharged me without anywhere to live. Fucking bitch, I wished somebody could put her in my situation. I'd have

209

loved to see her crack up like I did. Who the fuck did she think she was? Margaret Thatcher or something? I'd been evicted from Felix's and had spent a week down the Homeless Person's unit in Brixton. I lived with Sonia for a bit but she was sharing a room with three other girls in a hostel. At the weekend, we had to stay in a hotel at £80 a night because her flatmates didn't want me there. They felt uncomfortable with us smooching around and sleeping together.

After begging and crying for a week, I was offered accommodation in Streatham. I was too ashamed to see my family and, if I did, I might not have the strength to return to London, and Sonia and I might split up. She meant everything to me. If I hadn't been so persistent I would have been out on the streets. The people at the Homeless Persons Unit were wankers. They didn't give me any choice where I lived, kept postponing when I would move, wouldn't answer my questions and generally treated me like a piece of dog shit that they were scraping off a brand new pair of shoes. They were African, didn't speak proper English, seemed far less educated than me and determined what happened with my life!

My Case Officer phoned up Felix and tried to get him to let me move back in with him. This was the most humiliating experience of my life. I was crying on the other end of a bullet- and soundproof screen. This screen, as I understood it, was placed to stop assaults on the staff but symbolised how detached they were from their client's problems. It's one thing being impartial, but if they really don't give a fuck how can they do an effective job? They never believed anything I said, kept losing paperwork and were suspicious and rude despite me being as polite, calm and positive as possible.

When I got to the hostel in Streatham I was relieved to discover that I had my own room. People at the Homeless Person's Unit had told me fuck-all and, as far as I knew, I might have been sharing a room with a dozen crack and smack addicts. The room was small and basic and the area was a dump but at least I didn't have to embarrass myself

210

further by taking refuge with either of my parents and their partners or Sonia and her flatmates. I would rush to see Sonia every afternoon and wait for her in Bayswater.

My mum got me a mobile so she could monitor my mood and so that I could keep in touch with Sonia and my friends. It turned out to be really useful and would help Sonia locate me. I became more and more depressed and would only be happy in Sonia's company. I lived to see her and she must have presumed that I was better than I actually was. I stayed off the alcohol and sank into depression. I saw the tramps outside the hostel drinking cider and wasting their lives away. Everyday I would see the Irish man I had shared a room with in St. Thomas' begging for spare change and drinking the same 8.4% brands of cider that I used to drink in Manchester. Once I spoke to him and he didn't even recognise me. I wasn't going to end up like that. I had some dignity left.

At the time, I begged my psychiatrist to put me on some antidepressants. She would make fleeting remarks when I would say that I felt like jumping in front of a tube or out of a high rise building. I could see that she was trying to snap me out of it but I still think it was unprofessional. She was oriental and I couldn't tell if she was smiling at my predicament or if that was her natural manner.

I remember two occasions when my dad got angry with me. In the garden I told him that I was terrified of losing Sonia as the whole episode may prove to be too much for her to handle. He snapped and said: "For God's sake, she's only a girl." I said that I loved her and he said to pull myself together. The other time was when he gave me a lift to meet my brother and his new girlfriend, Angela, in Gloucester. It was the first time I'd met her. I was talking about how I needed to go on antidepressants but the doctor didn't want to risk it as I could go high. I continued talking about my depression. My dad shouted: "Bloody hell, can't you just snap out of it." I started to cry and said how I felt: I was too weak, I didn't know how much longer I was going to be around ... I just wanted to kill myself ... I was a burden to everyone I knew. I couldn't take it anymore. I didn't care if I

211

was dead or not.

My dad put his arm round my shoulders and patted me on the back. He looked horrified and said: "Jay, I'm there for you anytime day or night, OK?" I could stay with him when I wanted to and for as long as I wanted. He told me that things would be fine, that we could fight through things together. He said that if I didn't get put on antidepressants the next time I saw the psychiatrist then he would phone her and get things sorted.

I often wondered what Sonia would think of my brother and vice versa. It was a pleasure and a relief to discover that they both liked each other. My brother had spent the previous three years setting up his own business. As he became more enlightened, he became more ambitious. He set up a company that sold oil paintings and antiques. His ideas were innovative and he worked day and night to kick start his "empire", as he saw it, but he had a bad credit rating and always had problems getting a loan to fund the business. Therefore, it was always stopping and starting. He did not receive the enthusiasm that he craved for about his business from the family, except from me. I've also given him some valuable contacts along the way. Only time will tell if Dr. Crichton can one day pull it off. If he does not he can see enough beauty in the world to have a happy existence.

Trying to fund his business expenses and his other outgoings, however, he'd constantly badger mum, dad, me, Nan and grandma to lend him money for two reasons. Firstly, he thought he deserved it because of the way they treated him in the past. Secondly, he believed that lending money was the kind of thing that families should do for each other. I tried to stay out of that. I would never take sides when it came to the family. I just told my brother not to ask me again and to spend his money more carefully instead of buying things that he didn't need, all the time. I told him to get his priorities right.

The whole thing stressed me out too much. If I thought about my family too much I would become anxious. When I got anxious, my blood pressure increased. If my blood pressure increased for too long I would start going high. It was clear from the therapy I had gone through that I could cope with just about everything from everyday life except for my family. The memories of them, meeting them and seeing them in the places I used to be so often. I couldn't bear being forced to listen to their criticisms of, or worries about, one another. I wanted good news or no news. I wasn't strong enough to weave all the different strands and threads together.

My brother has such a deep love and compassion for art and beauty that it's sometimes hard to believe. He loves listening to Beethoven, looking at art and reading philosophy. He is remarkably well read and extremely romantic as a lover. He is always there to talk to if I need his help. He doesn't mind if I ring him in the early hours of the morning when I am upset or a bit high. Often, there even seems like there is a metaphysical connection between us because when I ring him up we are thinking of the same thing.

However, he is so interested in objects, the world, and the universe that he tends to speak an awful lot. Therefore, it can be very difficult to get a word in when you are in his company. He has a brilliant mind. Sometimes you just feel like writing down the things he says because they seem to have so much meaning and relevance to your life and the lives of others. He understands how the universe works and why people operate in the way that they do.

But he always goes from one extreme to the other. He can go from being the perfect gentleman to standing at a bar with no money in his pocket. One minute he can be at the proms in a tuxedo waving the Union Jack and behaving as an aristocrat, the next he can be walking round with a scruffy top, a pair of trousers with stains on them and holes in his socks.

Anyway, Angela was a 25 year-old, slim, Glaswegian sculptress whose mother looked after homeless people. When she met Harvey he was 29, and wearing a monk's outfit in the garden. Angela and her mother had come round to try and get my grandmother to take on a reformed prisoner as a

213

lodger. Angela, Harvey and me went out a few times and I was over the moon to see my brother so happy. I wished it could stay like that for him forever. Whatever the outcome, I was grateful to her because she has helped my brother love again. Going out with her had got rid of his misogyny and enabled him to be a romantic again. That meant my brother had got over his previous bad relationships and would find it easier to get another girlfriend in the future if he needed to. Then he wouldn't have to be alone in his old age like my grandma.

Harvey is one poor rich man and heartbroken true love. When I got ill it hit him hard. Funny thing is if we hadn't been through so much we wouldn't be as determined to succeed now. I am at ease with my family now and Harvey will be too, in time. Therefore my mum can stop thinking that "everything is her fault". Please mum, never even think of taking an overdose again because my brother and I are proud of who we are. You can enjoy life. So can dad. You deserve to. Take it from me.

Blood is thicker than water and I love all of my family. You can't choose your family, you just have to put up with them, and as friends come and go families usually stick around. They love you for what you are – not what you can give them or do with them. That's the ideal anyway and it's true most of the time with mine, thank God.

Anyway, the next time I saw my consultant after meeting my brother's girlfriend she put me on Efexor. This time I was sexually functional and it started working within a few weeks. I had clung on long enough to avoid ending up like Tim. There were times when I thought I was going to crack but the will to live beat the will to die. I told Sonia once that I would have killed myself had it not been for her. It was the most upset I had ever seen her. She said that it was not fair to put that kind of pressure on her. It was as if I was blackmailing her to stay with me. If she left I would kill myself and she would be to blame for my suicide. I was so depressed at the time that I thought what I was saying was true. Humans have a lot of resolve, though. Look how Robert

De Niro gets the gooks in the Russian roulette scene in *Deer Hunter*. He's pushed to the limit and comes through it. I wouldn't know if I would have survived without Sonia. Glad I never had to find out. Glad she never had to find out, either.

After four months on the antidepressants my life was bearable again. Sonia and I had our ups and downs but maintained a strong relationship. She went on holiday with her friends to Biarritz and I survived without her. That would have been unthinkable a few months before. My mood improved enough for the two of us to go to Corfu. We hired a car and I enjoyed driving around the snake-like winding roads. I harassed the council, my GP, consultant and psychologist to get me my own flat in Vauxhall. They eventually agreed and by 15 October, 2000 I had my own flat. There was nothing in it but I got a grant for £1,000 from the Social Fund to do the place up. That really helped and I owed a lot to one of the housing officers at the hostel. It was an Asian woman who worked in the office who told me that I could apply for a grant. Without her I wouldn't have known about it, and she was very kind and helped me fill out the form in detail. I saw her several months later and thanked her again. She said that she was glad to see me back on my feet again and pleased that I was "one of their success stories". And there weren't many success stories that came out of that hostel.

Chapter 11 – Dealing with it

So in October 2001, for the first time in my life, I had my own flat and my own space. I took pride in turning an empty house with no carpet or furniture into somewhere that actually expressed my identity. It also helps that it's only a 15 minute walk to the hospital, and on the first floor, meaning it's warm and less likely to be burgled.

Mum and dad came up to help me move in, and dad even helped me paint the lounge magnolia – he knows how good it is to feel secure and comfortable in the area that you live in, as much as I do. It was a new beginning and things were looking up. One thing is for sure, though, I don't think I'd be half as comfortable as I am at present without the time, effort and love that dad showed me when we were doing it up – Christ, I've even taken to DIY.

All in all, my life was getting better. For added peace of mind, the authorities reassured me that I couldn't get evicted from this flat, even if I went out of my mind. I went to my psychologist every two weeks and, after I had come to terms with the stigma attached to going to see a shrink, we undertook an intensive relapse prevention programme. Carol Busch, the aforementioned, is a middle-aged, erudite and extremely intelligent individual who helped me put my life and experiences into perspective. Importantly, we concentrated on identifying the early warning signs that I am going high, that I'm heading for another episode. We covered and examined nine signs in all:

The first sign is *energy*: more energy than normal is a potential danger, as is doing too many things at once and being disorganised, so be aware. The second sign of an impending episode is *sleep*: going to bed one to three hours later than usual, taking longer to get to sleep and sleeping less (five to six hours). Third comes *alcohol*: half a pint of lager makes me feel light-headed and confused and my heart rate increases. My mood changes and I can become depressed, quieter, more irritable, self-confident and grandiose. The fourth sign is *caffeine*: drinking even small amounts of coffee, tea or Coca-Cola make me feel anxious, and my heart rate increases. Five, *diet*: I eat less well with fewer home cooked meals and more fast foods – especially burgers. Sixth sign: *headaches* and *migraines* are more frequent. Seven is *social contact*: I become more talkative with friends and strangers, yet more intolerant and critical of others. I make more complaints about poor service. If I feel uncomfortable in social situations, I seek out reassurance by sharing my "crazy" thoughts with others. I worry more about what others think of me. Eight, *loneliness*: I feel increasingly lonely, and increase my contact with old friends and family; I try to make new friends. The final category, *sex*: I become more perverted, submissive and lose touch with reality, fixating myself with mistresses in my imagination.

The work I've done with my psychologist is long-term, and a good place to turn to if things ever became unmanageable. Combined with closely observing my medication levels it plays a key role in avoiding serious episodes and ending up "back in the bin". I will never know how bad my illness is compared to that of others but I'm not prepared to find out. I'm determined to do something about it. The boxer that had been hit so hard that he couldn't get back up has found new strength within himself and through the help of someone else:

Still seein' Sonia
bein' honest with ya
hope we can be together
forever and forever
your love is true to me
as mine will always be
so sorry to hurt you
what was I supposed to do?
hope we can get through it
I was evil when we met
for that I'll always regret
we're so close now
that I've taken this vow

always to be faithful
rather than be so hateful
you've been so loyal
removed my hate with toil
I was scared of life
been through so much strife
now I'm so much stronger
just hang on a little longer
I love you more than anything
our happiness is the key thing
thanks for your help and aid
for that you didn't get paid
I'll never forget your tender love
my wonderful magical dove ...

Through a wonderful woman from a different culture than his own this man has found a kind of humanity that is more sacred than he has ever experienced before. Meeting her and having her stick by him has made him face up to all the pain of his past, and for the first time he can be himself. He has discovered his own identity without the bullshit, and without all the pretentiousness, and whatever the outcome he will always be grateful to her for that. Sonia Fernandez Bascones has helped strengthen the resolve of Jason Pegler.

Pride, determination, frustration, anger and a desire to prevent the majority from bullying others will always give him extra resolve and he will fight on as long as he can. Although an outsider, he still believes he can be victorious in a fight with limitless rounds. Someone has to get knocked out unless both come to their senses and stop fighting.

He is fighting for mental health, fighting for those poor mad bastards who wander around the hospital wards wanting to kill themselves. He is fighting for those people who are immediately prejudiced against because of the colour of their skin. He is fighting for the memory of those Jews that were massacred in the Holocaust. He will relive all the pain from his past over and over again to try and help a fellow sufferer. Maybe he could even help a 17 year-old with manic depression accept their illness long before he had, and then

218

they wouldn't have to go through as much pain as he went through. That, indeed, is his goal, just to help one poor bugger, face up to their serious mental illness and enable them to get on with their life. Then, and only then, will all that reflecting and self-analysis be worthwhile.

Chapter 12 – Jaw trouble

By November 2000 things were looking up. I was getting settled in my flat and, as the days passed, I came to terms with my illness. Some days, of course, were harder than others. After all, I'd been depressed and still had to be careful and conscientious when taking my pills, and be able to identify any change in mood. For example, if I cut the dosage of my antidepressants too soon I'd be too depressed, but if I stayed on them for too long I could go high and relapse. And like any episode, it could prove to be too much, and the last one. Game over – you're history.

I had a supply of Valium to relax me when I was feeling stressed out. I knew I was far more vulnerable than people who didn't have bipolar effective disorder and I knew I would have to live my life in a way that would suit my condition. However, I also knew, importantly, that part of my illness was psychological so I could still live a decent life by refusing to give in. The ball, to a certain extent at least, was in my court. I didn't want to be so much of a hypochondriac that I couldn't fulfil my goals, ambitions and dreams. Each time I got knocked down I would get up again because I was a survivor.

The positive philosophy that I had made for myself was severely tested when I had another episode, or a serious blip as my psychiatrist called it, in December 2000. A noticeable difference this time was that I managed to avoid hospitalisation somehow. I had spotted it sooner than before and, thus, decreased the time of my hellish experience. I was hit just as hard but my relapse prevention work strengthened my ribs. I tried to be like the great Mohammed Ali when Joe Frazier hit him during their amazing fights. Ali said that Frazier would hit so hard that he couldn't feel anything. His body was totally numb.

The most disturbing fact, in my eyes, was that I'd finished the first draft of my memoir on 30 November, 2000 and suffered a relapse the following week. I had achieved my greatest ambition at that point in my life, yet relapsed almost immediately afterwards. Had writing so much about madness made me mad again? Well, it certainly hadn't helped, had it? I had put myself under a lot of pressure by writing 50,000 words in eight weeks. Considering the subject matter and my condition I had put myself under a great deal of strain. My mother had warned me but I had been fighting too hard. I'd been fighting too hard to catch up with my millionaire-aiming business friends, Mark, Sean, Felix and my brother. I'd been fighting too hard to catch up with my journalist buddy, Dominic, and ended up falling on my arse. My high level of expectation had been my downfall. I was my own worst enemy, putting myself under stress when it wasn't worth the risk.

The whole experience of writing the memoir had been a roller coaster ride that was different to anything I had previously experienced. I had started writing it in July 1998, the day after I left Barclays Bank where I worked as a Sales and Service Advisor. I'd been working full-time for nine months – six of them with Barclays – and the idea of the memoir came to fruition during that period. As my health improved I wanted to write more and more. I wrote 15,000 words in two weeks and was so upset, drained and enlightened by the end result that I couldn't add to it for two years. By the time I'd returned to it and finished the first draft, though, I'd let sleeping dogs lie. I'd found out more about myself and learned to face up to the bad things that had happened in the past. My anger, frustration, hang-ups, and bitterness had come out of the closet, and the ghosts from Green Lane, the rest of Gloucester, Manchester, and even some of those in London, had flown away. All in all, it had been a cathartic experience.

I saw my psychologist on the same morning and she congratulated me for finishing. I even managed to have a meeting with a junior consultant who educated me about the chemical aspects of the medication I was taking. Unfortunately, though, I would soon end up like Hamlet – taken over by my own antic disposition. Concentrating on the theme of madness had to some extent made me mad again. Mad as a hatter, in fact.

Why else had it happened? Wasn't it simple? My medication wasn't right and needed to be adjusted; it would take time and years of practice to be able to distinguish between feeling happy, or content, and actually going high. I knew I was going to have further relapses and I knew that it would be a long time before I would be able to see it all coming. The fact that, on this occasion, I had managed to spot myself going high and had got help straight away saved me months of hell – and possibly even my life. It saved me from topping myself like the popular Tim from Chelsea Charter Clinic. It saved me from becoming too introverted and giving up. It saved me from being chemically depressed to such an extent that I was a lamb to the slaughter. I'd been saved, but the feeling was just the same, the punch was just as hard and the impact was just the same. I was pitiful, weak and a blubbering wreck. I was like a smack head suffering from withdrawal symptoms and in desperate need of a fix.

Other stressors contributed to me going high again, the most noticeable of which was a massive argument I had with Sonia. We were very close by December 2000 and hardly argued. Sonia prefers to keep things to herself and I was always conscious of discussing things rationally rather than shouting, screaming and hurling abuse as my parents had done. Sonia and Anna (her best friend in London, 20 years-old, from Naples and in the first year of a marketing degree) were desperate to leave the hostel that they had lived in since April 2000. In fact, they had moved in on the same week that I had moved into hospital. I said they could leave the hostel and stay with me for a while until they found a shared house with some other people. I would look after Anna's belongings while she went back to Italy for three weeks. This would save her three weeks rent, and I could also save Sonia a couple of weeks rent as she was going back to Spain to see her family for Christmas. I really wanted to help them out, but as soon as I suggested it I started to get stressed out. I panicked. It may affect my benefit. Wouldn't the flat be too crowded? The flat would be a mess, and I knew that would stress me out just like when I used to clear up the mess of my friends in my room, all those years back when I was on acid.

I spoke to my psychologist who advised me to retract my offer, but I still wanted to help them out. They had been good to me and I wanted to repay their kindness.

On 1 December, 2000, a Friday night, Sonia and I went to a classical concert, Handel's *Messiah*, at a church in Sloane Square. Sonia won tickets through the Metro newspaper. During the interval, I bought Sonia a glass of wine and, while I sipped my orange juice, I asked her and Anna for £20 a week keep while they were staying in the flat with me. I knew I was over-vigilant with money and thought that the payment would compensate for the adjustment that I was making and make them concentrate more on finding a flat.

Sonia went ballistic and we left the church without seeing the rest of the concert. It was particularly upsetting as it had been a romantic evening up until that point. I realised that I had really hurt her pride, and became so frustrated when she wouldn't accept my apology that I shouted at her to fuck off. It was dark, and about ten seconds later I started looking for her but she was nowhere to be seen. I looked for her everywhere, shouting her name in desperation.

I eventually caught up with her back at the hostel in Bayswater at about 11.30pm. I told Anna what had happened and knew that I had upset her as well. I'd hurt her pride and I had done something selfish. Sonia didn't want to speak to me. We eventually went for a walk and she was so disillusioned with our relationship that night that she was considering finishing it. We both cried in the street knowing that things weren't as they should be between us, so I agreed to give her some space.

She agreed to let me stay with her that night and I left early in the morning as I wasn't going to beg her to stay with me like I had begged Meredith. I had my pride too, I thought. I also expected her to come to Dominic's sister's thirthieth birthday party later that evening. It would be nice to see Tara as I hadn't seen her for ages, and it would be a special social occasion where I would be able to introduce Sonia as my girlfriend. Sonia eventually did come and we made up.

Over the next couple of days, I spoke to my mum and dad and told them what had happened and they told me that I was in the wrong. Their judgement was enough for me to admit it.

After I'd finished writing my memoir my mood had become quite elevated as it was such an intense experience. The row with Sonia had increased my anxiety and I had been extremely lively at Tara's party. I'd drunk four bottles of Stella, which had been my limit for two years, but because of the strong medication I was on I was very drunk. I was drunk enough to really show off when dancing. I was dancing to some hip-hop, most notably House of Pain's "Jump Around", and the whole dance floor, around 20 people, were watching and applauding me for about two minutes. James Brown would have been proud of me. I don't think that I was manic then but this instance illustrates that a manic-depressive has to be very aware when they feel happy – there's a fine line between happiness and the very early stages of mania. I'd managed to keep my alcohol limit to no more than two pints in a day since the night I got kicked by the doorman on 17 March, 2000.

On 4 December I met a guy from New York on Oxford Street. He was working on behalf of Centrepoint for homeless people. He taught film studies at some film school in Bristol and gave me an address where I could have my first screenplay "A Can of Madness" critically reviewed. This eventually cost me £15 but proved to be worthwhile. On Wednesday 6 December, five days after our falling out, I invited Sonia out for a surprise. I booked top quality seats for a ballet about a mermaid in the West End.

We met at seven and I was crying my eyes out. I'd told Sonia that I couldn't go to the ballet with her because I was manic. I was afraid and would be unable to concentrate. I was ill. Fucking hell. Not again. When would this fucking nightmare end? I didn't have the strength. I couldn't go through it again. I was too weak. Why me? Why the fuck did it have to be me? Why the fuck couldn't it be someone else for a change? It wasn't fair. I was so glad that she was there. I don't know what I would have done without her. Without her love I was even more vulnerable. I would be even more useless. A lamb to the slaughter; "Meat is Murder" as Morrissey and the Smiths so aptly put it.

I'd seen my consultant earlier that morning and he had recognised that I was high and gave me some new pills: Diazepam, which is more commonly known as Valium, Risperidone, Zimovane, Droperidol and Procycladine. We'd arranged to meet again on Monday 11 December to see how much the new medicines were bringing me down. From then on Sonia was careful to note when I should take which medication and how much I should take.

I can clearly remember being high. My appointment with Dr. Richard Haslam was at 1pm on Wednesday 6 December, 2001, and I had gone to play squash with Mark in the morning. He lived in a posh flat in Clapham Common and was one of my best mates in London. I told him that I felt high and was worried I was going mad. I broke down in tears and told him that I was losing my mind again. Mark's response was to give me a caring pat on the back and ask me if I wanted a copy of the latest U2 album. The song, "A Beautiful Day", was playing in the background.

Instead of going to play squash straight away Mark set about cooking a superb fried breakfast. He put on MTV, made me a filter coffee and told me to relax. Mark was an excellent cook. He would often mix his coffee with brandy, and take breaks having a few drags on a Marlborough Light. He would therapeutically tidy his flat while cooking. He was 29, nearly four years older than me, and was from a wealthy background. He'd spent most of his life working in marketing and was partial to the odd drink or 10. He liked his pills and was into charlie when he felt like it. At the time he worked for an IT dot com that was really pissing him off because of its lack of ingenuity. By mid 2001 he ran an expanding software company that had been set up by his dad. It was a high pressure job where he was in charge of alot of people. He would often fly to Boston for business meetings but was there for me when I had problems. He moved in with an Irish journalist called Maria. She was good for him. They moved into a flat in Tower Bridge and then to Clapham Junction.

When I was watching MTV at Mark's flat in Clapham Common I practised the diaphragmatic breathing that my psychologist, Carol Busch, had taught me to try and relieve the stress that I felt. It was too late. I was as weak and as fragile as a little baby being raped by a paedophile. I sat down absorbed in the television and watched the most remarkable pop video I had ever seen. It was "Coffee and TV" by Blur and it made me cry and feel the most scared I had ever felt. The video shows a little caricatured carton of milk walking around a dangerous route. He catches sight of a pink female carton of milk and is clearly in love but she is run over by a car as they cross the road to meet each other. A tear of milk drops down his eye when he sees his love flattened and, at the end of the video, he is thrown in the bin by one of the band and is flown up to heaven with the help of an angel. I felt so upset when I saw her run over, and I actually thought that I was the carton of milk that was thrown in the bin. I wasn't happy; I was utterly miserable.

Mark arrived back with the greatest breakfast I had ever seen. It was fit for a king. Sausages, bacon, black pudding, mushrooms, grilled tomatoes, eggs, beans, fried bread, filter coffee and orange juice. I ate it like a tramp at Christmas who had realised they had been invited in for their last warm meal for a long time. I knew that this was a special occasion, and I was aware I would experience months of pain and suffering just as I had during my previous episodes.

Soon afterwards we walked to the squash courts and had a few games. Mark won four games to nil, although I scored about six points a game which wasn't too bad as Mark was pretty good. In fact, he'd captained his university at it.

I couldn't believe what happened next. I discovered I was sat next to Geoffrey from the old TV programme "Rainbow" on the train from Clapham Junction to Waterloo. He looked as pale and ill as I did. I remembered seeing him on an advertisement at about four in the morning a few weeks previously. The advertisement mocked him for not having saved a pension. Maybe Geoffrey was mentally ill as well. That was such a pity. Zippy, George and Bungle hadn't been real people and all that time Geoffrey hadn't known. No wonder he was so depressed now that he had found out.

I managed to get to the hospital in time to see Dr. Haslam. I ran all the way from Waterloo station to St.Thomas'. Dr. Haslam said he could tell I was high before I told him. Well, thank fuck for that. This was the first time ever that a medical professional had spotted that I was high relatively early. He should have been given a medal or something. I cursed the GP I had seen a few weeks before. My usual GP, Dr. Law, had not been there so I saw an Indian doctor. When I told him that I had been feeling high and that I had wanted to reduce my antidepressants, during an emergency-only Saturday morning appointment two weeks before, he told me to go home, chill out and drink some peppermint or camomile tea. Fucking bastard. That was another occasion when the system had let me down. Doctors just didn't listen to me. In hindsight, though, I thought of many reasons why: they didn't have enough time, there were too many patients, they had too much paperwork and they couldn't spend enough time one-on-one with a patient. Instead, they just rushed people through the surgeries. I felt like a clone going through the escalators on the underground at rush hour. The thing is, when some shit happens to you like that, you feel let down. You feel like they don't give a shit about you because you are mentally ill. You feel like you deserve to be ill because you're inferior to others. You don't feel human. You feel like a vagrant; like a useless motherfucker. Like a loser in every possible way.

This was the first time that I had been ill since I had known Dr. Haslam, with whom I had struck up a good rapport. We had had some fascinating scientific, psychological and philosophical discussions. It was the best relationship I had had with a highly qualified medic since Kath Porceddu in Manchester some years earlier. I was in his care and he set about planning his course of action to make me better.

First he put me on Zimovane which was a sleeping tablet. Sleeping is often the first thing to go when you go manic and it's vitally important to get back to a proper sleeping pattern as soon as possible. Then he decided to put me on Rispiridone. This was a typical anti-psychotic that also had mild antidepressant properties. I was to take 7.5mg of Zimovane every night. The Risperidone would start at 1mg twice a day for three days in the morning and the evening. After that it would increase to 2mg twice a day. He set up another back-up in case I still felt high. If I felt high at any time I was to take 5mg of Droperidol and wait half an hour; if I still felt high I could take 5mg of Diazepam, wait and revert back to the Droperidol. Each time I was to take one of these drugs, I had to take 5mg of Procycladine to counter any side effects.

When Sonia took care of me that night I found it difficult to go to sleep. In the morning I still felt high. Sonia took the next two days off work to be with me and escorted me to the hospital. Before we went we decided to go for a fried breakfast. Within five minutes of finishing it I was screaming in pain. My jaw was winding. It was a side effect of the Droperidol. The pain was just as excruciating as when my jaw had winded up in Coney Hill eight years before. I cried now just as I did before.

We rang the hospital and a consultant told me to take Procycladine tablets every five or ten minutes until the pain went away. I took three Procycladine tablets in ten minutes and on the way to Scutari Mental Health Clinic at St. Thomas' hospital the pain finally went away. I could see my jaw unwinding itself rapidly. The Procycladine had had an immediate affect.

We were advised to go to A&E and see the Duty Psychiatrist, but we weren't going to do that again. We'd spent two days there, nine months before, and still hadn't got anywhere. We demanded to be seen by someone at Scutari even though we didn't have an appointment. Eventually, we saw a psychiatric nurse called Jo Bowd. She told me I could take one more Proclycladine and to take up to four straight away if I felt any pain in my jaw again. She gave me some more medication, and Sonia and I went back to my flat. Sonia was so strong. I was dumbstruck that she was still with me when I was going to go through all this shit again. A lot of women would have got off the roller coaster rather than psyche themselves up for another ride. I saw another consultant on the next day, 8 December, while Sonia spent a few hours in bed with terrible stomach cramp. She wasn't as invincible as I thought she was – she was human as well and needed to be looked after once in a while just like anyone else.

Over the following week I settled down a bit but was still manic. This was the only time that I had been manic leaving me with no confidence whatsoever. It was turning out to be a completely different – but always harrowing – experience every time. I saw Doctor Haslam on Monday 11 and Wednesday 13 and saw my psychologist, Carol, on the Thursday. We all hoped that through my relapse prevention work I had prevented a serious episode occurring. We hoped that with the drug package Dr. Haslam had put together I could avoid going into hospital. Only time would tell. I was as emotionally weak as an eggshell that had been trampled on by somebody wearing steel-capped Dr. Martens, and Sonia stayed with me every night until I went to Gloucester on 21 December.

Despite my fragile condition I managed to attend a meeting with Victim Support on 12 December at Ladbroke Grove. One volunteer, Caroline, was very sympathetic and helped me fill out my appeal for the incident with the doorman that had taken nine months previously. I was convinced that the incident triggered all the horror that followed in the months afterwards. It was the same as not knowing whether my dad's treatment of my mum or my mum leaving home when I was 14 had affected my life and subsequently triggered off my illness. I don't blame either of them. Parents are only human and they make mistakes too. The most important thing is that I have. and will continue to

229

have, their support in the future because they love me and I love and respect them.

I can say what I like about my dad's behaviour towards my mum when I was little, but he never left me, he always stuck by me and there was always a room for me there, even if it did turn out to be the little bedroom. There was also always a room at my mum's. I used to stay there a lot when I was at university and I knew I could stay there again despite what my stepdad, Michael, had said when he was pissed up that night. Thing is, I didn't want to stay at either of their homes anymore. I wanted them to come and see me live my new life in London. I was making my own life in London. I had made a decision to stay in London after I had fallen ill the last time, and I had my own flat now.

As the depression took over I became more and more introverted and less and less active. My mood seemed to have slumped to an all time low, and my thought processes became lazy and monosyllabic. I was becoming terribly lonely whenever Sonia wasn't around. Thing is, I would still be terribly unhappy when she was with me, no matter what she said. Sonia had to go to work and I would meet her at the tube station every evening. We put the sofa bed up in the lounge and lay there watching TV all night. We would cuddle each other, praying that the pills would do their job. The moments when I felt the best were when Sonia hugged me as I cried my eyes out and reassured me that I would be OK and that we would be OK. She had to keep on reassuring me that I was not a burden to her and that I would get better one day. I had got better before, and I had been worse before for longer periods and battled through it.

I lost count of the number of times that Sonia echoed these remarks but they never seem to register when you've slumped into depression. You become oblivious to everything. You just want the pain to stop. You want to distract yourself but you can't because depression is like a python grabbing hold of you when you're asleep. It grabs hold of you and it takes a long time and a lot of assistance to get it off without cracking your windpipe.

On 16 December, 2000 it was our anniversary. So much had happened in the 12 months since we had met each other. Sonia had got more than she bargained for, but our love was still strong and she was still fighting for me. Someday, maybe, I want to return her loyalty and love and fight for her, and us if need be, in an equally powerful manner. We went for a Chinese meal in Clapham and, although I was very nervous about going out, we had a beautiful, romantic evening. We both loved the duck and pancakes with Hoi Sin sauce, and we both loved each other.

As I boarded the train at Paddington to Gloucester on 21 December I felt uneasy as I knew I would not see Sonia for over a week. She was going to spend Christmas with her family in Spain. This was the first time we would spend so long apart since we had started going out and, although I would desperately miss her, it was a good test of seeing how much we would miss one another. Sonia flew to Madrid the following day and met up with her family in Burgos. I spent a few days with my dad and saw my Nan, grandmother and brother before going to stay with my mum on Christmas Eve. I was getting worse. I spent most of Christmas Day reading Nietzsche's *Ecce Homo* which describes how he went mad, and read from start to finish a book by John Gray called *Men are from Mars, women are from Venus*. I thought it would help Sonia and me in our relationship. I felt that we were strong, but we had been through so much that I felt it was advisable to look at ways of avoiding any unnecessary problems that may have arisen. I needed to keep her. She was a gem.

My jaw ached on a few occasions and I took the Procycladine accordingly. I always made sure that I carried my drugs on me in case I needed them. It was nice to see my mum and dad but I was so weak and confused that the only spark I had was when I phoned Sonia and said "*Hola, esta* Sonia *por favor, soy* Jason" or when she called me from a phone box. Then my face as well as my heart would light up. I was happy that she was with her family and tried to keep myself together when speaking to her as I wanted her to enjoy her time.

I desperately wanted to meet her family some day, but this was not the time. Sonia had only told them a couple of months before that she had a boyfriend. They were Catholic so they needed time to get used to the idea. I liked the fact that we were from different backgrounds. It made life more interesting. However, sometimes I felt left out. I feared that they wouldn't accept me when I met them. Sonia had been accepted by all of my family. They all thought that she was great, but what would her family think of me? I mean, I was hardly the model boyfriend. I didn't have a job. I wore baggy trousers and had a mental illness. I couldn't even speak their language and I still picked my blackheads. I was from a different religion. I was a Christian. Even worse, I was a Christian who was probably an atheist when he thought about it. How could Sonia explain to her mum that she was in love with someone like that? How could she persuade her mum, dad and two brothers that she wanted to spend the rest of her life with a man who would hardly understand a word they were saying when they met him?

By the time I returned to London on 27 December I was in a really bad way. I spent the night round Mark's, took my sleeping tablets early and saw Dr. Haslam the next morning. He asked me what had happened and told me that my health had deteriorated. He attributed it to the stress of me seeing all the members of my disjointed family in such a short time. Was it my eccentric brother that had driven me further into the abyss? Had his ingenious mind been too powerful for me to absorb this time? Was I a failed hero like Ajax? Had I been embarrassed at not feeling like the most intelligent person in the room and lost my critical faculties even more because of this fierce psychological competition and rivalry that existed between us? Had an unwitting attempt at overhauling his mania backfired and increased mine? It probably had. Dr. Haslam's drug concoction had also not worked as well as we had both hoped. He couldn't explain why, in detail, as he admitted that psychiatry often had to treat people on a trial

232

and error basis. I had to be patient. I had to hang on in there. I had started an episode and it would take time for it to filter out, unless it took me over for good.

I spent the next day cracking up in front of Mark. As we walked across Clapham Common to Battersea on the icy path, a couple saw that I was upset but ignored me and walked pass with their dog. They were probably mental health nurses. Mark had gone on ahead and I broke up crying my eyes out. I told him that I was fucked. I said that I was depressed and I couldn't fucking handle it. He told me not to worry as Sonia would be back soon. I carried on crying out loud. He didn't know what else to say. Who would? I mean there is nothing that you can say to make a depressed person feel better. That's the problem.

I rang the hospital on my mobile and tried to get in touch with Dr. Haslam. As usual, he wasn't around. It was like the Coyote trying to get hold of RoadRunner. Fucking impossible. The man was never there and it would take him a week to get back to you, and then he would not get the message or would forget. As my credit ran down, 35p a minute on my Orange "pay as you go phone", one of the secretaries managed to get me through to the head of the Mental Health Department at St. Thomas' Hospital, Dr. Davies. I informed him of my discussion with Dr. Haslam that morning and he said they had discussed my case briefly. That gave me some reassurance knowing that there were two consultants who were concerned about my health.

I was told to go to a chemist and double my antidepressant dosage of Venflafaxine, that I had started that same day, from 75mg to 150mg. The chemist spoke to Dr. Davies on the phone and issued me with the drug. I was still terrified as they told me that the drug would not work for about two weeks. Fuck, how could I last that long man? I was fucked. Mark and I went into a bar next door. He drank a few pints while I had a few orange juices. I couldn't touch the booze at all as it would interfere with the medication. I had to be really careful this time and I had to be resilient for Sonia. She had proved her resilience and loyalty for me so I would do the same for her. I would show her some respect and reveal to her that I could be as responsible as she had been when taking care of me.

Sonia came back on 30 December and I met her at the airport. Months later she told me that she couldn't believe how bad I looked. Anna was away in Italy so I spent the night in the room that they shared. We slept and cuddled for 24 hours. We went back to my house for New Year's Eve. We fell asleep about eight in the evening and at 11.57pm woke up to the Queen song "We Are The Champions". As Big Ben chimed we ate grapes and cuddled each other in the Spanish tradition.

The next six weeks were masked with a terrible depression that clouded over me. All the colour went out of my face, my mind weakened and my personality lost all its charisma. I put on weight, slept in late and was terrified of being on my own. I only avoided hospital because Sonia stayed with me every night. Each evening after she finished work I would be waiting for her, without fail, at the tube station. I would be at Vauxhall most of the time but sometimes I'd meet her at Fulham Broadway. When we met at Fulham we would plan for Sonia to stay there but I would be so upset that we would get a taxi to my place. Each journey cost £10 and that was a noticeable hole in our financial budgets.

It wasn't really fair on Anna. She had moved to a new house with Sonia and wasn't getting to see much of her at all. (We were both pleased for her when she found herself an Italian boyfriend some months later. His name was Enrico and he was a nice bloke.) As the weeks went by I became so desperate for company that I would ring Anna as soon as I had crawled out of bed and spend as much time as possible with her, waiting for Sonia to come back from work. Anna was very understanding and would make me camomile and fruit tea which I brought round for her and Sonia. She proved to be a very good friend and I was lucky that all my mates stayed on the madness bandwagon with me early in 2001. I needed their empathy and I would always remember their friendship and loyalty at such a crucial time in my depression. Loyalty, love and respect from my friends, girlfriend and family provided me with the backbone to survive. Some credit was due to the barbarian instincts within me, although I was in such a state that I never really noticed these instincts surfacing.

I saw my psychologist, Carol Busch, on 8 January and begged for the session to be extended. She just told me to go to Scutari Clinic or A&E. Fucking hell. She talked all that positive, intellectual talk but when it came to the walk got in her car and brum brum brummed off. I was fucked, she knew I was fucked and, when it boiled down to it, I was just another patient. I wasn't her responsibility, I was just becoming an increased burden on her workload. The person who had been directing my life, thoughts, hopes and aspirations for the previous nine months had let me down. If she let me down like that then that meant anyone could. But was she really letting me down? Was this just another, but more poignant reminder, that I had to assume responsibility for my illness? We had set rules together, but as she said some months later: "Only you know how much you can bend them." I knew I could let myself down if I could not get hold of Dr. Haslam. He was the one who had the authority and expertise to change my medication if I got high.

One positive thing about Dr. Haslam was that he was very proactive whenever we met. The guy was fucking intelligent and he really did give a shit. I knew he had a passion for his research and, when I met him on 23 January, 2001, he wrote down a more detailed plan of action than before to show me how he hoped the drugs were going to stabilise my mood. I was on: Rispiridone 1mg twice a day; Venlafaxine 150mg once a day at dinner time; Sodium Valporate 600mg twice a day; Zopiclone 7.5mg a night. Dr. Haslam ran me through them all. Risperidone had some antidepressant effects but was prescribed to stop me going "high". It was a safety net. Venlafaxine was an antidepressant but ran the risk of making me high. Sodium Valporate was the real safety net for mania and depression. I was to continue on the same drugs and the same amount except increase the Sodium Valporate to 800mg twice a day.

The Risperidone had been added after I had relapsed. This, along with the increase in Valporate, meant that I had less chance of a future relapse. The drugs were experimental and their effectiveness was based on a trial and error basis. Combined with my relapse prevention techniques and finding the right drug combination I could minimalise or even prevent future relapses. I had done well to catch this episode early and extremely well to avoid going into hospital. It was tough but I just had to dig in deep and battle on until the episode had worn itself out.

According to figures published by Mind in July 2001, 40% of people who take antidepressant tablets experience sexual problems. The same is true with other drugs. I had become impotent and, by the end of January 2001, had terrible difficulty obtaining an erection. By February 2001 it was upsetting me so much and contributing to my depression that I told Dr. Haslam. He understood that my sexual dysfunction was affecting my moods, and we agreed to risk taking me off the Risperidone and switched me to two 100mg Quetiapine tablets a day. I was to take one in the morning and one in the afternoon. I could have gone high in the interim but fortunately didn't.

Within two weeks I was able to make love to Sonia again. This helped my mood and gave me some peace of mind. Sonia was incredible. I couldn't believe that she was still with me after she had experienced so much shit. We went to a couple of Manic Depression Fellowship meetings, and it helped the pair of us talk about the illness with other sufferers and carers. It made us feel that we were not alone. And we weren't alone. Scientists believe that between 1% and 3% of people suffer from it. Bare in mind that 13 million people in the UK are taking anti depressants (Samaritans 2004) and over 1 million people commit suicide every year (World Health Organisation 2002) and you begin to realise the scope of the problem. To some degree we all have mental health issues so why not be open about it and help each other.

Today's patients aren't like those poor sufferers who were thrown in the same prison cells as murderers as Foucault describes in *Madness and Civilisation*. We weren't alone but seeing the group was a sad experience in itself. The literature it collected on manic depression was really out of date. They didn't even have the right phone number or form to become a member. The leader of the MDF group, moreover, was hardly a role model as she admitted having great difficulties with coping with the illness from day to day and had some very peculiar ways of trying to cope with it. She regarded being high as being something special and couldn't accept the horrific side to it. The group itself was, on the whole, very timid and lacked inspiration, direction and positivism. They were scared to open up and when they did they were usually talking about how crap their life had been. They were wallowing in self-pity like I had done over the last seven years.

The strongest character there was an elderly woman of about 65 who had cared for her deceased husband for 30 years. I admired her grit and determination, and Sonia told me that the woman gave her a much needed insight into caring and provided her with even more resolve than she already possessed. Thing is, the old lady always stressed how much of a burden it was to look after her ingenious husband who had a professorship in medical science. That made me fear even more that the drug concoction I'd agreed to take with Dr. Haslam would have to work sooner rather than later or Sonia might fuck off and do one. I didn't want that, but I didn't want Sonia to see me as a burden as this old lady had seen her husband. That's one reason why we didn't go back. However, I was also getting better, and the shock of going there and seeing that life does go on after episodes made me accept it and kick start my life for the umpteenth time.

Although I was bitterly depressed and very fragile, my doctors, family, friends and Sonia encouraged me to escape from the prison that my home had turned into. Instead of hiding under the sheets in the bedroom then hiding on the sofa bed watching TV, sleeping all afternoon, watching my plants die and overeating, which included three giant Kit Kats a day, I actually went out. I met Dom a few times in Canary Wharf for lunch. He'd been living in Clapham Junction and Clapham South with his girlfriend Tiggy. She was a good influence on him and I was pleased to see him happier than when he was in Stockwell. I went to the cinema in the afternoons. I rescued my plants from certain death, put them closer to the window and they began to grow again.

Sometimes, I'd meet Mark for lunch in Clapham Junction. I also went swimming a few times with him or sometimes on my own. I met Felix for lunch and we became good friends again. Time had healed the wound. He had forgiven me for trashing his flat and I had forgiven him for evicting me. I mean, he had no option really. If my flat had been trashed like that I would have done the same thing. I wouldn't want a manic on the loose in my flat. Would you? When I was meeting Sonia I would get to Vauxhall tube station early and have a coffee. I started reading again. I started doing the Daily Star sports crossword, reading the tabloids, even the Evening Standard, and finally some simple novels.

The episode was fading away and although I had more scars I was used to having scars. I'd been in a lot of fights in my life and was a tough cookie, mentally as well as physically. One of the scariest statistics that I knew about manic depression was that between 13% and 16% of sufferers kill themselves, at sometime in their life, during an episode. Well, it hadn't been my time this time. I really got hold of my relapse prevention, sought to educate myself about the drugs I was taking and to maintain the good rapport that I had built up with my head consultant and psychologist.

Having a strong network of professional support is vital if you want to avoid hospitalisation. Nurses, doctors, whoever's path you cross, it's vital to get the most you can out of the system. Some of them are brilliant people and if you find a good one it's vital to stick with them if possible. They can help facilitate your struggle with mental illness and make the condition a lot more bearable. You can talk about when you think you are going high and plan with them when to alter your medication. Fine-tuning is essential when dealing with this sort of condition. GPs have to see far too many patients, but the Labour Government is actively recruiting more of them all over the country, during the first 10 years of the millennium. There is far too much bureaucracy in hospitals. Staff are forced to waste endless hours filling out forms and carrying out mundane procedures when they could spend that time giving quality care.

So much needs to be done. Governments need to do more. Mental Health awareness groups like Mind and the Manic Depression Fellowship need to be more proactive. More grants need to be available for people with mental health problems. Society needs to be educated to accept sufferers. The media has a responsibility to behave in a responsible, sensitive and impartial manner when dealing with the mentally ill. If they don't then they must be warned and punished. I am all for a democratic society and freedom of expression, but give people an inch and they'll take a yard. A free press is a great idea in theory but, if it persecutes innocent people, it must be held to account.

So the episode that had started in the middle of December 2000 had ended by the end of February 2001. Phew! Now that was the shortest episode that I'd ever had. I'd spotted one when I'd been with Gina but I'm not really sure whether that was an episode or not as I'd spotted it so soon. That time round, I'd found it hard to return to being a normal human being again, but this time it was much easier. I had my own flat so I knew I wasn't going to get thrown out of anywhere. I wasn't being pressured into anything by anybody as I had my own space. I had the security of being a council tenant, had good friends in London, my family to talk to and a girlfriend that I adored. I was proud of how I had come through another episode and as long as I could avoid getting ill my life was bearable.

Hell, even if I got ill every now and then, I would still have somewhere to live even if I trashed the place. Maybe even one day I could buy the flat? I would always be terrified of losing it but I had accepted what my illness would have in-store for me in the future and I wasn't bitter about it. I was alive and had two arms and legs. I could see, feel, touch, hear, smell and wasn't in a wheelchair. I wasn't one of those guys in the hundred metres in the Paralympics. I admired those guys, their determination and courage. I wouldn't cringe when I saw them on television as I would have before I was diagnosed with manic depression. I would even go so far to challenge people who took the mickey out of them, which I may not have done if I hadn't been diagnosed. It wasn't my job to protect them, they could do that themselves. I wouldn't feel sorry for them. They didn't want pity, they just wanted to be accepted like everyone else.

Everyone has a dilemma when they see a blind person about to cross a road. Should they offer to help him or her? Surely they look like they need help? I'm happy to help somebody like that but I'd wait until they ask for help. That's not me being selfish. That's me allowing somebody to have their own identity. That's all I want for mentally ill people and other minority groups – to be able to live as themselves in a multiracial and multicultural world.

The clouds eventually cleared, the sky had turned blue and I felt as free as the birds looked in Tim's picture in the art room in Chelsea Charter Clinic. I was still with Sonia. I regained my confidence and managed to interact with people again. I was given an opportunity. The man who believed in me proved to be a great councillor, anthropologist, philosopher and friend. Eventually we went down the gym together. He gave me lots of advice and was a pretty mean boxer. At last I had found someone to fight with who wasn't scared of me. We went boxing and I got fitter as time went by. I guess that the moment I we met signified the end of the latest relapse and a new period of sanity. Even though I finally realised that I went in and out of my mind everyday I'd learnt to live with my illness. I wouldn't know how long my good health would last but each minute would be a precious one and I would try not to take any of them for granted.

My dad helped me improve my flat and set up a great

office environment to work in. He really came up trumps. The BBC liked it so much that they made part of a documentary called *Smallpox* in it. I'd sent my first draft to several publishers and one of them wanted to publish it. I had to increase it from 66,000 to 100,000 words and knew that I would when the time was right. I saved up for a computer and buying it and improving my office area inspired me to continue with my memoir again. I got on the internet, discovered another world, took an extensive computer course to increase my IT skills and plugged my memoir to people who crossed my path (this was from August 2001 until spring 2002, but only when my health permitted it). My life was worth living again and I realised that in one way I was lucky. I had the opportunity to help people who were disadvantaged, especially those who had manic depression. If I could communicate myself to them then maybe they would feel better about themselves. My intention for writing the book would often reverberate in my mind: "Even if I could only help a 17 year-old with manic depression then that would make reliving it time and time again all worthwhile."

I now coped with stressors in an effective manner. My brother came to stay and we both managed to stay calm enough to have a great time together.

Tom also came to stay for a week. He had survived a suicide attempt some months earlier, and I was glad that I had spent some time and even more glad to see that he was back on his feet. He'd split up with Perry, which was a shock to me, and was now a free man, as he put it. His presence made me pause for a moment and think whether Sonia and I were with each other for the right reasons. Were we really doing the right thing? Did we really hope to spend the rest of our lives together? Was it worth working everything out and adapting to accommodate each other's needs? Could she forgive me for what I'd put her through? I knew I needed to give her time, space, love and understanding whenever it was necessary. I would have to listen more and be more considerate. I had to be open to criticism. Although our relationship was up and down and I sometimes felt like a yo-

yo I always wanted to fight for her. I never wanted to let her go and, to my delight, she felt the same. We could be rational and sit down and talk about things when other couples couldn't. I was very patient in the months that followed, even listening to her doubts over the relationship.

Then one day in June of 2001, as if by magic, I had a shift in attitudes, although fluctuating in and out of madness was to remain a daily occurrence. I stopped asking questions about my past and just accepted it. I'd realised that I'd come of age and that I wanted to enjoy the present and look forward to the future rather than dwell on the past. I'd finally grown up. I also matured in my attitude to Sonia. I knew she loved me and she knew that I loved her. She knew that I would do whatever was in my power to accommodate her wishes and keep us together. I admitted to myself that what would be would be. If we split up then there were plenty more fish in the sea, but I knew that I had a special catch and felt that I always wanted to keep hold of this one.

Sonia and I saved up and went for a holiday to Barbados in July. It was beautiful. The people were so friendly. I took Sonia jet-skiing and she clung onto my waist saying that I was great as we bumped up and down on the waves. We went on a safari tour and learnt about the whole history of the island. We went out on a catamaran and went swimming with the turtles. We even went snorkelling together and saw the tropical fish in the sea. It was so romantic. The place was so beautiful. The plants and wildlife were more beautiful and wild than anything I had ever seen before. We saw steal-drum bands playing, spent time with the locals and drank coconut milk from coconuts that we had got down from the trees ourselves. It was a much-deserved break for us both and we planned many more together in the future.

Conclusion – Looking forward

It's February 2002 and I haven't exceeded two pints of lager (or the equivalent thereof) in one day for 23 months, but I am still aware of my life struggle with alcoholism:

I have no shame for having a chemical imbalance in the brain

And as I sit and write I don't know how or when I'll go mad again

It could be now, it could be then, if or how it's made worse by society.

Despite the pain and hurt I'll succeed and maintain my sobriety

With my psychologist, Carol Busch, I've also set up my first Action Plan For Life helping me cope with, and respond to, the very early stages of going high. The plan is as follows:

Changes in medication: Stop Venlafaxine, increase Quetiapine, add Diazepam, continue with Sodium Valporate, take, or stop taking, sleeping tablets as appropriate.

Follow sleep rules to improve sleep pattern (go to bed before 1am and get eight hours' sleep).

Reduce stress: use relaxation techniques daily, stop multi-tasking, build quiet periods into each day for chilling out, avoid too much social activity – reduce, or cancel, social engagements if necessary.

Reduce or stop work if necessary. Focus more, when at work, on the job in hand rather than interacting with colleagues.

Use up excess physical or psychological energy by doing some physical exercise, again, when appropriate.

Stop intake of alcohol and caffeine.

Contact GP, psychiatrist and/or psychologist.

Contact close friends and/or family for additional support if needed.

On 3 October 2001 Sonia and I left London and flew off to Bilbao. From there we took the coach to Burgos where I was to meet her family for the first time. They were everything I hoped they would be, and more. They welcomed me with open arms and I felt comfortable and relaxed in their home. Sonia's mum and dad didn't speak English but her brothers could hold a conversation. Although I'd started two Spanish courses in September 2001, and I was keen to experiment with the language, Sonia had to do a lot of translating. We had a brilliant time having tapas; visiting the cathedral, local monastery, shops and cinema; walking along the river and around the historical city. Sonia's mum and sister-in-law were also great cooks which was a bonus.

All the anxiety we had as a couple about whether or not I would be accepted was blown away. They could see that I made Sonia happy. Staying with them also filled a void in my relationship with Sonia. I had a much greater insight into her past and could therefore assess her expectations for the future. The whole experience drew us closer together.

We looked through hundreds of photos together of her brother's wedding, when she was in America, her friends and members of the family. I was touched to see so many people love Sonia like I do. I saw the books that she had read, the things that she had kept in her room, her collection of Walt Disney cartoons and her brilliant drawings, which I knew nothing about before. I saw what she was like before she met me and that made me love her even more. I appreciated again how beautiful she really was.

In the hallway there was a huge picture of her when she was eight years old. To my delight and relief she looked as beautiful then as she does now. We only stayed for three nights but went back for nine days at Christmas. My Spanish is improving, and we get closer as the weeks fly by. We are as close as ever and are true soul mates. Like every couple we have our ups and downs and we don't know what the future holds for us. All we know is that we love each other and that we want to be together.

...

On 20 October 2001 my best friend from Manchester, Tom Robertson, was forced to end his life. He was suffering from depression and his pain was too much to bear. This was, and always will be, one of the saddest memories of my life. I wished I could have helped him more but I couldn't reach out far enough. Tom, the guy who had been so strong in helping me and others, did not have enough strength left for himself. I didn't find out until the day of his funeral that he had a mental illness. That meant that all those times he said that he understood how I felt were not just words of comfort but were actually true.

When I write now, sometimes I feel like I am writing for Tom. Through what has happened to Tom I've strengthened my resolve and am more committed than ever to helping people with mental health problems and others that are prejudiced against it. As long as I am able I will never give in. If Tom taught me one thing then that is to never give up what you believe in. We often used to talk about the memoir I was writing and its positive implications on the people I wanted to read it. I remember when he read the first draft. When I asked him what he thought he said with a smile "it's deep". One thing is for certain, whatever happens after its release, whether it's a flop or a best seller, I'll never lose track of why I wrote what I wrote. I wrote it to help people relieve themselves from suffering.

Being a manic-depressive has meant that I've grown up quicker than I wanted to, but I'm glad I lead my life the way I do. I intend to reduce the risk of any serious relapses in the future as much as is humanly possibly and let others read my heart instead of just pouring it out for my own comfort onto a keyboard and computer screen. I practise other mediums: novels, poems, comedy scripts, screenplays, raps, short stories and children's stories. It depends what mood I'm in. I empathise with people who suffer more than the average person does. Whether they're homeless, have Down Syndrome, are starving in Africa or Afghanistan, have been tortured or persecuted because of their beliefs I want to help. The only thing that had any significance in my life apart from Sonia, my family and friends the last time that I was suicidal in hospital was when I was reading Nelson Mandela's *Walk to Freedom*. It put my life in perspective. This hero had gone through more hardship than I had and he had overcome it. Therefore, when the cloud lifted, I could do the same.

Hell, health permitting I could conquer the world ... make it a better place ... be a successful person .... win the Booker Prize ... become an MP ... a member of the cabinet ... Prime Minister ... like Winston Churchill, the manic-depressive like me. A manic-depressive ... I've got more talent ... as I'm God ... better be the pope as well ... to help these mortals attain peace ... set up Chipmunkapublishing ... The Mental Health Publisher... Reduce Stigma and discrimination on mental health... stop the 1 million suicides that are committed every year... Create the world's first mental health brand. Oh, and be an astronaut ... and learn to fly ...

Better stop there for that's a manic mind after all. Wouldn't want to have another episode, now would I? ... And none of you want one ... that includes everyone, believe me.

Printed in the United Kingdom
by Lightning Source UK Ltd.
118372UK00001B/9